Always hungry, never greedy

Food and the expression of gender in a Melanesian society

MIRIAM KAHN
University of Washington

WAVELAND PRESS, INC.
Prospect Heights, Illinois

For information about this book, write or call:

Waveland Press, Inc.
P.O. Box 400
Prospect Heights, Illinois 60070
(708) 634-0081

70 - 014 - 916

Mai Wamira,
Agu gaegaena o vereu.
A tarataranuaiemi, nuanuau ega i na vuru.

Contents

List of plates, figures, maps, and tables   *page* vi
Preface, 1994   ix
Preface   xi
Acknowledgments   xix

Introduction   1
1. Ethnographic orientations   11
2. "Sorry my friend, no food"   33
3. "Famine" reconsidered   45
4. Tamodukorokoro: the monster within   60
5. Pigs and pork: the domestication of affinal tensions   74
6. Taro: the cultivation of men's "children"   90
7. Digestion and reproduction: parallel acts of regeneration   110
8. The language of feasts   123
Conclusion   149

Appendixes   157
References   174
Index   182

v

Plates, figures, maps, and tables

Plates

1. Alice walking to her garden	*page* 29
2. Women at village meeting	30
3. Women fishing in the river	47
4. Pigs being singed at a *torela* in Pova	83
5. Men turning soil in taro garden	105
6. Women weeding taro garden	107
7. Jeremiah and Malcolm	129
8. Osborne	129
9. Simon	130

Figures

1. Mean monthly rainfall, 1925–80	15
2. Fluctuations in annual rainfall, 1925–80	17
3. Population graph, 1896–1982	18
4. Population according to age and sex, 1978	19
5. Relative seasonal availability of foods	46
6. Hours spent on subsistence activities	52
7. Pig genealogy	79
8. Affinal pig exchange	80
9. Method of butchering pig	84
10. Hamlet genealogy	96
11. Taro with and without *anona*	97
12. Male and female taro	103
13. Stages of taro cultivation	108
14. Energy exchange between people and taro	113

15. Energy exchange between people and taro correlated with
    female and male categories   115
16. Schematic representation of continuity in nature and of what
    is named and categorized   117
17. Relationship of named categories to tabooed areas   117
18. Taboos in female and male areas of creation   120
19. Cultivation cycle and taboos   121

Maps

1. Papua New Guinea   xii
2. Wamira region   12
3. Wamira   21
4. Residential hamlet   94
5. Taro gardens   95
6. Structural relationship of Inibuena to Wamira   128

Tables

1. Structural breakdown of Wamira   23
2. Time spent on horticultural activities   53
3. Nutritional status according to weight for age   55
4. Nutritional status according to weight for
   height and height for age   55
5. List of taboos   116
6. Incorporation and transaction modes of feasts   126

Preface, 1994

Only eight years have passed since the publication of *Always Hungry, Never Greedy: Food and the Expression of Gender in a Melanesian Society*. Yet much has changed since then—in the lives of Wamirans, in theoretical developments in anthropology, and especially in my own thinking about the topics of food symbolism, gender issues, and cultural elaborations on the control of desires and passions. Reading over my book several years after having written it, I am overcome by mixed feelings of nostalgia about my friends and family in Wamira, pride at the fieldwork feats I accomplished, and embarrassment about the intellectual flaws that were so permanently committed to paper. In many ways, only eight years ago already seems like ancient history.

My aim now is not to rewrite chapters from a past era of my life, for that would entail composing an entirely new book. The motive for coming out with a paperback reprint is simply to make the already existing book more accessible and affordable. I was deeply gratified by the many colleagues who commented favorably on my book, and especially on the quality of its ethnography, when it first came out. They expressed their desire to use it in undergraduate classes, something that was not possible in its previous format. Thus, it remains—a piece of my former life and that of the Wamirans—exactly as I originally wrote it, with all its lumps and bumps.

The book still stands, most substantially and effectively, as a contribution to the demonstration that food is both a physical necessity for survival and a culturally elaborated symbol for matters of human concern. I aimed for a culturally sensitive examination of Wamirans' theories of consumption and needs. I indicated ways in which the general structure of ideas evident in Wamira about food and sex, and about production and reproduction, can be compared to similar ideas in other parts of Melanesia. In addition, the book was an initial probe into the politics of gender and the light these politics shed on social concerns about control and restraint. Ideas about food and gender are the conceptual anchors of a complex of ideas about human character and the dilemmas involved in coordinating individual desires with the social good.

Because one of my original motives—and a philosophy I always embrace—was to write not only for anthropological specialists, but for people everywhere, I intentionally kept the book short and held details of data to a minimum. Yet I now realize that keeping things simple and accessible may obscure—even falsify—the science and elegance of analysis. Occasionally there is insufficient evidence to support my symbolic analysis, and a dearth of emic statements to back up some of my conclusions. More data are needed on theories of substance and substance exchange, and on the claims that matrilineages and patrilineages have on individual Wamirans.

The greatest flaw from an analytical point of view, and a common thread in some of the written reviews of my book, is my oversimplification of what I interpreted as a clear dichotomy between female and male realms, and my association of the female realm with things natural or "real" and the male realm with things cultural or symbolic. Not only does this represent an incomplete analysis, but it is also a dichotomy that is contradicted by my own data. Female and male realms are occasionally separate; yet they are often intertwined. By emphasizing how cultural meaning is constructed out of men's perceived needs and dilemmas (men's need to escape affinal obligations, their need to master women's sexuality, etc.), I downplay women's dilemmas and the ways in which these, too, are elaborated on in cultural and symbolic ways. By naturalizing the domain of women and restricting symbolic practice to men, I thereby render control an entirely male agency.

Changes in my ability to grasp the complexities of Wamiran life eight years later are matched by changes in the lives of the Wamirans who appear in these pages. Alice, my Wamiran "mother," has traveled back and forth between Wamira and Port Moresby where her grandchildren clamor for her nourishing love. Alice's mother, Sybil, sadly, is no longer alive. In a recent letter I received from Alice she reports in her usual letter-writing style. She says she is fine, mentions people who have died, elaborates on the seasonal food available, and laments the "big sun" and the "hard work" of village life. This particular letter is full of photos of her new house that was recently constructed in the village. She is seen sitting with friends under the shade of a chestnut tree next to the house. Her hair is noticeably grayer. "Don't cry for me when you see that I have gotten old," she writes.

In the past eight years, as my anthropological experiences and outlook have matured, so too have Alice's experiences and understanding of her world. As we each grow in our own ways, the bond between us that was established when I first entered Wamira in 1976 is still strong. One thing a simple reprint of a book can never convey is a sense of the ongoing nature of fieldwork. Anthropological fieldwork starts out as a goal-oriented task for the student, designed to turn her or him into a professional anthropologist. In reality it accomplishes much more. In the process we become part and parcel of many lives and places in a deepening lifetime experience.

Seattle, Washington

Preface

I first arrived in Papua New Guinea in June of 1976. My original, although since then somewhat altered, intention was to learn about indigenous horticultural ritual in a taro-growing region, focusing on the human qualities attributed to these tubers. Influenced primarily by Hallowell's (1955) ideas on the "behavioral self" and F. Panoff's (1971) work on vegetable metaphor, I hoped to find a culture that viewed the horticultural realm as metaphor for the human one, and to arrive at general Melanesian concepts of "human being." On the suggestion of William Clarke, then at the University of Papua New Guinea, I decided to visit the northeast coastal region of mainland Milne Bay Province (see Map 1). With the exception of Seligmann (1910), who visited the region in 1905, no major research had been done in the area, and little was known about it anthropologically.

My decision to work on the northeast coast was reinforced by conversations I had with people from the area while I was still in the capital city of Port Moresby. Those with whom I spoke informed me that, indeed, taro was the most important food consumed. It was the only crop still cultivated according to traditional lore, and the item most passionately exchanged at feasts. As one man explained, "Although the villages have been missionized for a long time, taro gardens remain almost entirely traditional." He described how introduced clothing or tools were not allowed to come in contact with the growing taro. One university student lamented to me how, upon visiting her village, she was not allowed to work in the taro garden because she wore Western clothing instead of the traditional skirt made of shredded coconut leaves.

Intrigued by what I heard, I flew from Port Moresby to Alotau, the capital and largest town of Milne Bay Province, and then proceeded by boat around the coast to the Anglican mission station of Dogura, where I was given temporary accommodations. While I lived at Dogura, I explored the region and

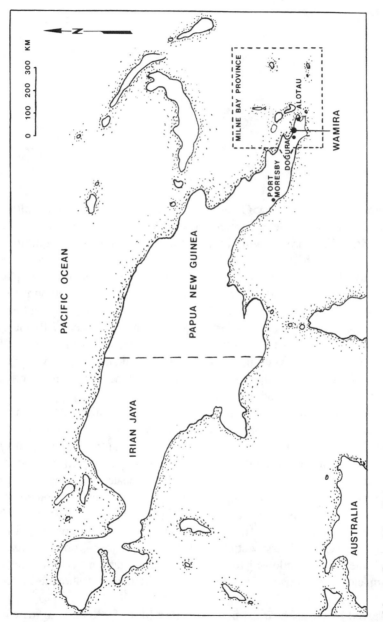

Map 1. Papua New Guinea

visited numerous coastal and inland villages, explaining my presence to the inhabitants and noting their receptiveness to my living among them. I finally decided to work in Wamira, a large, sunny coastal village less than an hour's walk east of Dogura.

My choice of Wamira was based primarily on three factors: First of all, having a population of about four hundred people, it was the largest village in the area. Because of its size, the residential hamlets were divided into two named wards. I envisioned a form of dual organization and decided, correctly as it turned out, that such a factioned village might offer interesting research possibilities.

Second, because of its location in a dry belt, Wamirans, as well as the other villagers along the northeast coast, had developed an intriguing irrigation system for growing taro on their parched savanna. Of those systems presently in use in Papua New Guinea, the Wamiran one is the largest in terms of kilometers of canals and hectares of land used. Furthermore, not only did Wamirans irrigate their taro gardens, but they alone utilized an aqueduct as part of their irrigation scheme. To my knowledge, it is the only indigenously conceived aqueduct in Papua.[1]

My third reason for deciding to settle in Wamira was a practical, linguistic one. Wedau, the language spoken in Wamira, was documented (King 1901) and had become the lingua franca of an extensive region because of its early use by the missionaries. There were clear methodological advantages in learning a language that I could also employ in neighboring villages to gather comparative data. As it turned out, I spent three months away from Wamira, living in the nearby villages of Boianai and Garuai, and making various trips along the coast, into the mountains, and one to the offshore island of Goodenough. On all these occasions I could communicate in Wedau. It was only as I stumbled through gardens in these other villages, and shared in the people's lives, conversations, and feasts, that the ideas I had been wrestling with in Wamira were put into a clearer perspective.

The choice of a fieldsite often follows matters of the heart as well as those of the mind. Influential in my choice of Wamira was what I perceived as its idyllic setting and the generous hospitality of the inhabitants. I was charmed by its spacious, brilliantly blue, seaside location, and reassured by its proximity to the mission station with an airstrip, wharf, hospital, post office, trade store, and several Europeans. The ultimate magnetism of Wamira, though, was the friendliness, warmth, and lively character of the people who, in addition, seemed eager to help me with my work.

Loaded down with a boatful of possessions, I moved into the village. I had been told that initially I could stay in the village resthouse that was built for

---

[1] I do not deal specifically with the irrigation system here. For more detail consult Kahn (1984, 1985).

official visitors on overnight trips. I found upon arrival, however, that the house's condition was deteriorating. Several Wamiran women, upon trying to repair the sagging house, decided and then communicated to me that I could not stay there. Furthermore, they were distressed by my desire to live alone and tried to explain to me that I needed to live with people who could teach me the language, help me with my work, and most important, cook for me and care for me. As I stood next to the sagging house, surrounded by my goods, Alice Dobunaba quietly but decisively stepped forward. (When I was in Port Moresby, I had met her daughter, Felicia, who had given me a letter of introduction which I had previously given to Alice. As a result, I later learned, Alice felt responsible for me.) She led me to her house and explained that for the time being I should live with her family. She cleared a space in the back of the house for my belongings, rolled down a mat for me to sit on, and gave me some food. My friendship with Alice, her brother Aidan, and their old mother, Sybil, grew; I ended up staying with them for the first year of my initial two-year stay in Wamira.[2]

From the moment I moved in with Alice and her family, I was visited and surrounded by people eager to watch me, touch me, understand me, help me with my work, cry for me when they felt I should be homesick, and laugh at my clumsy attempts to learn their customs. I was as fascinating to learn about for the Wamirans as they were for me. Like anthropologists, they arrived at my door with questions about life in America, wanting to look at photographs of my family and at maps of the world, and to hear about American food and eating habits, television, skyscrapers, rockets, and men on the moon. For instance, a leader of the village, clutching a pencil and paper, wanted to write down my answers to his weighty questions. He began by probing my mind for an explanation for what he heard was a major problem in my country, namely tensions between black and white people. One teenage girl, home in Wamira for the weekend, immediately interviewed me for her high school newspaper because to her I was "the most interesting person in the village" (Giurina 1976).

Throughout the first few weeks, as I struggled with the language and generally acquainted myself with the physical and cultural landscape, I remained attached to the family with which I lived and hovered close to Alice, somewhat like her shadow. Gradually, as I learned more of the language and customs and recognized and knew more Wamirans, I was weaned from Alice when she, as well as I, knew I could get around on my own.

I slowly began to turn to what seemed uppermost in the Wamirans' minds, namely cultivating gardens and sharing and distributing food, particularly taro

---

[2] Alice's husband, Campbell, was living and working in the town of Lae during my residence with Alice and her family.

and pork. Within the first few days, in an attempt to explain Wamiran customs to me, Alice often uttered the phrase "taro is our life." In the meantime, much to my annoyance and wonder, I was kept away from the taro gardens. Each time I asked whether I could go along to see them, I was showered with excuses such as, "The sun is too strong and you will get hot," "The grass is too high along the path and you will cut your legs," "You should stay in the village and rest," or "Not today, maybe next time." After two months of waiting patiently, I was surprised one morning when I was suddenly told, "Okay, take your notebook and come along to the taro garden." Later I learned that only at that time had I gained enough of their trust to be shown some of the customs that were most sacred and private for them.

From that day on, I spent much of my time accompanying families to their taro gardens, mapping, observing, weeding, learning, and generally asking what must have seemed to them to be ceaseless irrelevant questions. Almost a year passed until I was allowed to witness the women's taro-tending ritual, and eighteen months went by before I was permitted to observe a man planting taro. But, precisely because I was an outsider, eventually I was able to learn much about individuals' taro gardens that Wamirans keep secret from one another. My return from someone else's garden at the end of the day was always met with queries about the size and abundance of the taro I had seen. Much of the information I gathered was based on my intimate exposure to several families' taro gardens – something impossible for any one Wamiran.

For the entire time I resided in Wamira, my main methodological style was one of following the natural rhythm of their life – days of seeming inactivity punctuated by the bustle of feasts, dances, meetings about sorcery, garden activities, fishing expeditions, weddings, funerals, gossip, and arguments. I soon learned that I gathered data most productively when I adjusted to Wamiran interests rather than to my own. For example, I learned most about dancing during a day of dancing festivities, and about house construction when a house was being built and I could help with sewing its walls or thatching its roof. I recognized early on that to pound Wamirans with too many questions only met with unenthusiastic and oblique responses. They shared information with me willingly, but only when *they* were ready and interested in doing so.

In the beginning, my data were undeniably influenced by the fact that I lived with one family. I was adopted into their matrilineage, expected to associate with their kin, and exposed to their – and not many other people's – lives and points of view. What I gained in firsthand observation of private life and in the comforting feeling of being included in a family, I lost in breadth and diversity.

After I had lived with Alice's family for one year, however, the people in my hamlet, Inibuena, decided to build a separate house for me to accommodate a friend of mine whose visit was approaching. They built a spacious house for me directly next to Alice's. During the second year, although I had my own house, I continued to eat together with, and be strongly associated with, Alice's family.

In retrospect, I seem to have benefited from the best of both vantage points. I had the early experience of living closely with a family, sleeping and eating side by side with them, and being allowed to share in what goes on behind the walls in a society where private life is very different from public life. Later, I also experienced privacy of my own at a time when my research questions and interests were more focused and I needed space of my own into which I could invite my friends and in which I could spread my work. During the second year I made up for the lack of diversity I experienced in the beginning and worked with numerous people, conducting structured interviews to check the validity of previously gathered data. During the two years of my first trip to Wamira, my time was divided equally between the two living arrangements, each carrying its own advantages and disadvantages.

In March of 1978, I left Wamira to return home and write up my research on horticultural ritual and food symbolism. Spurred on both by a theoretical interest I had developed in the irrigation system, as well as by my homesickness for Wamira and Papua New Guinea, I returned to Wamira for a second visit from August 1981 to March 1982. I was warmly welcomed upon my return and was treated with increased respect because not only had I "come home," but, as Wamirans continually informed me, I had become "a very important person." For them, the change in my status from student to teacher indicated the mark of a prestigious and influential person. They correctly felt responsible; they were proud that they played such a large part in elevating me so within my own society. This time, the people of the entire Rumaruma ward of the village built a new house for me which I shared with my original Wamiran family. My new rank, of course, demanded that I give accordingly in return. For example, the same situation that in 1976–8 called for my presenting a pig and twenty kilograms of rice, in 1981–2 necessitated an entire cow and at least three times as much rice.

I again settled comfortably into my home in Wamira, where I was helped with my work even more generously and patiently than before. This time, I wanted to investigate the ecological context of their food world, and analyze what I perceived as sociopolitical constraints on agricultural intensification. As I gathered ecological data, I still paid close attention to the symbolic and communicative values of food.

In addition, I had a new, more practical, role. The Milne Bay Provincial Government asked me to advise them on matters of irrigation and agricultural development in the province. Rural developers were interested in using the Wamiran irrigation system as a model for building other irrigation systems in drought-affected areas. I felt pleased that my research could be put to such a use, and thought the Wamirans would be proud that the local government valued their ancient system. When I told this to the Wamirans, however, their response, although in keeping with the Melanesian emphasis on exchange in human relationships, only served to exemplify the frequent misunderstandings and frustrations among anthropologist, villagers, and local government. Wamirans told me that they did not want the government to use their ancestral secrets to help other Papua New Guineans until the government first helped them. What they requested from the provincial government was the installation of running water for drinking and washing. In the meantime, they showed me every possible pitfall the government would encounter in trying to develop Wamiran-style irrigation systems elsewhere. For example, they stood waist-deep in the river behind their irrigation dam and asked me to take photographs so that I could demonstrate to the rural developers that such deep rivers, which the other areas lacked, were necessary for building an irrigation scheme.

While remaining frustrated in these limited attempts to "help," I was able to deepen my relationship with the Wamirans and gather the ecological data I needed. I left Wamira again in March of 1982. As I was getting ready to depart, one man said:

By now you have really learned everything about us. You do not need to come back for such long visits. Just return for short trips when you feel there is a little more you need to find out. We know you will be back. The reason is that you will always be homesick for Wamira.

He was right. I shall "always be homesick for Wamira." As Chateaubriand has said, "Every man carries within him a world which is composed of all that he has seen and loved, and to which he constantly returns, even when he is travelling through, and seems to be living in, some different world" (1803). The traveling of an anthropologist in many ways is a constant voyage in search of oneself in a personal, cultural, and global context. Prolonged stays in other places – such as mine in Wamira – lead to imaginary journeying in which we find roots for ourselves, beyond time and space, and beyond cultural constrictions. In a Proustian manner, each journey I make evokes all that I am and have been and all the places where I have left a small part of myself behind.

And as my Wamiran friend also anticipated, there will always be "a little more" I shall need to find out. After two and a half years of living among Wamirans and learning from them, there is much that still escapes me. No matter how much I learned and came to feel "inside" their life as opposed to "outside" it, I am far from understanding all there is to know. I learned and accepted Wamiran customs and followed the rules. I became increasingly accurate in predicting people's behavior. During my second trip I often obeyed the cultural rules instinctively and unconsciously, which made it easier to feel at home, yet harder to notice cultural differences and learn about them. The longer I lived in Wamira, the more I could understand such nuances as the warmth or coolness of a gesture or the seriousness or jesting quality of an insult. I began to internalize symbolic behavior rather than merely imitate it. Yet, even after two and a half years, although I often thought and occasionally even dreamed in their language, I never came to conclusions by the same patterns of thought as the people among whom I lived.

It is for both theoretical and empirical reasons that I attempt to analyze the food-related universe of the Wamirans. Food is important to Wamirans because it serves as a medium in which to think and communicate. It is the main focus – to the point of what outsiders might call an obsession – in the Wamirans' lives. It is also that which still remains most elusive and intriguing to me. Food, in addition to being a nutritional morsel, provides a total system which is explicitly followed by Wamirans to inform them of who they are and how they should relate to one another. This quest for knowledge and understanding of who one is – full of its dilemmas, contradictions, and ambiguities – is not only a Wamiran passion, but a pursuit that ultimately concerns us all.

Acknowledgments

Over the past years, I have received generous help and support from many individuals, all of whom in some way figure prominently, although silently, in the pages of this book. Margaret Mead first aroused my interest in the South Pacific when I worked for her at the American Museum of Natural History in 1970–1. Two years later, when I started graduate school at Bryn Mawr College, Jane Goodale acquainted and captivated me with the charms and complexities of Melanesian ethnography, encouraged me to do fieldwork in Papua New Guinea, and then patiently and supportively directed the writing of my dissertation. Also at Bryn Mawr, Frederica deLaguna conveyed to me a love for anthropology which has stayed with me ever since. For their helpful criticism during various stages of writing this book, I particularly thank Debbora Battaglia, William Davenport, Marilyn Strathern, Ward Goodenough, Harriet Whitehead, Michael Young, Robert L. Rubinstein, Richard Jordan, Paula Rubel, Judith Shapiro, and Wendy Weiss.

On my various stopovers in Port Moresby, Ann Chowning, William Clarke, Andrew Strathern, and Daniel Vasey were generous colleagues, as were Anthony Forge and Michael Young when I visited Canberra. Especially profitable was Michael Young's visit while I was in Wamira, the concern he showed for my work, and the many conversations we shared about it. His persistent curiosity and encouragement while I was in the field often opened my mind to new ways of contemplating my data.

Numerous individuals assisted me in Papua New Guinea by showing interest in my work, commenting on my field reports, and supplying me with some of the information that appears in this book. I am particularly grateful to the Reverend Archbishop David Hand, the late Canon John Bodger, Bishop Rhynald Sanana, the late Father Robert Barnes, Father Randolf Orori, Manming Hung, Ben Minken, Lesley Slade, Emily Clarke, and Pamela Banks. Above all, for giving me their friendship when I was notably far from home, I am especially thankful to Prime Minister Paias Wingti, Billai Laba, Jelilah Unia, Eve Scott, Hilary Monsell, Anthony and Jen Crawford, Steven and Margaret Raw, Philippa Gold, Sara Richards, Rae Pannel, and Audrey Payne.

My greatest obligation is to the people of Wamira. To Alice Dobunaba, Aidan Gadiona, and Sybil Gisewa, I owe my happiness while I was in Wamira, for they became my family in a way more loving and permanent than the two and a half years I was "adopted" by them suggests. I am beholden to Alice's daughter, Felicia Dobunaba, for having introduced me to her family and for allowing me to share them with her. To all the people of Inibuena who built my house and gave me land, who included me in their discussions and feasts, and who assisted me daily with my work, I express immeasurable appreciation. Invidious as it seems to single out names, I must mention several individuals outside of Inibuena (some of whom, sadly, are no longer living) to whom I wish to express special gratitude: Patrick and Laura Davora, Napoleon and Grace Boloti, Zelma Petari, Violet Kirirua, Belemy and Rachel Maibani, Barnabas and Maggie Badirega, Mark and Mary Badirega, Hobart and Lilias Dote, Stevenson, Edward and Clothilda Maikaina, and Kipling and Coralie Dobunaba. I warmly thank Biddy Gugara of Boianai, Mary Sybil Tauradi of Garuai, Elijah Gadiona and Campbell Dobunaba of Lae, and Johnson and Miriam Orere of Alotau for taking me into their families, nourishing me with their food and their kindness, and teaching me about their village and its customs when I was away from it.

The research trips upon which this book is based, and the subsequent periods for writing up the results, were made possible by generous financial support from the National Science Foundation (grant numbers BNS-80-05243 and BNS-82-05462), the National Institute of Mental Health (grant numbers 1 F31 MH 05331-01 and 5 F31 MH 05331-02), the Wenner–Gren Foundation for Anthropological Research (grant number 3089), the Institute for Intercultural Studies, the American Friends Service Committee, and the Jewish Communal Fund of New York.

The computer center at Byrn Mawr College, and particularly its director, Jay Anderson, deserve special acknowledgment for their help in untangling the minor catastrophes I occasionally created.

I thank my husband, Richard Taylor, whose careful and perceptive reading of my manuscript helped refine substantive problems, as well as poorly constructed sentences, in a final quest for clarity. Even more bolstering, however, was his unfalteringly good-natured and loving support during my various outbursts of irritability and self-doubt.

More than anyone, I thank my parents, Ludwig and the late Tatyana Kahn, for their continual understanding and support, for encouraging me to go to the far unknown despite their parental concern, and, most of all, for their love.

Introduction

While conducting fieldwork in Wamira, I received the most helpful clues from my guides, the local inhabitants. They invariably and unanimously pointed me in one direction: food. My Wamiran "mother," Alice, always eager to help me with my work, explained more than once:

Food is our life. We plant our crops. Next we harvest them and hold feasts. Then we plant them again. That is how we live. You should pay close attention to our gardening and our feasts for then you will learn everything there is to know about us!

Taking my cues from those who know best, I embark in this book on a description and analysis of Wamiran food-related behavior and thought. I have focused on food in an attempt to understand and share, if not everything, at least as much as I can, about the Wamirans. I try to unravel the meanings attributed to such cultural phenomena as daily behavior associated with food, food-related mythology, horticultural ritual, and food displays and exchanges. In particular, I examine concepts of food and hunger as *cultural* constructs. As I demonstrate, the Wamiran preoccupation with food and hunger has little basis in ecological fact. Rather, food is an important mode of symbolic expression. It is used to convey a variety of beliefs and feelings about things and relationships that are not-food. Specifically, Wamirans use food as the vehicle with which to communicate gender qualities, control ambivalent relations between men and women, and manipulate political rivalries among men. With food they objectify their emotions.

In their use of food, Wamirans display an overriding cultural emphasis on control. This passion for control parallels their definitions of human nature; they see human beings, and especially themselves, as innately selfish and greedy. They integrate this understanding of their biological needs and desires with their social values, which are those of sharing with and caring for one another. Thus, they feel that individual needs (perceived by Wamirans as

1

"greeds") must be controlled for the good of society. It is in their control of food, and their beliefs about food, that Wamirans symbolically tame their biological desires in socially acceptable ways. For Wamirans, food is the symbol, and a digestive idiom the metaphor, by which they define themselves as biologically needy yet controlled – in other words, human yet social – beings.

Food: good to eat

Anthropological approaches to the study of food have traditionally fallen within two camps, namely, a materialist approach which searches for causal relationships and a mentalist one which is interpretive.[1] Materialists locate the causes of human food-related behavior in the satisfaction of biological needs and the functioning of total ecological systems, of which human organisms are seen as one element. Harris, for instance, argues that the cow is sacred in India because its survival permits the agricultural masses to use the animal and its products most efficiently in their farming (Harris 1974:11–32). Or, he argues, pigs are taboo for Jews and Muslims because these animals, which are unable to perspire, are thermodynamically ill-adopted to the hot, dry climate of the Middle East, which lacks the mud in which they can wallow (Harris 1974:42). Harner suggests that Aztec sacrifice of humans existed as a means of distributing protein among the privileged classes in the valley of Mexico (Harner 1977). Turnbull, although generally not a materialist, indicates that physical hunger was the cause of the breakdown in sociability among the Ik of the Kenya–Uganda border (Turnbull 1972). Even Richards, in her pioneering and comprehensive food-oriented study of the Bemba of Northern Rhodesia, wanted "to prove that hunger was the chief determinant of human relations" (Richards 1939:ix).

Materialism, however, has its limitations. Materialists seem to neglect the fact that religious taboos, sacrificial rituals, and even seemingly unsociable behavior, in fact, may have meaning for a society and may meet more than biological needs. Why, for example, did the people of the Middle East not simply delete pork from their diet without creating a religious taboo? Why did the Ik not develop other solutions to ward off starvation, such as increased sharing and caring for one another? Or, why would there not have been an easier, more efficient way to distribute protein, if that is what was needed, than to toss the arms and legs of sacrificial victims down the temple sides for the Aztec privileged classes to consume? Sahlins, taking an approach that

---

[1] For an up-to-date bibliography of various approaches to food in a cross-cultural context, see Freedman (1981). Arnott (1975) and Farb and Armelagos (1980) deal specifically with the anthropology of food, and Goody (1982:10–39) presents an historical overview of anthropological approaches to the topic.

emphasizes cultural meaning, notes that Aztec culture was believed to be reproduced by human sacrifice (Sahlins 1978:47).[2]

Cultural materialism, in addition, is plagued by logical inconsistencies.[3] Although providing causal explanations, it fails to explain why one particular cultural elaboration develops, as opposed to another. It also fails to deal convincingly with questions of what constitutes total adaptation. Questions such as adaptation to what, and for what elements of a society, often remain unanswered. For instance, the Indian cattle taboo could also be analyzed as a means of increasing the number of impoverished farmers. Yet it is unclear why this would be a society's most "cost-efficient" objective (Sahlins 1978:52).

This is not to deny the contributions and strengths of the ecological, materialist perspective. Much can be gained from ecological insights and approaches. In Melanesian ethnography alone, anthropologists who have described and analyzed food ecologically have increased our understanding of such topics as tropical agriculture, population dynamics, nutritional needs, and biological explanations for food taboos. For example, we have learned about the adaptable and expandable nature of shifting horticulture (Barrau 1958, 1965; Bayliss-Smith and Feachem 1977; Bonnemaison 1974; Brookfield and Brown 1963; Brookfield and Hart 1971; Brown 1978; Clarke 1971; Serpenti 1965; Spriggs 1980, 1984; Steensberg 1980; Waddell 1972). We are now also aware of the relationship between the introduction of the sweet potato (*Ipomoea batatas*) into the New Guinea Highlands and the expansion and migrations of populations (Golson 1976, 1977; Watson 1977). We are cognizant of the relatively low dietary need for protein among native Melanesians (Ferro-Luzzi, Norgan, and Durnin 1975; Hipsley and Kirk 1965; Norgan, Ferro-Luzzi, and Durnin 1974). And we understand that taboos on the consumption of animal protein, which result in child malnutrition, may be an adaptation to an environment of endemic malaria (Lepowsky 1985). In a more theoretical vein, we have seen how the pig feasting ritual may be analyzed as a mechanism for the distribution of protein, land, and people (Rappaport 1968).

In my own analysis of the Wamiran data, I find that an ecological approach alone does not provide sufficient insights into food-related behavior and complaints of hunger. As will be seen in Chapter 3, I apply basic ecological

---

[2] A charming illustration of the human need to create "extra life" around essentially practical behavior occurs in Myerhoff (1978) when Schmuel Goldman explains the custom of drinking tea with a spoon in the glass. The original practical reason, he says, is to keep the glass from breaking when the boiling water is poured into it. But, as he goes on to relate, "We always made other explanations in my little town. . . . We were growing boys, very interested in sex. . . . The spoon that is the man, the glass the woman. We bring them together. . . . We did these things because we could turn everything around and give it extra life. . . . When I drink my tea with the spoon in it, all those things from my childhood come along with me . . ." (Myerhoff 1978:67).

[3] For some of the general criticisms of cultural materialism, see Sahlins (1976, 1978).

principles to the Wamiran situation. As a result, I find that the Wamiran environment, although fickle, is not one of scarcity. Indeed, Wamiran statements about "hunger" do not refer to nutritional deprivation, but rather are metaphorical comments about control. In short, an ecological analysis does not demonstrate why Wamirans are overly concerned with food, nor does it give us insight into the numerous cultural uses to which food is put.

Food: good to think

From an opposing perspective, mentalists examine human food-related behavior by classifying and interpreting cognitive constructs believed to be held by the people involved. These anthropologists give us an understanding of the many elaborations and permutations played out by human beings in the social and symbolic uses to which they put food. Lévi-Strauss, for example, examines the symbolic value of cooking styles, searching for patterned homologies between these and social occasions (Lévi-Strauss 1965). He also proposes that some animals are "good to think" (and taboo to eat) because of the structural relationship between natural species and social groups (Lévi-Strauss 1962b). Noting that social groups are interlocked by exchanges of women and food, he explores the empirical connections between marriage rules and eating prohibitions and proposes that the "connection between them is not causal but metaphorical" (Lévi-Strauss 1962a:105). Others, such as Leach (1964) and Tambiah (1969) expand on the associations between food categories and sexual categories. They link these subtle mental structures to symbolic oppositions and mediations as well as to the idea of taboo.

   Symbolic interpretation lends itself to a multitude of approaches. Ethnoscientists, such as Frake (1964), draw parallels between a people's food-related language and their conceptual world. Several anthropologists examine the symbolic value of particular food rituals, such as eating biscuits in Britain (Douglas and Nicod 1974), or the American custom of eating hamburgers at McDonald's (Kottak 1978). Others analyze ideas of substance and self in terms of food. For example, Hanks reports that some Thai villagers believe babies grow within the mother's stomachs where they sit eating the rice the mother swallows. They believe that body tissue is made of rice and that mother's milk is blood purified by rice. "Thus the rice growers' image of man becomes rice itself" (Hanks 1972:22). According to Gregor, the Mehinaku of Brazil correlate beliefs about the human body and its secretions with their ideas about manioc. Mehinaku women, in processing manioc, "create semen" for men to ingest. The manioc produced by women and consumed by men is thought to be ejaculated during sexual intercourse and returned to women in the form of new life (Gregor 1985).

   Mentalists, who classify and relate the classifications to the deeper structures of the mind, however, like materialists, may be accused of reductionism. For people like Lévi-Strauss, human behavior and social details appear to be irrelevant because they feel that universal laws are not proven at the level of fact, but at that of structure. In bypassing historical developments and the specifics of human behavior, Lévi-Strauss, in fact, whittles away the element of meaning.

The reductionist tendencies of Lévi-Strauss give rise to a more fundamental problem. He converts cultural phenomena to structures of the mind, and the human mind to cells and chemical reactions. In reducing the mind to chemistry, Lévi-Strauss dissolves the processes of thought into biology or nature. Yet, as he himself has stated, it is precisely because of the mind and its consciousness, that human beings are set apart from nature. Thus, one is confronted with the following logical dilemma. On the one hand, he defines biological factors out of the explanation. Yet, by ascribing symbolic behavior to the deeper structures of the mind, he reduces mental ideas to biology because the mind itself is a biological phenomenon. Thus, for Lévi-Strauss, the dialogue of thought, although topically existing between biological nature and historical culture, is located within nature only. One may even read Lévi-Strauss as asserting that nature speaks through the human mind without the human's awareness or consciousness. For example, he demonstrates "not how men think in myths, but how myths operate in men's minds without their being aware of the fact" (Lévi-Strauss 1964:12). By reducing the human mind to chemistry, Lévi-Strauss creates a human being who cannot see or know itself as a cultural being. In doing so, he demolishes the entire dialogue of human consciousness.[4]

Criticism of Lévi-Strauss aside, symbolism has been a richly rewarding topic of study, particularly in Melanesia where food has received great attention. Many view food in terms of the important social role it plays in Melanesian exchanges; it is an item of wealth, an indicator of social status, and a symbol in defining and manipulating social relationships (Bell 1946; Hogbin 1970a; Johnson 1982; Lea 1969; Malinowski 1922, 1935a, 1935b; Oliver 1955; Powdermaker 1932; Reay 1959:95; Rubel and Rosman 1978; Rubinstein 1981; Schieffelin 1976:64; Schwimmer 1973; Wagner 1972:49; Young 1971). Ethnographers also indicate the existence of metaphors between human beings and food, particularly between humans and taro, yams, or sago palms (Fortune 1932:94–5, 108–9; Gell 1975; Gerbrands 1967:29–33; Kaberry 1941:356; Malinowski 1935b:92, 104–6; F. Panoff 1970; M. Panoff 1968; Whiteman 1965:106). More specifically, yams and pigs are interpreted as phalluses and symbols of male prestige (Forge 1965; Kaberry 1941; Tuzin 1972; Young 1985). Vegetative models for social relationships, notions of nurturing, grow-

---

[4] See Giddens (1979) and Paz (1970) for a general critique of Lévi-Strauss, and Goody (1982:17–29) for specific criticism of Lévi-Strauss's approach to food.

ing, and the regeneration of society are also analyzed (Gillison 1980; Jones 1980; Meigs 1984; A. Strathern 1977; Weiner 1978, 1979).

Well aware of the advantages and limitations of the materialist and the mentalist approaches, here I have chosen to analyze food symbolically. I have opted for symbolic analysis because such an approach better answers the question with which I am concerned, namely, why are Wamirans so preoccupied with food? Symbolic analysis furnishes insight into conscious and unconscious knowledge as reflected in beliefs and behavior associated with food, and the mythology, ritual, and exchanges surrounding it. Although my approach is a structuralist one, I modify it considerably in an effort to shun reductionism. Unlike Lévi-Strauss, I include the specifics of human behavior; I avoid reducing the individuals involved to chemical reactions devoid of history and affect.

In my treatment of myths, for instance, I juxtapose the cultural themes embodied in them against the backdrop of food-related behavior. I view myths as "objectified thought," as crystallizations of cultural themes and social experience, in much the same way that Burridge (1969) and Wagner (1978) have interpreted myths. Because the particular myths I discuss are communally owned and known, I cannot, as Young (1983) does, view them as political instruments or symbolic resources for the construction of personal biography. My method of decomposing mythical structures and themes, however, is similar to Young's.

A symbolic approach to food, in addition, sheds light on contemporary concerns with gender and gender relations in Melanesia. One such concern is with antagonism and separation between the sexes, visible in beliefs about female pollution and such cultural artifacts as female menstrual huts and male cult houses. This theme of antagonism pervading intersexual encounters dates back to Read's work (1954) and has been discussed in the literature ever since (Meggitt 1964; Sillitoe 1979). Another concern is with men's symbolic expression and imitation of female reproductive powers (Herdt 1981, 1982; Hogbin 1970b; Meigs 1976). There is also well-defined discussion about male means of achieving and displaying power in warfare, big-man politics, and the accumulation and distribution of wealth (A. Strathern 1971, for example). Anthropological descriptions and analyses of the delicate balance between the sexes stem mainly from work done in the New Guinea Highlands and the Sepik River area. Little work that focuses specifically on expressions of gender identity or gender relations is available from the Papuan coastal area (with the exception of Weiner 1976, 1978). Yet, an analysis of Wamiran food symbolism indicates that similar cultural themes of ambivalent relations between the sexes, male imitation of female productivity, and competition among men are present. The main difference between Wamira and the other regions is that in Wamira the expression of gender and gender relations is more subtly buried in their cultural symbols. How men and women present taro, for instance, is not as conspicuous as a male cult house or a menstrual hut.

The struggle to control one's appetite

Human beings everywhere grapple with questions of identity. In part, our task of defining ourselves consists of distinguishing those aspects of our being that we interpret as biologically determined from those that we view as socially conditioned. A definition of self as a socially tamed form of biological needs renders us both natural and socialized, or hungering and controlled, simultaneously. Living in a social world, we must continually balance individual needs with those of society. The more we fear our individual needs, the more we control them socially.

In Western culture, people have become most vociferously aware of their being and have made themselves the focused object of rational inquiry and categorization. For example, we separate "man" from "animal" and, in the West, devote much time and study to probe "man's" relationship to his "animal" ancestors and tendencies. The Western Judeo-Christian myth of Adam and Eve, for one, illustrates how these historical definitions may explain human nature in terms of the taming of biological needs. From this preoccupation with objectifying ourselves stem entire intellectual traditions such as those of human psychology and social philosophy. Indeed, the very discipline of anthropology may be viewed as an outgrowth of man's capacity "for becoming an object to himself and contemplating his existence as a being living in a world conjunctively with beings other than his kind" (Hallowell 1965:25).

In Melanesia, people also define themselves as beings who have socialized their natural human impulses. However, Melanesian methods of self-reflection are less academically defined than those in Western society.[5] In cases where people are less lugubrious about these matters, we can learn how they think about themselves and their relationships, and why they behave as they do, by understanding other subtle, complex, and highly communicative cultural phenomena. Daily interactions, myth, ritual, marriage proscriptions, and economic and social exchanges are all ways of regulating human impulses and social relations, and form part of a grand attempt at social ordination. In Melanesia, male initiation, for example, is seen as a mechanism whereby men can control their biological essence (Newman and Boyd 1982:176–7). Myths, for instance, indicate that men who are unable to control their gustatory and sexual appetites may lose access to both food and women (Schieffelin 1982: 178–9).

[5] The struggle to balance human beings' animal and social sides has been analyzed for several non-Western cultures. See Geertz (1972) for Southeast Asia and Nadelson (1981) for South America, as examples.

The production, distribution, and consumption of food generally provide conspicuous and richly resonant systems of symbolic communication about biological needs and social relationships. To exist as a species, all animals must eat. But it is only the human animal who elaborates upon the essential task of eating and transforms it into more than a technique for survival. Some of the most cognitively complex and emotionally laden symbolic systems that inform human beings of who they are, are based on this biological need for food. Humans participate in all the dialectical, emotional, and philosophical dilemmas gustatory pleasures involve: lusting and controlling, being autonomous and dependent, desiring and fearing. These contradictions and ambiguities continually call into question, and yet confirm, human definitions of themselves as both biological and social beings.

In this book I analyze how Wamirans define themselves, and communicate and manipulate their identities, especially of gender and sexual relationships, through the medium of food. Symbolically, through their use of food, they tame biological needs and desires, and control ambiguous relationships, in socially acceptable, tangible, and communicative ways.

Wamira: "famine," food, and feasts

In Chapter 1, I outline the ethnographic data necessary to understand the subsequent analysis. This includes a discussion of the setting, climate, demography, political structure, lineages and marriages, and relations between the sexes.

Next, in Chapter 2, I describe the food-oriented universe of the Wamirans. Images of food and hunger are uppermost in their thoughts and continually influence their behavior. They see their environment as one of scarcity and deprivation, a parched savanna that offers them nothing but perpetual "hunger"; they perceive their fellow villagers as motivated by untrammeled greed.

As an objective corrective to their views, in Chapter 3, I present and analyze the environmental setting over the past century. After assessing their available food supply, measuring the time they allot to food procurement, calculating their soil content, crop yield, caloric intake, and nutritional status, (and after eating with them for two and a half years), I conclude that, although they live in an unpredictable environment of seasonal extremes and periodic droughts, they are *not* nutritionally deprived. Such perpetual environmental instability, I suggest, may influence their general emphasis on control, and their use of food as a mechanism for maintaining control.

In Chapter 4, I examine the symbolic relationship between food and sex and indicate how control in the realm of food is used to express control in the realm of sexual relations. I do so by analyzing the Wamiran myth about Tamodukorokoro, a monster who, according to them, could have brought them abundant food had they not, being torn between feelings of desire and fear, chased him away. The Tamodukorokoro myth, in Wamiran eyes, renders abundance unobtainable and undesirable. At first glance the myth appears to be etiological; Wamirans refer to it to explain their state of "famine." My analysis, however, indicates that the myth is not about food and famine. Rather, it elucidates the ambiguous nature of sexual relationships: ambivalence between men and women, and competitive tensions between men.

I deal with pigs and pork, the Wamirans' main source of meat, in Chapter 5. I analyze behavior related to the exchange of piglets for domestication and the exchange of pork for consumption. I suggest that pigs are concrete symbols of female sexuality, which men control metaphorically to escape the affinal "double bind." Men, in this matrilineal society, are confronted with a dilemma: They must marry women to produce children, yet the children acquire their mother's, not their father's, lineage substance. Thus, in gaining access to a woman's productive powers, men lose their substance to matrilateral kin. Symbolically in the realm of pig, men attempt to master female sexuality which, in reality, they can never possess. Moreover, in exchanging pigs and pork, they express and control the tension-riddled relationships among them which arise from their unequal relationships to one another as husbands or brothers to women.

I deal with taro, their main vegetable food, in Chapter 6. In their cultivation of taro, men completely avoid the affinal "double bind" by metaphorically producing their own "children." Whereas women are seen as reproducing society naturally by giving birth to children and perpetuating matrilineal groups, men reproduce society culturally in the cultivation and exchange of taro. Wamirans view female reproduction of children and male production of taro as parallel activities. Energy spent on taro production is seen as having the same source (and symbolically parallel results) as that spent on sexual reproduction. It is in the cultivation of taro that a symbolic balancing of male and female creative powers is achieved.

The production of taro and the reproduction of human beings are seen not only as parallel acts, but are thought also to be interrelated. Processes of growth, withering, death, and rebirth are not self-contained within each form; the growth and death of each are directly connected with, and dependent on, the death and growth of the other. Because of this interconnection, strong taboos, which I analyze in Chapter 7, intervene in overlapping or competing categories. Both Lévi-Strauss (1962a) and Leach (1964, 1976) have discussed the human process of naming artificial categories in order to punctuate the continuum of reality. As I demonstrate, Wamirans categorize their world very differently from Westerners. Only by rethinking Western categories, such as those of food and person, of production and reproduction, or of digestion and regeneration, can we understand the Wamiran perception of their universe and of themselves. If we view them as interrelated rather than as separate, we see, as Wamirans do, that they are not necessarily opposed to one another.

The categories that Wamirans carefully separate, however, are those of female and male. Sometimes in concert, sometimes in conflict, men and women always appear interlocked in a temporarily asymmetrical, but ultimately balanced, continuum of life.

In Chapter 8, I unite the two key foods, pork and taro, and analyze political displays and exchanges of them. These exchanges are occasions when men continue their process of masculinization by displaying their knowledge of horticultural magic and defining their social positions to one another. I present details of a sequence of feasts and demonstrate how tensions between men are expressed and resolved at these times. I include my farewell feast in 1978, which was a fiasco partly because, in hosting the feast, I unwittingly usurped male power. Fortunately, I was able to compensate for my naive attempts at sponsoring a feast when I returned three years later. As I was told to explain at my welcome meeting in 1981, "I have returned to feed you properly." This meant that I would let politically prominent men conduct my welcome feast within the accepted cultural framework, thus rendering the symbolic messages clear (and unthreatening) to all.

I conclude with a chapter on the symbolic meaning of food and famine in Wamira and on how Wamirans' definitions of themselves as hungry but controlled beings fit into the larger Melanesian picture. Also, on the basis of insights gained from Wamiran data, I make some observations about the symbolic ways in which personal identities, as well as ambiguities and tensions in relations, are defined and controlled in Western society.

1. Ethnographic orientations

The village of Wamira lies in Milne Bay Province at the extreme southeastern tip of Papua New Guinea's mainland at 10.1 S latitude – 150.2 E longitude (see Map 2). It is located directly on the southern shore of Goodenough Bay, midway between the rounded mouth of the bay at Sirisiri and the long spindly strip of land that juts into the sea at East Cape. In the center of this coastal stretch between Sirisiri and East Cape, directly adjacent to Wamira, protrudes Cape Frère, a mountainous promontory. From Cape Frère eastward, one encounters a contoured coastline pocketed by graceful bays with bushy velvet peaks rising above them. From Cape Frère westward to the village of Boianai, a coastal stretch of about thirty kilometers, which includes Wamira, the geography changes drastically to one of extreme dryness and desolation. Le Hunte, upon visiting the area west of Cape Frère, called it an "indescribable nightmare of barren, broken, wilderness of peaks and precipices" (*British New Guinea Annual Report* 1900/01:13). Massive mountains tumble into the sea. Occasionally, where a large stream cascades down their crevices, an extensive alluvial plain has formed as the river opened its stony bed into the ocean. In the relatively uniform setting between Cape Frère and Boianai, four such plains exist. Each is the site of a village located on a large grassy plain etched by a river and backed by rain-sheltering mountains. Because of the unique dry belt in which these villages are located, each village must irrigate its taro gardens. It is in the eastern part of this dry area along a beach of gray pebbles, white coral outcrop, and beach-creeper scrub, that the village of Wamira spreads for somewhat over two kilometers.

The geographical and historical setting

If one stands on the Wamiran shore and scans the horizon, the feeling of spaciousness is overwhelming. To the north, the bright blue sea opens mag-

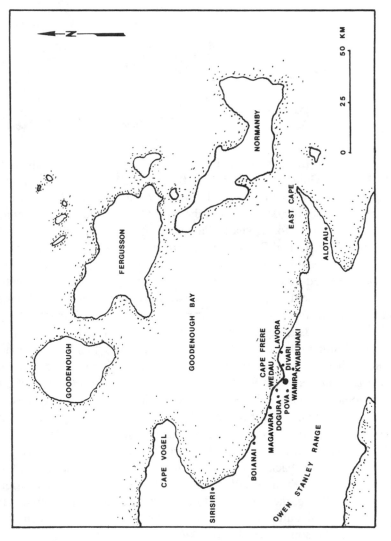

Map 2. Wamira region

nanimously under an often equally brilliant sky. To the west, the arm of land at Cape Vogel sweeps around the bay and tapers into the sea. To the east, massive Cape Frère looms like an elephant climbing out of the sea, the changing sunlight creating shadows on the barren folds of its body. On exceptionally clear days, the silhouetted shapes of Goodenough, Fergusson, and Normanby Islands, eighty kilometers across the bay, sit upon the horizon. South of Wamira, the alluvial plain extends for about two kilometers before it rises into graded slopes. Beyond the hills, along whose bases slither snakes of irrigation channels, tower higher mountains with distant spiny ridges clad in dense foliage. These climb inland to form the first ascending ridges of the Owen Stanley Range which reaches up to 3,000 meters in the interior. The grassy plain (primarily *Imperata cylindrica*) is dotted with green patches of banana gardens and occasional clumps of scraggly eucalypt trees. Green only during the short rainy season, the plain is bristly and golden-brown for months on end. If one scrutinizes the plain behind the village, one can discern heads of people, burdened with heavy loads, walking under the scorching sun on their way to and from their gardens.

Wamira lies within relatively close walking distance of a number of smaller villages. The villagers in this surrounding region visit, trade, and occasionally feast with one another, the few connecting social links between them being those of marriage (about seven percent of Wamirans are married to spouses from villages in the immediate vicinity). About four kilometers to the east of Wamira lies the small village of Divari, strewn along the sandy strip that is caught between the precipitous base of Cape Frère and the open sea. Wamirans are fond of the Divari people and, for no apparent historical reason, occasionally refer to Divari as an extension of Wamira.

Three kilometers to the west of Wamira lies its closest neighbor, the compact village of Wedau, on the pebbly, tree-shaded coast. In the past, the people of Wedau and Wamira were continually locked in feuds, usually over precious irrigation land. Jealousy and hostility still persist between the two villages.[1]

Four kilometers inland, nestled among coconut palms, is the lowland village of Pova. The people of Pova enjoy friendly relations with the Wamirans. Kwabunaki, a small hilltop village, lies in the mountains above Wamira. The Kwabunaki people, who speak a different language and practice "mountain" customs, are targets of drollery for Wamirans, who laugh heartily as they relate how the bush people in the chilly mountains have strange customs. According to Wamirans, the Kwabunaki people live in wobbly houses raised

---

[1] According to folklore, the mutual antagonism between Wamira and Wedau accounts for the respective village names today. The Wedauans disparagingly called the Wamirans owners of "dirty canoes" (*wa* means "canoe," *mira* means "dirty"). In response, the Wamirans shouted out that the Wedauans had worse than dirty canoes, namely only rickety rafts lashed together with cane (*wei* means "this," *dau* means "raft").

on posts, sleep in a circle around a central fire with their feet propped up over the flames, and pad the top of their heads with leaves to cushion the heavy loads they carry down from the mountains to the local market.

Directly above Wedau, perched on a lofty plateau with a commanding view of the region, lies Dogura, the Anglican headquarters for Papua New Guinea, and definitely the main agent of change in the Wamirans' lives. Today, however, with government appropriation of former mission activities, Dogura stands primarily as a monument to a previous era of colonial prosperity. The station was first established when Albert Maclaren and Copland King landed on the shore between the villages of Wamira and Wedau in 1891. The main area of the plateau, an old battleground from the days of cannibal warfare, remains an open field, now used instead for sports activities, dancing competitions, and church festivities. The field is flanked by the various buildings that constitute the mission station: a large trade store, a small branch of the Bank of New South Wales, a post office, a radio room, the Diocesan office where the administrative work of the mission is conducted, and numerous old rambling, fiberboard, iron-roofed buildings, the most classic of which is Dogura House, once the mission library. Most of the eastern and southern sides of the field are ringed by the buildings of St. Barnabas Hospital, founded in the 1940s. Across from the hospital is St. Paul's Community School for the children from the nearby villages of Wedau, Pova, and Magavara. Further behind the field lies Holy Name High School, founded in the 1950s. Below the mission station is an airstrip where small planes land almost daily. Next to the airstrip are thatched market stalls which burst into activity on Wednesdays and Saturdays when women from the surrounding villages sell their garden produce to the station residents.

Dominating Dogura plateau, as a majestic landmark visible from great distances, is the monumental white-walled, red-roofed Cathedral of St. Peter and St. Paul which, when completed in 1936, was the largest cathedral in the southern hemisphere. It presents a somewhat disproportionate and discordant edifice, towering above the village huts and nestling against the backdrop of grassy Papuan hills. By all outer appearances, the proximity of the mission station has greatly influenced the lives of the Wamirans. Upon closer inspection, however, one soon realizes that the awesome concrete cathedral has cast but a thin shadow over the true soul of the villagers.[2]

Climate and seasons

Wamira is marked by seasonal climatic extremes (to be discussed in detail in Chapter 3). The year is divided into two seasons, the dry (*omra*) when, according to Wamirans, "the sun rises over the open sea" and the weather is

---

[2] See Kahn (1983) for more detail on the process and results of Anglican missionization.

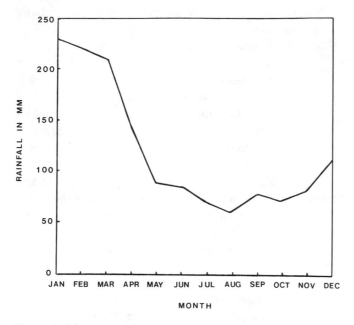

Figure 1. Mean monthly rainfall, 1925–80

"hot and dry," and the wet (*bodu*) when "the sun first peers over the profile of Cape Frère" and the days are "cold and damp." Only the amount of precipitation changes from one season to the next. Although Wamirans characterize the seasons as "hot" and "cold," the temperature remains fairly constant. The mean annual temperature is 27°C, the lowest at night about 17°C, and the highest at noon 35°C (Papua New Guinea Bureau of Meteorology 1978).

Along the coast from Cape Frère to Boianai, the dry season is unusually long, lasting from approximately April to December. An average year brings only around 1,400 millimeters of rainfall (see Figure 1).[3] During the dry season, it is not unusual for three or more months to pass with uninterrupted scorching sun (McAlpine, Keig, and Short 1975).

Seasonal extremes are great. What in the dry season appears to be a slight indentation in the village gravel, with the coming of the rain transforms itself into a raging river that roars around rocks. An otherwise stone-dry river bed may suddenly rise to two to three meters; people who go off to their gardens in the morning may be trapped there for the night. Gardens that are close to the river get inundated to such an extent that all the crops die. During this

[3] See McAlpine, Keig, and Short (1975) and Papua New Guinea Bureau of Meteorology (1978) for comparison with other regions in Papua New Guinea. Only the Port Moresby coastal area and the Markham Valley suffer from an equivalent lack of rainfall.

period when the rain "pays back" the sun, Wamirans tend to stay indoors
and pass the time by weaving mats, making baskets or string bags, visiting,
and playing cards. Outdoors large waves crash and pound on the beach, eating
away at the coastline, carving out and uprooting the coconut palms that are
thrown out to sea. Hazardous travel between distant villages or to Dogura is
kept to a minimum. During the 1981–82 rainy season alone, four people died
after having been swept out to sea while trying to cross rivers along the coastal
strip between Boianai and Wamira. By the end of March, the rain gradually
ceases and what seems like an unending progression of brilliantly sunny days
begins once more.

In addition to classifying the seasons according to the rain, Wamirans reckon
seasonality by the direction of the prevailing winds. The seasons of the winds
fall into four categories. At irregular intervals during the wet season, *kari-
wabu* blows from the north across the sea and is followed by days of rain.
From May to August, *rauanaga* whistles cool air down from the mountains
in the south behind the village. Following that, from October to December,
lavarata gently puffs from the west, a time when the air is calm, the sea
rippleless, and the general atmosphere sultry. *Barubaru* occasionally wafts
from the east but brings no major alteration. All of these changes of the elements affect even such minor decisions as where people go to wash and
which paths they walk on. In short, the composition and flow of their lives
change seasonally with the rains and winds.

Although seasonal extremes are great, their effect is minimized by the fact
that they are predictable. Having by far the greater impact are the sporadic
and fickle annual fluctuations. Because details on these droughts and famines
are presented in Chapter 3, suffice it to say here that annual fluctuations can
be catastrophic. Annual fluctuations (illustrated in Figure 2) bring unpredictable droughts when even irrigation is impossible and crops die. In the past,
increased trade between villages was the only means of warding off starvation. Since contact, there are new methods of combatting hunger; now during
times of scarcity, store-bought foods, and in extreme cases government relief
food, are at a premium.

Language

Because linguistic fluency was mandatory for my grasp of Wamiran ideology,
and because linguistic analysis occasionally accompanies my interpretations,
I briefly discuss language here. A detailed description of the language appears
in Appendix A.

The language, an Austronesian one, was given the name "Wedau" by
early missionaries. It is the common language of about 2,500 people whose
native homes are the coastal villages of Wedau, Wamira, Divari, and Lavora.

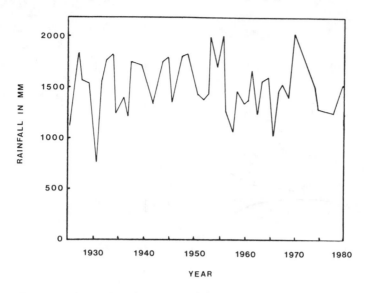

Figure 2. Fluctuations in annual rainfall, 1925–80

The language varies slightly among the four villages, the people of each claiming that only they speak "real" Wedau.

Wedau language belongs to the larger language family of Taupota, which includes the three additional languages of Taupota, Tawara, and Garuai spoken to the east along the coast. As one moves east within the Taupota language family, one encounters gradual shifts in vocabulary due to slight phonological and morphological changes between neighboring villages. In classical "dialect chain" fashion, although intermediate forms are different only by small steps, the farther one proceeds in distance, the more unintelligible from Wedau the languages become. A major divergence in language family, however, exists between the coastal and mountain villages. Mountain people inland from Wamira, such as those in Kwabunaki, often speak languages (although still Austronesian) in which one dialect is unrelated and unintelligible to the people of the neighboring settlement.

When the missionaries first arrived in 1891, they mastered Wedau within a few years. After learning Wedau, they taught the local people to read and write, so that today nearly all Wedau speakers are literate in their own tongue. In 1901, Copland King compiled a Wedau dictionary and grammar, most of which is fairly accurate today. Because Wedau was the language learned by the missionaries and used to preach in church and teach in school, it soon became the lingua franca of the larger geographical area that extends along the coast and into the mountains. Pacification by mission and government at the turn of the century enabled the villagers to travel safely within a fairly

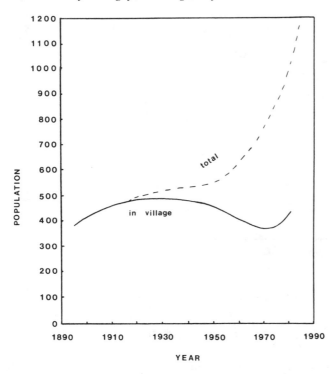

Figure 3. Population graph, 1896–1982

wide geographical region. The simultaneous spread of Wedau as a lingua franca permitted them to communicate more effectively with one another on their journeys.

Today, Wamiran school children are taught in English by teachers from other regions of Papua New Guinea. Most of the children, however, unless induced by the teacher, are too shy to speak spontaneously in English.

Population

The population of Wamira, although large compared to the surrounding villages, nonetheless is moderate in size. As illustrated in Figure 3, from 1896, when the earliest population figures were recorded, until today, the population within the village has remained relatively constant, hovering around four hundred. Since contact and the first recording of population figures, however, there has been a threefold increase in total Wamiran population, due to the cessation of warfare and cannibalism and to improved medical services. The excess population, which increased exponentially, is drained off by migration from Wamira. Thus, the total Wamiran population in Papua New Guinea today is about 1,200, only one-third of which lives in the village. Another

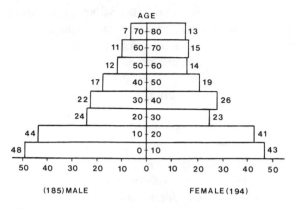

Figure 4. Population according to age and sex, 1978

third (mainly women) has married into other villages and resides with spouses, mostly in Milne Bay Province or neighboring Oro Province. Yet another third (men, women, and families) lives in towns such as Port Moresby, Lae, Alotau, and Samarai.

From a tabulation of the village population according to age and sex, it is evident that those who permanently live in Wamira comprise a fairly representative sample (see Figure 4). The relatively few men and women in their twenties reflects the migration to towns.

The Wamirans' long contact with mission schooling has given them a superior education and much experience operating within the "European" world. As a result, their only "cash crop," in their otherwise desolate area, has been the export of human labor to towns. The migrants, in turn, supply villagers with cash. Wamirans who have migrated secure jobs on wharfs, in stores, banks, hotels, hospitals, and schools. As early as 1959, sixty-two percent of Wamiran males were absent from the village as a "result of the very high degree of education available through the Anglican mission" (*Baniara Patrol Report* 1959/60:7). "Taxation . . . [was] deemed responsible for a large percentage of the temporary absentees" (*Baniara Patrol Report* 1959). The high degree of education and the income from town dwellers that trickles back to the village resulted in the labeling of Wedau and Wamira as "elite villages" by a patrol officer who, for instance, counted thirteen radios in Wamira in 1973 (*Rabaraba Patrol Report* 1973/74).

The Wamiran town dwellers, although physically absent, have an important presence in the villagers' lives. It is clearly the wage earners in town who provide the primary source of monetary income for the villagers. Each family has at least one member working in town who is the sole provider of its income. These migrants usually come home only at Christmas, a time that is embraced with much joy by those in the village because, among other reasons, the holiday guests arrive laden with store-bought goods and food.

Although two-thirds of all Wamirans live outside the village, the village remains a stronghold of traditional custom and pride. For instance, although primary school is seen as the first step toward a town job and future income, it is fairly common for families to keep some children out of school to "learn village ways" and continue the traditions. As a result, the gap in the amount of education and material possessions between villagers and town dwellers is wide and continually increasing.

Yet, the feeling of loyalty to the village by the town dwellers is substantial. For example, the landing of a boat from Lae or Alotau at the wharf near Wedau never fails to bring goods from kin in town. Frequent jaunts by villagers to their relatives in town are also common, once the town dwellers have paid for the villager's passage. The sad irony, however, is that Wamirans cannot all come back to their village. Not only would there be no space for them were they to return, but, having become dependent on a cash economy, they literally could not "afford" to live in the village without remittances from town.

Political structure

Political structure is reflected in the geographical layout of the village. Wamira is bounded on the west and east by the Wamira and Uruam rivers, respectively; to the north and south, by the sea and the mountains. Wamiran land, thus circumscribed, comprises a total of about six hundred hectares and is roughly square in shape (see Map 3).

Wamira is divided into two wards: the original old village at the western end called Damaladona or Wadubo (*wadubo* meaning "old"), and Rumaruma (which acquired its name from the word *rumei,* meaning "to scout around"). Damaladona has a little over one-third of the village population (about 143); Rumaruma holds somewhat less than two-thirds (about 236). Rumaruma originated several generations ago when the growing population of Damaladona "scouted around" and settled in what up until then had been Damaladona's banana garden area (thus indicating that the population was expanding even prior to contact).

Antagonism and competition exist between the two wards. Although previously united, both geographically and politically, the wards now find it hard to unify themselves as "one Wamira." They occasionally even refer to themselves as "Wamira Number One" (Damaladona) and "Wamira Number Two" (Rumaruma). Most traditional activities, such as gardening, feasting, and dancing, are conducted separately, side by side. Their traditional dancing, for example, is of two such distinct styles that the village cannot dance as one. Although each ward knows the dances of the other, they claim they cannot dance together because "there are too many people and they would knock

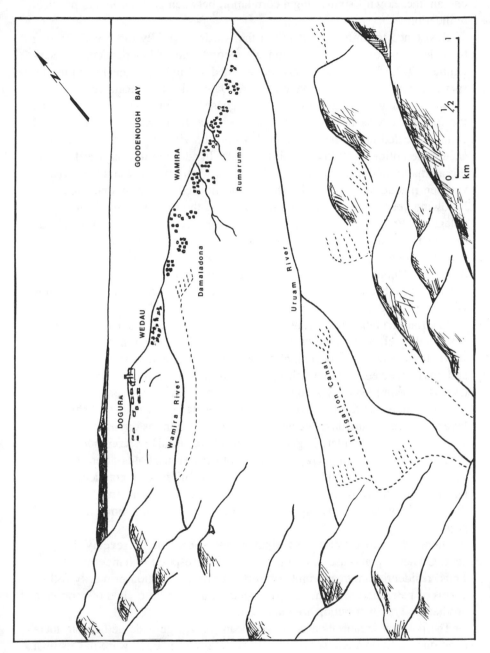

Map 3. Wamira

one another down" (indicating a correlation between group size and political unification).

Resistance to unification between the wards is vividly displayed. During the celebration of Papua New Guinea's second year of independence in September 1977, the Anglican mission decided to highlight the festivities by sponsoring a dance competition at Dogura. Damaladona and Rumaruma danced as two opposing teams along with several coastal and mountain villages. When the first prize was bestowed upon the two wards of Wamira to be shared equally, heated arguments developed within the village. Neither ward could accept the notion of "tying" with the other. In addition to each ward receiving a small amount of cash, the village as a whole was given an indivisible wooden plaque that was to be shared and housed within Wamira until the following year when it would be passed on to the new winners. After many village meetings and much altercation, Wamirans requested to return the plaque to Dogura because they found no neutral ground on which to display it. Damaladona opted to house the shield inside the Wamiran church, as this was their only "neutral" territory. Yet Rumaruma objected because the church itself, although erected on land that had been given to the mission, stands within Damaladona boundaries.

The fragmentation present between the two wards exists at each successive structural level. Within the two wards, the household dwellings are scattered in eighteen named patrilocal hamlets (*melagai*) that are located along the coast and are connected to one another by narrow paths. Hamlet allegiance is extraordinary, and jealousy among hamlets, even within one ward, is rife. Six of the hamlets are further divided into smaller named divisions. There, too, loyalty to one's immediate locale, such as the division, as opposed to a wider area, such as the hamlet, is great. A household usually accommodates one nuclear family with an average of four children. Households often include a grandparent or grandchildren, and occasionally children or grandchildren of family members who are living in town. (See Table 1 for a structural breakdown of the village according to wards, hamlets, divisions, households, and population.)

Hamlet residence follows a verbalized patrilocal rule by seventy-five percent. Ownership and use of taro garden land correspond to hamlet residence. Thus, residential units and units of horticultural production primarily follow norms of patrifiliation, although patrilineages as corporate units of economic production and distribution are unnamed.

The political organization offers no means of village-wide unification; there is no one traditional leader for the village as a whole. Each ward has its own leader respected for his general wisdom and horticultural knowledge, but whose role in organizing large groups is limited to the ward level.

In daily activity the most prevalent form of leadership is that of headman at the hamlet level. A hamlet headman inherits his rights and duties primarily

Table 1. *Structural breakdown of Wamira*

VILLAGE	WARD	HAMLET	HAMLET DIVISION	HOUSE-HOLDS	POPU-LATION
W A M I R A	D A M A L A D O N A	GABOBORA	—	1	6
		IRERE	—	7	24
		DAMALADONA	Gora / Gado / Damaladona	6	17
		GORETANA	—	2	15
		KWARARA	—	2	7
		GERAMTITI	—	1	2
		ANIMALA	—	6	42
	R U M A R U M A	KOBARA	Pudi / Aruati	6	30
		GOMIRA	Gomira / Guga / Uriuria	7	24
		LOIMARA	—	4	9
		AGAMORA	—	4	20
		INIBUENA	Akirani / Diguma / Iriki / Tutuvuna	19	80
		WERAU	Werau / Bebelari	6	28
		TOPANA	—	1	3
		GARALA	Imara / Labolabo / Inairu	11	52
		RABENA	—	1	9
		DARAWAVUNA	—	2	8
		AMOVUNA	—	1	3
		TOTAL		87	379

through partrilineal primogeniture, but then must live up to his status by exemplary behavior that demonstrates a deep understanding of traditional (mainly horticultural) customs. He is the individual responsible for initiating the various stages of the cultivation cycle and calling the feasts which mark their completion. He must motivate the members of the hamlet to work by providing, or prompting the hamlet members to provide, the food which is seen as necessary compensation for their labor. A headman's prolonged absence from the village, or the infirmity of his old age, may call for his younger brother or his father's younger brother's son to step into his place to organize activities while he sits by in a supervisory capacity.

The traditional form of leadership has been amplified, but not entirely supplanted, since 1964 when local government councils were established. Since that time, Wamirans elect one village councillor every three years. The councillor usually is chosen for his experience with white people and knowledge of government ways, rather than for traditional respect he holds within the village.

The problem of village unification present in traditional political organization is also found in the introduced system of village councillors. For example, the councillor elected in 1976 continually complained about the unwieldiness of his job. He held several meetings to encourage Wamirans to elect a second councillor, thus hoping to have one for each of the two wards. The local government council did not agree to this idea, and in 1981 an identical request for two separate councillors was still being voiced by the 1976 councillor's successor.

Lineages and marriage

Marriage and matrilineal affiliation (*dam*) are the only social links that cross-cut the geographically separate units of residence, horticultural production, and political organization. Lineage exogamy is prescribed and, thus, matrilineal groups are geographically dispersed throughout the village. These named lineages, of which there are about twenty, distinguish themselves from one another according to their geographical place of origin, each one tracing its historical roots to a different locale. The fact that Wamira was settled by groups congregating from diverse areas results in a lack of any unifying mechanism also at the level of ancestral affiliation. Each matrilineage has its own group of animals, usually birds, lizards, snakes, or fish, which are taboo to its members. In the past, each had its prescribed exchange partner at revenge death feasts (*banivi*), which are no longer practiced today.

The matrilineages form corporate groups at important periods in the life cycle such as marriage, house building, and death. They unite only for those feasts that celebrate stages in the life cycle. In contrast, patrilineal groups (i.e., residential and horticultural units) unite for several types of food distributions, and especially for those marking stages in the gardening process.

Although lineage affiliation is the primary link across otherwise separate and often antagonistic geographical and political units, those bridges formed at marriage, and rekindled and redefined at death, are neither strong nor numerous enough to permanently bond the village together as one unit. This is for two reasons. First, once a woman marries, she severs most ties to her natal family, including those to residential and horticultural land. She remains on her husband's land even after his death. She returns to her natal land after his death, only if she bore no sons and thus has no male anchoring her to her husband's land.[4] The second reason why bonds of matrifiliation fail to create an amicable link across village wards is that 82.5 percent of Wamiran village

[4] Burial originally took place in one's natal hamlet, but now occurs in the village cemetery.

women (83 percent for Damaladona and 82 percent for Rumaruma) marry within their ward (18.5 percent marry within their hamlet). Thus, even marriages and deaths, with their accompanying rituals, exchanges, and feasts, fail to bring together people of the two wards very often.

Relations between the sexes

Public relations between men and women are reserved, segregated, and devoid of physical contact. It is men who publicly call large meetings, orate authoritatively, settle disputes, and organize communal activities and feasts. In the past, it was also men who waged what Wamirans regarded as the most virile of activities, namely warfare. At all these times, men are physically segregated from women. During public events, women observe attentively from the sidelines and actively participate only when requested by men to do so. Women often phrased their role during public disputes as being "like dinghies behind a boat." "We are only women," they would say, "and so, we do not lead, we follow." Turning to me, they would say, "Like you, we are only passengers."

These distinct roles between the sexes are reflected in spatial arrangements at public gatherings. At meetings or food distributions, women sit in concentric circles around the men, who sit in the center from where they rise to orate. Groups of women on the periphery fan out in increasingly wider circles that decrease in the amount of interest shown to the matters at hand. On the far fringes children romp and play.

It must be noted, however, that sex is only one of several lines along which groups are defined. Wamirans always separate into groups in public: according to sex (for which there is no term other than those for "men" and "women"), age (*kimta*), and residence (*melagai*), a topic that will be discussed more fully in Chapter 8. For example, at gatherings not only do women sit together, but women of one age group from one hamlet sit next to one another.

When women are in the company of other women only, they behave quite differently from when they are with men. Together with one another, fishing, washing pots or clothes at the river, planting sweet potatoes in a communal garden for the "women's club," or walking to market, women joke and banter, gossip, giggle, and laugh. Men, however, especially when in the company of other men only, are endlessly concerned with the minutiae of village life, such as who gave what to whom, and why.[5] Chapter 8, in which I discuss feasts, illustrates this aspect of men's affairs.

---

[5] As I discuss in Chapter 4, Wamira used to have men's houses (*potuma*) but otherwise did not exhibit any of the characteristics, such as initiation, menstrual huts, or ideas about pollution that coincide with the existence of men's houses in other regions such as the New Guinea Highlands (Hays and Hays 1982; Herdt 1981, 1982).

In their view, men work hardest because they are responsible for such monumental tasks as turning the heavy sod to make new gardens, or transporting cumbersome tree trunks for the building of new houses. Women, when asked, report that it is really they who work hardest, carrying food from the garden and firewood from the bush, sweeping the house and village, cooking, fetching water, going to market, and so on. After describing how they toil day after day, in a low whisper they add, "But men think they work harder, so we let them think so."

Relations between men and women appear respectful and ordered on the surface. A closer view, however, which is presented in the remainder of this book, reveals that sexual relations are full of tension, suspicion, and jealousy. As genealogies revealed, adultery was common in the past, although it is less prevalent now. Once I knew Wamirans better, I was often told, "Men and women fight all the time. Men sleep with women other than their wives. Women leave their husbands and sleep with other men. Men and women are always jealous."

A passionate people

Individuals possess a delightful combination of personal qualities. They are reserved, polite, and extremely respectful, as well as outgoing, lively, and even boisterous. They often joke and laugh, especially at their own human foibles, shed empathetic tears readily, and argue loudly and aggressively. The liveliest times occur when they are engaged in communal work. Then both men and women banter jovially, often lapsing into a local mountain language or Melanesian Pidgin (otherwise not spoken in Wamira) which, for them, provides comic relief.

They turn themselves and what they consider their pitiable lot in life – especially vis-à-vis the "good life" they perceive in town – into the brunt of most of their jokes. For example, toiling in his garden, a man once called to the woman working the neighboring plot, "Oh, when I was in town, I had gigantic, plump sweet potatoes, but here I have none." The woman shouted back, "You are in Wamira now, don't think of the town and all the food. Don't think of the buses and the taxis. Don't think of the tea and coffee breaks." She wrapped a banana leaf around her leg to keep the flies away from a sore, and they jested about her fancy "village" bandage that was different from the ones they could buy in town.

Or, once during the rainy season as I sloshed through the mud on a path, I met a young man who joked, "This black sticky stuff on the ground is not really mud. It is tar for the new highway we are building to take us to town!"

What they perceive as the wretched combination of a dry climate and inadequate food provides tangible substance for jokes. On one occasion, Rumaruma women were harvesting sweet potatoes that they had planted communally to sell in the market for cash. Upon unearthing the potatoes, the women tossed them into a huge mound in the center of the group. One prankster, with an improvised mango-pit badge, parodied a government official who had been sent to check on theft. When she danced up to one old woman, the suspect shamefacedly uncovered two withered potatoes, each barely the size of her little finger, and lamented that she had been hiding them for a scrumptious dinner for herself.

A story that always entertained listeners was about a Wamiran man who, on his way to Dogura, accidentally slipped in the mud and dropped his pot of food. Out tumbled his boiled sweet potatoes and taro. What made the listeners roll with hilarity was the fact that, being impoverished and hungry, he proceeded to gather the muddy food, take it to the river to wash it, and then put it back in his pot.

Wamirans clown around whenever possible, and a dance or party is an excellent opportunity for buffoonery. During a festive gathering one man suddenly appeared with a rag tied around his loins, grotesque designs painted on his buttocks, and a makeshift spear clutched in his hand. After prancing around "native style" for a while, he quickly disappeared and came back wearing his stiff white Australian navy uniform and waltzed "European style."

Villagers shed empathetic tears as readily as they burst out in gusty laughs. Their weeping is spontaneous and contagious. Shortly after settling in the village, I went with several women to gather firewood. They joked at my ineptitude at chopping down the small tree and my inability to carry large piles of firewood in the basket that hung from my head. They decided that at that time I should carry only a small bundle, and build up my strength gradually over the next months. Equipped with my tiny bundle slung from my head, I walked back to the hamlet with them. When several of the older women saw me approaching, they came out and shed tears at the sight of a white woman carrying a bundle of firewood, however small, a sight they had never seen. As they gathered and wept, moved by their tears, I began to do the same. When the younger women with whom I had gathered wood saw my tears, they too began to cry. In no time, we were all sitting on the ground laughing at our teary-eyed gathering triggered by a miniscule pile of firewood.

To argue, especially loudly, is also a favorite Wamiran pastime. Every personal dispute blossoms into a major hamlet affair, with everyone gathering to sit on the tree stumps and rocks along the side of the hamlet, listening, and shouting out their opinions.

The personality trait they most proudly display is that of extreme politeness and respect for one another. In the beginning of my stay in Wamira, each time I went to the river to fetch water and wash, I was followed by a cheerful throng of children who tagged along to watch me perform such strange rituals as washing my hair or brushing my teeth. One day they insisted on carrying my bucket of water as we walked home from the river. They began to tease me about the clumsy way I carried my bucket, my strange washing habits at the river, my inability to converse properly in their language, and the like. Suddenly, my mood swung to one of annoyance. I snatched the bucket from them, telling them I preferred to carry it myself rather than put up with what they claimed was "help." I went home, not giving the episode further thought. Later that evening, we heard a knock at our door. There stood all the children who had followed me home from the river, wanting to apologize. One by one, they shyly approached and shook my hand, mumbling in carefully practiced English that they were sorry for having teased me!

The combination of characteristics that make up the "Wamiran personality," which indeed differs from even that of the neighboring villagers, is delightful. Yet, beneath the politeness and laughter also lurk the suspicions, jealousies, fears, and hostilities referred to earlier. I save the discussion of these for later. They emerge gradually in my analysis, just as my understanding of them emerged slowly in the course of my fieldwork.

Daybreak to darkness

A typical day in Wamira begins when birds start chirping and roosters begin crowing long before the first light of dawn rises across the sea. Wamira awakens slowly as people emerge from their houses, the roof beams of which sag slightly under the thatch, and the sides of which lean jovially with the individuality of the coconut fronds that are woven into walls. In Wamira, the spacious houses, when new, have an air of freshness and neatness, but they age within a few years as the thatch begins to rot from the rain and the walls become blackened and battered from the snouts of pigs snuffling around their bases.

As the sun rises from the sea and the sky grows pink, the pigs, as if in slow motion, rise from their slumbering postures and begin to grunt about the village in search of food. Human shadows can be seen as people stroll on their way to "the bush" among the straight and sturdy tree trunks, some of which are covered with pale-green lichen, others dark with gigantic buttressed trunks. The women are the first to work, cleaning the village by gathering the dry fallen breadfruit or mango leaves into baskets. They scratch at the gray pebbly surface of the ground as they sweep, bent at the waist, one arm folded behind their back, with their brooms of bundled coconut-leaf ribs. They light fires on the edge of the hamlet, and flames blaze as the dry leaves and rubbish curl up into smoke. Young girls, proudly carrying on their heads dishes and pots from the previous night's meal, walk off to wash them at the creek that trickles alongside the hamlet. Pounding sounds reverberate as someone chops wood from an old tree stump next to his house. Occasionally, from a distant corner, South Sea guitar music can be heard on a radio.

The sun rises still higher and filters through the canopy of tropical leaves that covers the village. By now, inside the houses, women have carefully peeled

1. Alice walking to her garden

and cut up taro, sweet potatoes, or other root crops and placed them in pots of boiling water. One woman steps outside and, with a few skillful smacks of a machete around the circumference of a coconut, cracks open the shell and catches the streaming liquid in a dish for the pig. She sets up her stool for scraping coconut, and soon the rhythmic sound of coconuts being scraped resounds throughout the village as other women do the same. Another woman, finished with her scraping, retreats into the house to squeeze the coconut cream over the food. A few minutes later, her hand stretches from the door of the house as she flicks over the dish and taps it on the bottom to get out the remains of used, grated coconut meat. With the clink of the dish, the pigs and dogs, chickens and roosters, scurry to peck up the white flakes that lie scattered on the ground. The woman's hand disappears inside the house, where she dishes out the steaming food for her family. They eat indoors in private.

During the day, usually only a few people linger behind in the village. Men and women who have garden work to do leave early. The women wear shredded-leaf skirts and carry garden baskets slung from their heads down their backs (see Plate 1). A group of young men, swinging machetes in hand, go upstream to clear the irrigation ditch. Others are off to the river with their

2. Women at village meeting

friends to fish. Some of those who stay behind meander around, quietly in-
specting their food trees, contemplating whether the breadfruit are growing
well or whether it is time for their son to climb the coconut palm. Others, in
search of areca nut or pepper leaf (to be explained in Chapter 3), stroll away
to visit friends. Still others spread their woven pandanus mats outside, where
they sit down contentedly to roll their morning tobacco.

Every few weeks, one hears the early morning sound of a conch trumpeting
through the village and knows that a meeting is being called. By the time the
conch is blown for the third time – at least an hour or two after the first
blast – people start gathering. They sit down leisurely, according to hamlet
clusters, the women on the periphery with their legs stretched out in front of
them (see Plate 2). Some women knot fishnets, the bases of which are strung
tautly to their toes. Others shred coconut leaves for making skirts. A few
deftly roll twine on the calves of their legs and knot it into string bags. They
shout across to one another, joke, and laugh. Some local gossip is tossed back
and forth – there will be a wedding next weekend . . . Someone's pig ran
into a new garden yesterday and ruined the taro . . . A woman shouts to a
young child to fetch areca nut from a friend. The men, especially the more
influential ones, sit with an air of importance on mats spread in the center
under the shade of a mango tree. The village councillor sits in the middle of
the mat with his shiny badge proudly pinned to his T-shirt.
    When enough of the crowd has assembled, Moses, whom the villagers
have voted the *komiti* (committee), stands up and with a friendly grin ad-
dresses the crowd that has assembled. In typical fashion, he speaks in euphemisms.

Those of you who have radios heard last night. Some of you don't have radios so you didn't hear. Some of you have radios but no batteries so you also didn't hear. But those of you who heard know. On the radio they said, "*Komitis* are power" [*he* is powerful and what he is about to say is of significance]. I heard it with my own ears. And if you have a radio then you heard it too.

Yesterday someone's pig went into the new Mututavi gardens and rooted up someone else's taro plants. If pigs go into the taro garden, you are to spear them. We made our new gardens and we planted our taro. Never mind the pigs. We don't eat pork every day. We eat taro. If the pig ruins the taro, kill the pig. You heard me. And you heard the radio last night. *Komitis* are power. . .

Before Moses gets any further, someone else, in fading shorts, and with plaited grass bands decorating his upper arms, jumps up and shouts out that the pigs should be inside a fence, and that it is the fault of the owner for not keeping them penned in. He is told to sit down and be quiet. "The *komiti* is talking. Others are to listen now and speak later." Other men get up and raise their voices aggressively. The meeting proceeds for hours. The women continue to knot their nets and bags and talk among themselves. Some voice their opinion when the men call on them to do so. After a few hours, women murmur from the sidelines.

You men talk too much. We heard you. Sit down and be quiet. Look how late it is. We have to go to our gardens. Tomorrow is Saturday, and where is our market food? Too much talk, too many different opinions. We want to leave.

Some people get up and walk off. The meeting slowly disbands. A few men remain, continuing to squabble and shout.

On a more typical day, however, the village seems deserted until the late afternoon when people return from their day's work. Women walk back along paths behind the hamlets with their heads bent down under the weight of firewood or garden food piled in their baskets. Sometimes their husbands accompany them, occasionally carrying heavy timber for the building of a new house. The women unload their burden and dump out the chopped wood to dry in the remaining sun. They take the food into the house to peel, clean, and cook some of it.

Outside her house, Sybil sits attending to a small pot of food she is cooking for her pig. She blows the fire and pokes the sticks further in as they burn down. She is deaf and a figure of fun for the children. As she stoops down to pick up some leaves to cover the pot, her backside bumps up against a tree trunk, and, thinking someone has come up behind her, she jumps around in fright. The children giggle. She pretends to be angry with them, but soon giggles too.

As the sun sinks behind the trees and into the hills, an orange dusk settles over the village. As darkness comes, people light their kerosene lamps and fires. In our house, Alice sweeps the mat covering the pebble floor, lays down the plates, and sets out the steaming food in bowls: a bowl of sweet potato and plantain, another of breadfruit and more plantain, and a small dish with fish and greens. She closes the door and we sit down and quietly eat. Soon Sybil, Alice's mother, dramatically swings open the old metal door on its creaky hinges and enters the lamplit room, which glows in browns of coconut frond walls, sago stem partitions, pandanus mats, and fishnets, baskets, leaf skirts, and firewood hanging from the walls. Sybil complains of the heat in the house and props the door open. Alice tells her to close it because of the pig. "Never mind the pig," Sybil says, "I already fed him." As we sit and eat, the pig pokes his muddy snout over the ledge of the door and grunts into the house. Sybil shouts, "Io! That pig! His character is no good. He's starting up again!" She strategically places herself inside the door, a slab of wood in her hand to smack his snout each time it peers over the doorway. Aidan, Alice's brother, tells her to shut the door. Sybil tosses a sweet potato out the door, and the pig runs after it. When we have finished eating, teenaged Un-uba, a niece visiting from a nearby village, swiftly removes the plates and sets them aside. We carry our mats outside and sit down.

In front of individual houses, small groups of families and friends form around lit fires. Friendly shouts float across the hamlet. "Hey, where are you going? Are you off to look for young men?" Some girls come giggling through the darkness. Two men walk in the shadows of the trees, going in search of areca nut. Some men sit in front of the headman's house, discussing their gardens and the work that must be done the next day. A young man takes his fishing line and goes to meet friends at the river. Someone else shouts from in front of his house that he is out of tobacco. Everyone talks back and forth into the night until the late moon slowly climbs up over the sea. As people retire to their houses, the village becomes peacefully quiet, the only sound being the twang of guitar music that drifts up from the beach where young people have gathered to sing and dance beneath the stars.

2. "Sorry my friend, no food"

In this chapter, I describe Wamirans' perceptions of and attitudes toward food and hunger.[1] As much as possible, I let the Wamirans speak for themselves. I rely heavily on verbatim statements and narratives in order to convey as vividly and accurately as possible the extent to which Wamirans are food oriented. They possess a fantasy life rich in food imagery. Their statements are consciously verbalized and express the essence of what it means to be a Wamiran. My selection of food as the dominant frame of reference and medium of communication is far from arbitrary; it is one that profoundly infuses and directs their life.

Wamirans, when asked, always refer to their land as being plagued by "famine," and to their condition as one of perpetual "hunger." The hunger they suffer, though, is metaphorical and does not refer to a physical condition. In discussing hunger, they do not reach any consensus about the amount of food available in relative terms. Indeed, responses to my queries were ambiguous, perhaps precisely because hunger refers to a complex set of social behaviors and emotions. Wamirans emphasize the fact that human beings need to eat in order to survive and restore their physical strength. But this need, for them, is perceived as greed. They feel that people are innately hungry beings and, thus, in need of external forms of control over their rapacious natures. In keeping with these ideas, they have developed rules of social etiquette. Generosity, for instance, is the most highly valued of virtues. Prescriptions for sharing food are closely articulated and adamantly adhered to. Yet, strategies for concealing food are equally elaborate. Both the public shar-

---

[1] Although several of the food-related customs portrayed here are widespread in Melanesia, the extent to which they totally permeate behavior is atypical when compared to other Melanesian groups. Whenever I traveled to other villages, I realized that, because of their many laws and customs about food, Wamirans had acquired an extensive reputation even among Papua New Guineans for being exceptionally food oriented.

33

ing and private concealing of food are social mechanisms to control what Wamirans perceive as their "hungry" natures.

For a Wamiran, the dynamics of social relationships are expressed, interpreted, and manipulated in terms of food. Metaphorical statements made about the presence or absence of food convey nuances about social cooperation or conflict. Whereas "hunger" implies need, neglect, and antagonism, "enough food" indicates cooperation, sharing, and amity. In either case, the statement is about social relationships and emotional feelings, not about nutritional deprivation.

"Kapore, why did you come?"

Wamirans continually complain of "famine" and lament what they perceive as their impoverished lot in life. This attitude is so pronounced that it was evident to me within the first few days of my arrival in the village. As individuals crossed my path each day, they shook their heads, clucked their tongues in dismay, and muttered *"kapore,"* a phrase that I later learned conveys an extension of human sympathy and commiseration. The reason for this expression of compassion, as I came to understand, was that not only had I, inconceivably, left family and friends far behind, but I had abandoned what they considered to be a land of riches, luxuries, laborless living, and, above all, bountiful food. They could not comprehend that I had made a personal choice to leave the "good life" behind, and that I indeed wanted, and was happy, to be in Wamira. Rather, they continually questioned, *"Kapore,* why did you come? Wamira is a good place. The people are kind, respectful, and friendly. But it is a dry land with too much sun and no water. There is 'no food.' '' For the entire time I lived in the village, Wamirans described their situation as one of "famine" (*gomara*). Indeed, *gomara* appeared to be the normal condition.

Only gradually did I come to understand that other, more subtle, messages were embedded in such statements as "there is no food." For instance, I later learned that "food," to a Wamiran, refers primarily to taro. Taro alone is considered satisfactory food because, in contrast to other comestibles, "it sits inside one's stomach like stone." Thus, the difference between times of abundance (*maura*) and times of scarcity (*gomara*) hinges upon the amount of taro available. There are no degrees of abundance or scarcity; it is an either-or situation. As one man explained, "If there is taro then we have *maura,* if there is no taro then there is *gamora.*"[2]

---

[2] This is similar to the Kapauku conceptualization of " 'hunger' as a state when there are no sweet potatoes in the human stomach" (Pospisil 1963:373). It is also reminiscent of the Hadza's perception of meat. "The Hadza place such emphasis on meat as proper food and treat vegetable foods as so thoroughly unsatisfactory in comparison that they are apt to describe themselves as suffering from hunger when they have less meat than they would like. In fact, there is never any general shortage of food even in time of drought" (Woodburn 1968:52).

In addition, to say that one has "no food" may mean that one has some (whether taro or other food) but does not have enough, or does not want, to give any to others. As one man told me, "When we say there is 'no food,' we mean there is just a little for ourselves but not enough to share with others."[3]

It is also understood that sometimes one does not reveal all that one possesses, but harbors that which is most valuable in order to display it on the proper festive occasion. In the words of one woman, "We say we have nothing or we only have a little when in reality we have some. We say this so that people don't know. But they know. When the times comes, we bring out all we have." This discrepancy between the alleged paucity of daily existence and the display of abundance flaunted on ceremonial occasions was noticed in 1919 by the Resident Magistrate. He commented that "it is only when a reunion or other festivals are expected to eventuate that they [the villagers on the northeast coast] will cultivate anything like a large garden" (*Papua Annual Report* 1919/20:52).

Although they paint portraits of themselves as hard-toiling, hungry individuals (who are also "kind, respectful, and friendly," they never fail to add), Wamirans seem relatively content with their state of "famine." As one Wamiran man related,

In Wamira there is perpetual famine, yet every day is a happy one. If someone says, "Work and then I shall feed you," everyone gathers together to work because they want to get fed. They are forever looking for food but they are happy. That is why people are always down on the beach playing, singing, dancing, and laughing. . . . There is no food in the house to keep them indoors cooking!

In reminiscing about his recent visit to Boianai, where the inhabitants boast of an abundance of food, he showed further condonation of the Wamiran state of poverty when he added,

In Boianai there is lots of food, but the people are not happy. All they do is go to their gardens and cook and eat. They cook in huge pots. They eat the food and get hungry again. But they are not happy. At night it is so quiet that when I visited, I had to turn on my radio to hear a human voice. Imagine, I had to sit outside and talk to my radio!

Wamirans offer an explanation, grounded in mythology, for their life of "famine." However, for a presentation of the myth, the local exegesis of it,

---

[3] These general customs of food reciprocity with their inherent paradoxes are discussed for other societies by Sahlins (1972). For example, among the Ituri Pygmies, when men return from the hunt, "men and women alike but particularly women, may be seen furtively concealing some of their spoils under the leaves of their roofs, or in empty pots nearby" (Turnbull 1965:120). In discussing this conflict among the Bemba of Rhodesia, Richards says, "The young girls at their initiation ceremonies are in fact taught to hide a little food for their husbands at night . . . and I have often seen women take a pot of beer and conceal it in a friend's granary on the reported arrival of some elderly relative" (Richards 1939:202). For the Maori, Firth notes that a favorite proverb is "Broil your rat with its fur on, lest you be discovered by someone" (and have to share it) (Firth 1926:247).

as well as for a more analytical interpretation of their "famine," we must wait until Chapter 4.

"There used to be more food . . . there used to be less food"

Initially taking Wamiran statements about famine and hunger at face value, I tried to elicit oral history about amounts of food in the past. My queries, however, yielded answers that stunned me by their ambiguity. Not only did individual perceptions differ, but often two accounts by the same person contradicted one another. Moreover, the expressions used to describe amounts of food were full of inversions and oppositions.[4]

On the one hand, some individuals described an abundance of food in the past and compared it to a paucity of food today. Nostalgically recalling the days when her father was alive and gardened, one older woman said to me:

If you had been here when he was still living, it would have been very different. You never would have to eat sweet potatoes. Taro, sugarcane, and "pitpit" [*Saccharum edule*] were plentiful. He had so many yams that he stored them inside the house on the shelf in the back. There were so many breadfruit on the trees that they rotted. The whole village stank from the decaying food.

In contrast, another older woman talked of the continual famine she remembered from her youth:

Long ago famine was very bad, but now there is none. People went out in search of food during the day. They only ate licorice root, wild chestnuts, *natuela* [*Cycas* palm fruits], and wild yams [all food generally despised and eaten only in times of famine]. There was so much famine that coconuts never ripened on the trees. People climbed the trees and picked the nuts when they were still green. People were always hungry.

Regardless of which memory people have, they are eager to supply reasons for the increase (or decrease) in amounts of food. Individuals who, like the first woman quoted above, recall a past of abundance often attribute the present lack of food to new gardening tools and techniques. They blame the disappearance of food on the influence of imported technology. In the words of one woman:

Before, people used to turn the soil with wooden digging sticks and it was good. There was lots of taro. Now people also use metal garden forks, and some of them have rust. The taro plants disappear because they smell the rust on the fork.

Similar ideas pertain in the realm of fishing:

People used to catch fish with only their fishnets. There were many fish in the rivers. Today people wear diving goggles and put their heads in the water to look for fish.

[4] Firth, in discussing the Tikopia, observes the same wealth of linguistic devices. "All such situations [food related] are expressed in a body of linguistic material rich in metaphors and circumlocutions" (Firth 1939:38).

When the fish see the goggles, they get scared and swim away. That is why there are no fish today.

One man who noted the current scarcity of taro attributed this to the coming of white people. He sighed:

There used to be lots of taro, but now there is none. When Albert Maclaren and Copland King arrived [1891], there still was lots of taro, but by the time Henry Newton was Bishop [1899], the taro was gone. If all the white people would get up and tell us why there is no taro, we would know, but they don't know why the taro stopped. Now the taro is finished and we are pitiful.

Those who are of the opposite opinion, namely that food supplies are increasing, ironically give the same reasons as those quoted above, but with a different twist. They say that the use of Western implements, such as garden forks, fishing rods, or goggles, makes gardening and fishing easier, which, they say, explains the abundance of food today. Some individuals note that new foods, whether they are introduced crops such as watermelon and tomatoes, or store-bought goods such as rice and tinned meat, arrived more recently and, therefore, there is "more food now."

These opposing viewpoints are also supported by reference to the use of sorcery. On the one hand, Wamirans who perceive that taro is less abundant blame this on the increase of new sorcery brought back from town. For such imported sorcery they possess no countermagic. On the other hand, individuals who see a present abundance of taro attribute this to the fact that there is generally less use of sorcery now than there had been in the past.

Ambiguity and inconsistency reign whenever individuals describe the amounts of food available, perhaps precisely because hunger refers not only to a lack of food. As we shall see later, hunger is not simply a concept that relates to the physical condition of an individual, but rather is a metaphor employed to describe complex emotions, to control human desires, and to order social relations.

"Cockroaches always scurry around, looking for food"

The fact that food is the pivotal point in Wamiran life is emphasized by the way that people, places, and events are defined and described in terms of food. People are judged "good" or "bad" according to whether they share or hoard food. "Good" people are generous; "bad" people are stingy or greedy. In fact, the two most popular negative adjectives for describing people are "stingy" and "greedy." "To be stingy" is *am bou,* which means "to eat in an incorrect fashion" (i.e., not to share one's food). "To be greedy" is *am dewadewa,* which means "to eat a lot." Significantly, these adjectives continue to employ the root *am* ("to eat"), even if they refer to avarice in connection with non-food-related things, such as money, material possessions, or knowledge. Thus, people who are miserly with their money are also "*am dewadewa.*"

Nicknames for people and names of pets also derive their content from ideas about food. For example, Kaku, the nickname of the leader of Ruma-ruma ward, means "cockroach" and was said to be humorous because, in contrast to leaders, "cockroaches always scurry around looking for food." One dog was called "market," a pig "rice bag," another "ice cream," and yet another *voladaga,* which means "a pauper who has neither food nor possessions."

Places and events are also distinguished by food. Noting whether food is present or absent is a common descriptive mechanism and is illustrated by examples of the word *labalababa,* one of the most frequently used qualifiers in the Wedau language. The verb *laba* means "to look for food" when indicating any type of vegetable food other than taro. *Labalababa,* which is derived from the verb, can best be translated as "undefined" or "without meaning." Food that is *labalababa* refers to anything other than taro. One does not give food *labalababa* (for no reason). One does not make a taro garden *labalababa* (without following the prescribed rules). As a visitor approaches, one informs him or her that one is sitting *labalababa* (without any food to give). If one walks to market without carrying any food to sell, one goes *labalababa.* A house without a hearth is a house *labalababa.* And, to go to sleep *labalababa* is to go to bed without eating an evening meal.

In myths and stories, changes in time or place are punctuated by comments about food or eating. For instance, a new day or different location is indicated by phrases such as, "They went to sleep. . . . The following day they got up, cooked some food, ate, and went to the garden . . ." Or, a sense of geography is conveyed by reference to acts of eating. It is common, in relating a myth, to say "When he got to such and such a place, he sat down and ate . . ." This narrative style is typical for Wamira, in general, where people, places, and events are identified in terms of food.

"Our bodies are like fires"

Wamirans are acutely aware of the physical necessity of food for a person's survival and often cite the following statement. "Our bodies are like fires that cannot burn without fuel. If we do not eat, we have no energy to work. If we work, we immediately have to replenish our strength by nourishing our bodies with food." The expression used when eating after working is "to revive" the person (*vilawana*). It is extended to include items such as tobacco which, like food, are "eaten."

This idiom about physical need is used to justify social behavior, especially as it relates to work habits, even if from an outsider's point of view the eating seems unnecessary and the work seems economically "unproductive." For example, the residents of one hamlet decided to organize themselves into a work group. They planned to make sun-dried copra and, by selling it, produce income with which they would purchase metal drums and construct ovens to produce later the more lucrative smoke-dried copra. Each day, while half the members of the group cracked open coconuts, the other half went to the store to buy (on credit) rice, tinned fish, sugar, and tea to feed the workers. When they received their earnings for the bags of sun-dried copra, they paid their debts at the store and "ate" the remainder of the money; i.e., they converted it into food to reimburse themselves for their work. Two years passed in this fashion as the people of the hamlet remained without sufficient capital to buy their drums and build their smokehouse. Although they expressed great concern as to why they were not accumulating any capital, they knew of no other way to conduct their business. For them, sufficient "profit" lay in the social and cooperative aspects of gathering communally to work and restore their physical energy.

Hunger, to a Wamiran, indicates need, neglect, and antagonism. To care for someone is synonymous with feeding them; to feed them indicates that one cares for them. In explaining his concern for his older mother, a man once commented to me, "Of course, I love her. If I didn't she would be hungry all the time." Because hunger is viewed as an outcome and expression of the unwillingness to invest in social relationships, there is shame in asking for food. One never asks for food directly but makes statements such as "I caught a lizard" (*umara a vunui*), meaning the pickings are slim. The standard response is "the bivalve used for scraping taro is wasting away" (*kepo kiraiai*), meaning there is no food in the house. Not yet knowing the meanings or nuances of such circumlocutions, I made several mistakes in the beginning of my fieldwork. One old woman occasionally came to me asking for malaria pills for her headache, which I dutifully dispensed. After several months, Alice overheard the transaction and, once the woman left, explained that what she really wanted, but was too ashamed to ask for directly, was food.

In sum, Wamirans formulate their ideas about human needs specifically in terms of food and hunger. Hunger, which is perceived more as an emotion than as a physical state, indicates need, neglect, and antagonism. "Enough food" suggests cooperation, sharing, and amity.

"What meat did he eat that made him sick?"

Need, in Wamira, is perceived as greed. Fears of greed are so great that numerous mechanisms exist to control gluttony and avarice. One response to the perceived problem is an attempt to control human appetite. The ability to control one's own appetite is a highly respected virtue. To be able to control the appetite of other people is the talent only of respected leaders who, for instance, may place secret hunger suppression magic in food at feasts they sponsor.[5]

Ravenous appetite, or the lack of control over it, is often believed to be the cause of personal misfortune. Illness may be attributed to overindulgence, especially of meat. For example, the back pain of an old woman was ascribed to her sojourn with kin in a nearby village where there was "lots of food" and where she "ate too much." In another case, when a young man spontaneously developed two large boils on his leg, the general response was, "What meat did he eat that made him sick?" Or, whenever Alice was sick, I was reprimanded by others that I "had given her too much meat!"

Another manifestation of greed, the failure to share food, is a vice thought to have equally drastic consequences for the stingy person. Fortunately for those who fail to share food, the outcome of their unsociable actions can be retracted if they reverse their behavior. By giving food to the person one willfully neglected, one can regain one's normal health. For example, a young woman had been to her garden to dig up taro for her family. Although an older woman caught a glimpse of her placing the taro into her garden basket, the young woman failed to give any to the onlooker. That night the young woman's knee swelled painfully, and by the next day she was unable to walk. Suspecting the cause of her discomfort to be due to a bewitching by the jealous onlooker, the young woman presented the onlooker with some of the taro. According to the young woman, the pain in her knee disappeared immediately.

Situations where uncontrolled hunger, greed, and stinginess result in mishap are, I feel, more imagined than real, as is evident in the following case. Alice's mother, Sybil, had been deaf since childhood. She related the cause of her deafness to me in the following manner. When she was a child, she lived with a woman called Kakamo in order to help her around the house. One day Sybil arrived home from school feeling hungry. When Kakamo told her to go wash the pots in the creek, she refused, saying she was too weak from hunger. Kakamo shouted at her, saying there was no food in the house. When she still refused to wash the pots, Kakamo took a handful of pebbles and threw them at her back. When Sybil went to sleep that night Kakamo bewitched her and made her deaf. Alice, as well as Sybil's friends, explained to me that the real reason for Sybil's deafness was that her friends put pebbles into her ears. Which of the two accounts is accurate seems immaterial. The significant fact remains that, despite evidence to the contrary, Sybil is convinced that her deafness is a result of having been bewitched as a response to her greed and her complaints of hunger.

Numerous myths and stories reflect precisely this theme of the fear of greed

---

[5] See Young (1971:175–7) for a comparison with Goodenough Island.

and gluttony and a need for control over these human vices. One myth relates how two women were cooking green leaves (*gova*). One of the women, by the name of Marakwadiveta, sent the other, Maradiudiva, to fetch saltwater, and in her short absence devoured the greens. When Maradiudiva returned with the saltwater, she became angry with Marakwadiveta, turned herself into stone, and drowned herself in the sea. One folktale tells of two small boys who were angry because each day their mother ate up their taro and fed them only the discarded skin instead of the inner corm. Indignant, they turned themselves into birds and flew away. Yet another describes the wrath of a young girl when, day after day, her parents ate her ginger root and then fabricated tales of relatives who came and consumed it. Dejected, the girl threw herself into the sea and was dismembered by a crocodile. When I once remarked on the recurring theme of one person's deprivation due to another's gluttony, a woman explained to me, "Suspicion that others are greedy and are not sharing their food is what stories are about because that is what our life is about."

Greed appears to be an inescapable force; its locus is omnipresent. Wamirans fear not only the greed that lurks within themselves, but also that which exists within their fellow human beings, even, as can be seen from the examples of the myths and stories, one's closest kin.

"We are not like white people, we share our food"

Proper social behavior is dictated by verbalized rules which balance ideas about need with fears of greed. In fact, one may accurately say that Wamiran social etiquette centers on, and can be translated into, rules about sharing food.

Generosity is accorded the highest social value; social sanctions for sharing food are great. Any food that appears in public must be shared with as many people as see it. The Wamiran assumption is that the onlooker feels hungry and, if not given any food, would feel slighted and jealous. As a woman explained to me, "We are not like white people, we share our food. If we are eating and someone sees us, we have to offer the food to that person." A person may remain hungry all day because "too many people came into the house," meaning the food was left hidden because the person did not want (or have enough) to give any to the visitors.

This emphasis on sharing was brought to my attention within the first week of my arrival in the village.[6] Carrying a basket of food and not yet knowing the customs, I unintentionally walked in front of a man sitting outside his house. Upon arriving home, I was immediately asked, "What will you give

---

[6] Schieffelin (1976:46–52) notes that the basic theme in Kaluli relationships is expressed by the giving and sharing of food.

him now?" I was reprimanded for not having avoided his house to prevent him from seeing me with the food. Because I ignorantly strode right by him, I had to return and share the contents of the basket with him. "Our life is like that" was the explanation.

The most impolite behavior possible is to intrude on someone who is getting food, cooking, or worst of all, eating, for those observed immediately must surrender some of the food. A person never knocks on the door of a house without first stopping and listening for sounds of what is going on inside. The clinking of pots and dishes or the scraping of spoons are all signs for the would-be visitor to disappear again. When, for no apparent reason, a person arrives at someone's house, the household members later gossip, "I don't know why he came. Maybe he was hungry" or "I gave her food, but she said she would take it with her. Maybe her children were hungry." Once, when a young man arrived at our house, walked right in, and sat down, the response upon his leaving was,

What is wrong with him? He has no manners. He has no brain. He walked right in and sat down in the middle of the house. He should know to sit in the doorway. He sat in the middle and ate all the pieces of pineapple. He should have taken only one piece and then said he had enough.

Not only must public food be shared, but it must be divided equally. Upon visiting Wamira, a missionary, pleased with what she interpreted as indigenous good will, noted this concern with equitable distribution:

Another aspect of their feasting rather surprised me. We go to a feast generally to consume as much as we possibly can, whilst they spend most of their time in doling out and dividing the food into equal parts onto leaves, tin plates, or into coconut cups. . . . Probably this is more Biblical than our method. (Somerville 1976:18)

Now the Melanesian pidgin expression *wanwan* (to give equally to each), is used in referring to this method of food distribution. For example, if six people are present and six areca nuts are available, they are shared out *wanwan*, meaning that each person receives one nut. On one occasion this method of allotment was used for liquor, where one bottle of gin was equitably shared among some twenty to thirty men at a party. There was one shot glass, and, one at a time, each man was handed the filled glass to empty before picking up his guitar or preparing himself for singing. They downed their liquor *wanwan*, amidst joking about the resemblance of the situation to the parceling of medicine at the hospital. Even a small group of children on their own, when confronted with a piece of fruit or a biscuit, say, "There are many of us, let's *wanwan* it."

"We are only eating pigs' food tonight"

As seen above, rules for sharing food are meticulously cited by individuals. The other, more private, reality reveals strategies for deception and, naturally, is muted. Although less flaunted than rules for sharing food, strategies for hiding food are equally elaborate. For example, people never reveal that they are going to their garden. Wearing a traditional shredded-leaf skirt that must be worn in the taro garden, and carrying a garden basket slung from her head, a woman says to those she encounters that she is "just going for a walk." One also never mentions what is in one's garden. If talking about taro, one refers to it as "sweet potato" or "tapioca," the two most despised foods. The word *awanaina* is an expression that means to do something in a devious way, not exposing it for others to see. (*Awanaina* is also the name of the linguistic device people use when they say "tapioca" and really mean "taro," i.e., a euphemism used to obscure.) Before leaving the garden, a woman goes to great lengths to cover the sight of food in her basket with large banana leaves. Taro, if for household consumption, is transported surreptitiously either under the cover of banana leaves or in the darkness of night. "We do this because if others see what we have, we have to give them some . . ."

Noncommunal fishing is also done in a clandestine manner and is said to be "lucky." "If you tell anyone where you are going, you will arrive home with nothing. If you sneak out quietly and no one knows, then you will catch fish and come home with many." The "luck" was explained to me in the following manner: "We don't tell anyone when we go fishing because if we do, then we have to share the fish we catch with those who know."

It is not uncommon for someone to have a system of bags within bags to conceal her or his most prized possessions. When someone once asked an old woman for areca nut, she said she had none, as she opened her bag and spilled the contents to "prove" it. Out rattled the mortar and pestle for mashing her areca nut, her empty lime tin, her areca grater, and what looked like an old piece of rag – an unsuspecting-looking, crunched-up bag inside of which was the nut the other person wanted.[7]

Should a knock be heard at the door while a family is eating inside their house, a common reflex is to open the door with one hand as one quickly pushes the bowl of taro (or tin of meat, dish of green leaves, etc.) behind one's back or behind the house partition with the other hand. One then points to the tapioca and exclaims, "We are only eating pigs' food tonight." If meat or fish is being eaten, the person munching on the meat is advised, "Don't throw the bones out the door, or the dogs and pigs will gather and everyone will know we are eating meat."

The practice of concealing food also pertains to food bought from the store. If a bag of sugar is purchased, only a small portion of it is placed into a sugar container; the remainder is concealed somewhere in the back of the house.

---

[7] This is similar to what Malinowski observed in the Trobriand Islands. "In the Eastern end of New Guinea a type of large basket, with three layers, manufactured in the Trobriands, was especially popular among people of consequence, because one could hide away one's small treasures in the lower compartments" (Malinowski 1922:97).

Each day, as the sugar in the container is used up, it is replenished with another small amount. When, early in my stay, I remarked on what seemed to me unnecessary maneuvering in replenishing the stock, I was told, "We don't put much in the container in front so that when someone comes to ask for sugar, we show them the container and say, 'Sorry my friend, we have none.' " When I once gave a man a spoonful of powdered milk, he requested for his coffee, I was adamantly instructed, "If anyone comes and asks, 'Do you have any milk?' you have to say, 'No, the milk is finished.' That is how we do it."

Although my descriptions may seem to indicate that people often deceive one another, in fact, no Wamiran secrets have been revealed. Indeed, the hiding and hoarding of food are lucidly patent and socially sanctioned. Everyone knows what lurks under the banana leaves that cover the garden basket, or behind the partition in the house. The symbolic statement is understood by all to be "we have some, but do not have enough [or do not want] to give you any."

Ideals of generosity, rules about hiding food, and statements about hunger, are all mechanisms to control the fear of greed. Not only do Wamirans say "Sorry, my friend, we have no food" each time anyone arrives at the door, but they also explain that if they were to give food, they would trigger an avalanche of uncontrollable lusts and desires. Thus I was instructed, "Don't give people too much or they will be back for more." Only after I had lived in Wamira for many months, did individuals explain to me that the anxiety was not really about a scarcity of food. One older man pulled me aside and explained, "We are really afraid of too much food! Were we to have even a little more, there would be no controlling the desire and greed that would set in among us and rip us apart!" At that point I began to probe deeper into the meanings they ascribed to "hunger" and "famine."

3. "Famine" reconsidered

One of the principal points of this book is that the Wamirans' concept of "famine" is symbolic and cultural, and is not supported by an analysis of their ecological situation. Thus, before moving to a symbolic analysis, in this chapter, I present and analyze a variety of ecological data to demonstrate that the "famine" they depict and deplore is not a verifiable expression of nutritional deprivation. With this purpose, I am concerned more with a general understanding of their ecology rather than with a precise analysis of energy expenditure and biotic relationships.

The data I gathered on seasonal availability of food, time allotted to food procurement, soil content, crop yield, caloric and nutritional value of food consumed, and the nutritional status of Wamirans, all suggest that the state of "famine" Wamirans lament does not refer to nutritional deprivation. Occurrences of drought and food scarcity over the past century, however, suggest that Wamirans do live in a capricious environment. Although their environment generally offers them enough food, it sporadically and temporarily presents them with an insufficient supply.

When confronted with a generally sufficient but uncontrollable and unreliable environment, the human need for a psychological coping mechanism is perhaps as great as the need for a purely physical strategy. For Wamirans, an ideology of "famine" seems to provide just such a mechanism for dealing with the anxiety, ambivalence, and insecurity that fickle surroundings generate. I feel that their perception and description of their environmental setting as one of "no food," rather than being an accurate physical portrayal, provides them with a mode of long-term psychological adaptation to an erratic environment.

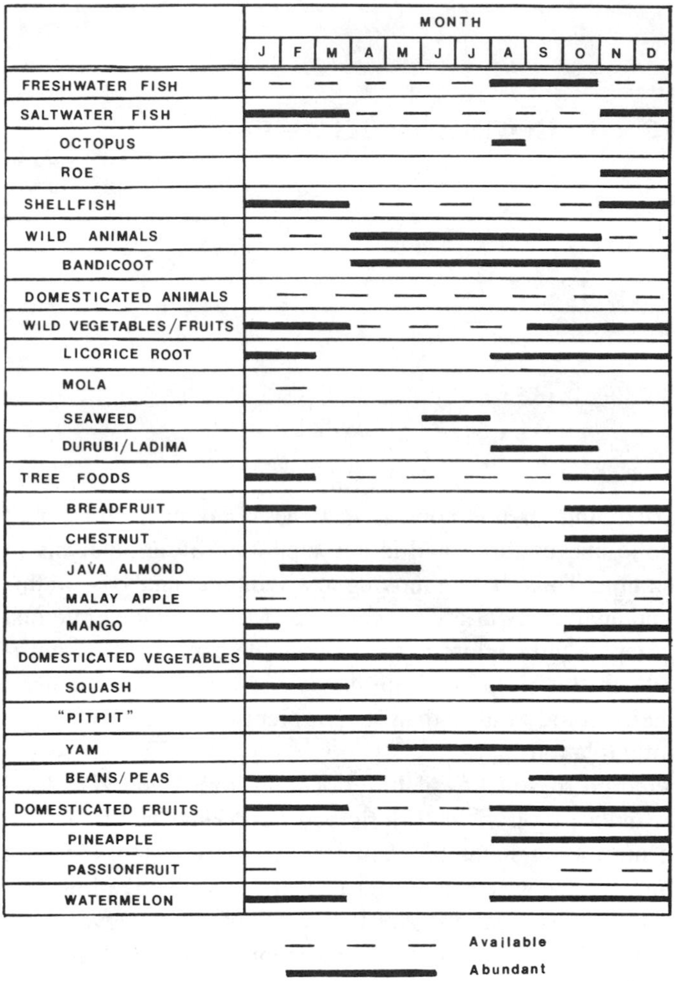

	MONTH											
	J	F	M	A	M	J	J	A	S	O	N	D
FRESHWATER FISH												
SALTWATER FISH												
OCTOPUS												
ROE												
SHELLFISH												
WILD ANIMALS												
BANDICOOT												
DOMESTICATED ANIMALS												
WILD VEGETABLES/FRUITS												
LICORICE ROOT												
MOLA												
SEAWEED												
DURUBI/LADIMA												
TREE FOODS												
BREADFRUIT												
CHESTNUT												
JAVA ALMOND												
MALAY APPLE												
MANGO												
DOMESTICATED VEGETABLES												
SQUASH												
"PITPIT"												
YAM												
BEANS/PEAS												
DOMESTICATED FRUITS												
PINEAPPLE												
PASSIONFRUIT												
WATERMELON												

— — — Available
▬▬▬▬▬ Abundant

Figure 5. Relative seasonal availability of foods

Available food

Wamirans divide their food world into two categories: *tia* (animal foods) and *lam* (vegetable foods), a distinction which I follow below in describing the seasonal patterns of their food supply and the type of labor necessary to secure it. A complete list of foods eaten, together with their local names as well as their zoological or botanical names, is presented in Appendix B. Although seasonal differences exist in the food supply, there is no annual "lean" time. As Figure 5 indicates, at any time during the year a varied diet is always available.

3. Women fishing in the river

The category of *tia*, or animal food, which constitutes about three percent of the total calories consumed, has fish as its most stable element. Over twenty types of freshwater fish are named, most of which are inconsiderable in size. These small fish seem disproportionate to the amount of excitement that accompanies the task of catching them. River fishing is a lively communal activity, and every woman in the village usually participates. The best time for river fishing is during the dry season. Toward the end of it, in August, women fish almost daily. To do so, they use nets that are twined and knotted from plant fiber and suspended on curved branch frames. Before fishing, women dam the river by placing a wattle of stones and mud across the river at a point where it forks or divides around an island. After thus diverting the water into one of the channels, they concentrate their efforts in the shallower channel, overturning rocks on the river floor as they walk from the mouth of the river upstream. The women form a continuous line across the river from one bank to the other (see Plate 3). As each woman scoops up the fish in her net, she tosses her catch, according to customs of sharing food, into the basket which dangles from the hip of a friend. Thus, when a woman arrives home with her basket of fish, the majority of her fish have been caught by other women.

Now and then, women also fish with a hook and line from the beach at night. As mentioned in the previous chapter, this solitary type of angling is considered to hinge on "luck." If anyone else knows that a person is thus engaged, it is believed that the fish will not bite. One's luck is considered at its best when the moon is "dead," and the person fishing is shrouded by the pitch black of night.

Men fish mainly from the sea and do so all year round. Most male fishing techniques, other than the "lucky" ones, are preceded by the observance of food taboos and are accompanied by magic. To fish, men use a variety of techniques. Most often, they hold a hook and line from the beach or from an outrigger canoe. Occasionally, they sink a seine net for a day or two before hauling it in. They also use pronged fishing spears. One man inherited a unique fishing skill that consisted of lowering a large clam shell secured in a netted bag into the sea from the side of his canoe. He placed bespelled bait inside the clam shell and, upon raising it, inevitably found it swarming with fish.

Over fifty types of saltwater fish are named, including sardine, flying fish, sunfish, mangrove jack, perch, sweetlip, whitebait, cod, striped butterfish, dart, whiting, shark, and turtle, which Wamirans also classify as a fish. Roes from flying fish, in season only from the end of October to December, are a savory delight and are gathered by women when the roes float ashore. Eel is a favorite and, although eaten only by men, is hunted and speared by both sexes. Eel are of both the freshwater and saltwater varieties. Included in the latter category is octopus, a special delicacy which is washed ashore in August.

Shellfish, such as shrimp, prawn, crab, crayfish, snails, and clams, are available throughout the year, and are most abundant during the wet season. Both freshwater and saltwater shellfish are caught by women who fish individually or in small groups.

Wild animals, which used to be caught by communal fire drives, trapping, and spearing, are now primarily hunted by shotgun. Hunting is dwindling in importance as animals are "not as numerous as they used to be." Hunting is still always accompanied by magic. Some of the animals hunted are wild pig, wallaby, bandicoot (during the dry season only), and nontotemic birds. Before contact with Europeans and the cessation of warfare, human flesh was also a primary source of meat. Certain snakes, when encountered accidentally and killed, are wrapped around a pole and brought back to the village as food. Large mango ants are considered a delicacy and are eaten alive together with seaweed, which is placed at the base of a mango tree to attract the ants. Wamirans relish the prickly feeling in their throats as the ants bite and sting when they are swallowed.

The main domesticated animals in Wamira are pigs, of which there are about two hundred. The people of Damaladona do not keep pigs because their gardens are close to the village and unprotected against the marauding animals (timber for the construction of adequate pig-proof fences is scarce). The people of Rumaruma, whose gardens lie farther afield, raise pigs. Pigs are fed the peelings from food and the leftover coconut meat after the cream has been squeezed from it. Young male pigs are castrated to guarantee their hardy growth. Thus, domesticated sows mate with feral boars. A small number of families keep chickens. The eggs are usually taken to market, and the bird itself is eaten only on festive occasions. Dogs and a few cats, which are not eaten, are owned and left to scavenge on their own. Dogs were originally kept by Wamirans to be traded as food to inland and island people. Cats are prized because they kill rats that raid household food baskets at night.

Two government cattle projects have been established in Wamira since the early 1970s. In each case, the government lends a number of cattle to an individual in exchange for the use of his land and labor in caring for the livestock. For each *bulamakau* the Wamiran slaughters and sells (usually to the mission for church festivities), part of his income goes to the government to repay the loan, and the remainder is kept as personal profit.

Lam, or vegetable foods, make up about ninety-seven percent of the total calories in the Wamirans' diet. There are numerous undomesticated vegetable foods that may be foraged by anyone who so desires. Among them are many varieties of wild yam, arrowroot, pandanus fruit, *durubi* (a red, tart, cherry-like fruit), licorice root, *Cycas* palm fruit, *mola* (small arboreal seeds), wild chestnuts, and numerous varieties of green leaves and seaweed. Most of these are seasonal and constitute an insignificant portion of the diet. Wild yams, licorice root, *Cycas* palm fruit, *mola,* and wild chestnuts are gathered only in times of dire need; some of these famine foods are toxic unless processed in special ways. For example, *Cycas* palm fruit is toxic when raw and must be soaked in water for several days before it can be pounded into flour, made into cakes, and cooked. *Mola* require husking and boiling for many hours before they can be eaten. The raw plant or fruit of the wild chestnut, if brought in contact with a person's skin, causes a severe skin rash.

A category that is intermediate between wild and cultivated plant foods consists of numerous large leafy trees within the village. As Wamirans are quick to point out, these are not just ordinary trees, but are personally owned and produce foods that constitute an important part of the diet. Not only does the coconut palm provide food and drink; its leaves provide house walls, skirts, mats, and baskets; the husks from its nuts are fuel for fires; the shells from the nuts are used as drinking cups; and coconut cream squeezed from the grated meat is used to anoint one's body. It is also a daily, and in Wamiran eyes mandatory, condiment for all foods. Another tree is the breadfruit. When in season from November to February, breadfruit constitutes about thirty to forty percent of the vegetable diet. Other seasonal food-bearing trees in the village, but of less dietary significance, are the chestnut (*Inocarpus fagiferus*) which produces food from October to December, the Java almond (*Terminalia catappa*) from February to May, the Malay apple (*Eugenia megacarpa*) from December to February, and the mango (*Mangifera indica*) from October to January. Trees of these last four species are often so old that the individuals who planted or owned them have passed away and contemporary usage rights extend to all hamlet members, or to anyone who comes along and picks the fallen fruit or nut from the ground. Only a member of the original owner's immediate family may climb the tree to gather fruit still clinging to the branches.

All other fruit and vegetable crops are cultivated in one of two types of family gardens: banana gardens (*peipei*) or taro gardens (*wapu*). The most common garden foods include banana (*Musa sapientum*) or plantain (*Musa paradisiaca*), of which Wamirans distinguish about twenty varieties, and taro (*Colocasia esculenta*), the more than sixty types of which Wamirans distinguish by the color of the stalk. Banana, plantain, and taro are planted continuously without seasonal differences in growth or yield. Many other vegetable crops also grow year round, among them the following: Giant taro (*Alocasia macrorrhiza*) is planted only rarely, and then it is placed among the coral near the beach or in a swampy area alongside the river. In the gardens one finds wild taro, also called elephant yam (*Amorphophallus campanulatus*), sweet potato (*Ipomoea batatas*), and tapioca (*Manihot esculenta*). Many varieties of yam are in season from May to September. The most common are the greater yam (*Dioscorea alata*) and the lesser yam (*Dioscorea esculenta*). Eight kinds of "pitpit" (*Saccharum edule*) and more than twenty varieties of sugarcane are in season from February to May. Squash, available from August to March, corn, papaya, and numerous varieties of beans, peas, and greens are also planted. Other foods, such as oranges, lemons, limes, pineapple, watermelon, tomatoes, scallions, and peanuts have been introduced and are grown now as well.

Imported foods are purchased from local trade stores with increasing enthusiasm whenever money is available from sales in the market or from relatives in town. These foods are seen less as a means of supplementing the diet nutritionally than as a way of augmenting the prestige of the consumer. In their contemporary desire to emulate the Western world, Papua New Guineans strive to attain whatever Western goods reach their stores, regardless of the quality. For example, it is not uncommon for a Wamiran to sell freshly caught fish to a European in the market and to use the earnings to buy a tin of Japanese imported fish in the store. For a villager, the tin carries prestigious value that far exceeds its taste or nutritional value.[1] The most commonly bought foods are rice, tinned fish, tinned meat, tea, sugar, biscuits (and to-

[1] The increasing incidences of obesity, malnutrition, and metabolic diseases among Pacific Islanders as a direct result of changing diets and life-styles are well documented (Coyne 1981; Parkinson 1982; Thaman 1982).

bacco). A weekly tabulation of trade store purchases among forty-seven households is presented in Appendix C.

Stimulants and intoxicants enjoyed by Wamirans are tobacco (introduced by the first missionaries in 1891), beer (introduced more recently and now brewed in Papua New Guinea), and their traditional areca nut. After meals, Wamirans carefully shred trade store sticks of tobacco and roll the shavings in strips of newspaper. Today, more and more people use store-bought cigarettes. Areca nut (*Areca cathecu*) is chewed together with pepper catkins, leaf, or stem (*Piper betle*) and lime obtained from the burning of clam shells. Areca palms are purposely planted and are extremely scarce and cherished. Wamirans veil young nuts with plaited coconut fronds to make it clear to others that the nuts are not to be stolen. Pepper plants are likewise rare. When asked as to why they do not plant more areca palms or pepper plants, a Wamiran's typical response is, "If we planted them, the fruits would be stolen." Most of the areca nuts and pepper that Wamirans chew are bought from the mountain people at the local market.

There are seasonal fluctuations in the availability of traditional food supplies. Because seasonality varies among the foods, the result is general sufficiency and variety throughout the year. The labor necessary to secure or produce the food, although time consuming, is engaged in willingly. Moreover, as I now show, the amount of work involved is not unusually great.

Labor input

The time devoted to subsistence practices indicates that Wamirans spend amounts of time comparable to other horticulturalists in similar settings. For purposes of comparison with other societies, my calculations of time allotted to producing food are broken down into all types of subsistence activities (horticultural activities, domesticating pigs, fishing, climbing food trees, gathering wild foods, and going to the market and the trade store) and horticultural activities only (work on the irrigation canals, garden cultivation, harvest, and walking to and from the garden). I gathered data in two complementary ways: from nine households (a total of eight male and nine female adults) for two weeks, as well as from one household over a two-month period. Time was measured during both the wet and dry seasons.

Figure 6 illustrates daily fluctuations in time spent on all types of subsistence activities for one man and one woman over a two-week period. The average daily amount of time spent on subsistence activities for an adult man is 3.8 hours (3.1 of which are on horticultural activities) and for a woman 3.5 hours (3.0 of which are on horticultural activities). For the remainder of the day, several hours are spent visiting friends, where Wamirans sit and talk

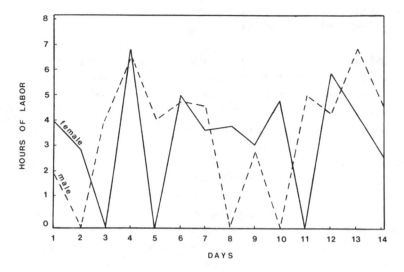

Figure 6. Hours spent on subsistence activities

about village matters and events. Time is also spent in gathering the necessary materials for, and making such items as, shredded-leaf skirts, string bags, baskets, and sleeping mats. Washing pots and clothes, bathing in the river, cleaning the village, collecting firewood, and cooking, as well as resting and sleeping during the hot noon hours, occupy the rest of the time.

In general, Wamirans spend the same amount of time on horticultural activities as other horticulturalists in tropical environments for whom comparable data are available. As Table 2 indicates, the figures I gathered for horticultural work (3.1 hours per day for men, 3.0 hours per day for women) fall within the range recorded for other groups (2.0–3.3). Thus, we can conclude that the Wamirans' perception of famine is not accompanied by an increase in labor.

Soil content and crop yield

I took eight soil samples from various gardens in Wamira (one in 1976 and seven in 1982), the results of which appear in Appendix D. Daniel Vasey, an anthropologist specializing in tropical agriculture, who looked at the results from the 1982 soil analysis, commented that they were all "fairly fertile" (Daniel Vasey, personal communication, 1983). Andrew Wood, a soil-scientist-geographer, commented in the following way on the analysis of the sample I took in 1976:

In general the soil is quite a fertile one with a suitable pH and adequate nitrogen content for taro growth. Cation exchange capacity is high and the soil appears to be

Table 2. *Time spent on horticultural activities*

GROUP	HRS/DAY	REFERENCE
WAMIRA	3.1 (male) 3.0 (female)	
BOMAGAI-ANGOIANG (New Guinea Highlands)	3.2	Clarke (1971:173)
RAIAPU ENGA (New Guinea Highlands)	3.0	Waddell (1972:88-97)
KAPAUKU (Irian Jaya)	3.2	Pospisil (1963:422)
IBAN (Borneo)	3.0	Freeman(1955:89-90,92)
HANUNÓO (Philippines)	3.3	Conklin (1957:150)
KUIKURU (Brazil)	2.0	Carneiro (1961:49)

able to retain nutrients (particularly calcium and magnesium). Potassium seems rather low and this could be limiting, though it could be increased by the addition of wood ash. Available phosphorus is also fairly low though I think potassium is more critical for taro growth than phosphorus. (Andrew Wood, personal communication, 1979)

Thus, soil does not appear to be a limiting factor in the cultivation of taro.

Indeed, as my calculations indicate, the average crop yield in Wamiran taro gardens is comparable with that from other areas in Oceania. An irrigated taro garden in Wamira produced an average of 17.9 metric tons per hectare per year, and a taro garden irrigated by the aqueduct on the open plain yielded 23.2 metric tons per hectare per year. Spriggs gives comparative figures, one of which is an average of 19.4 metric tons per hectare per year for gardens in

Lakeba, Fiji, where the irrigation system is most similar to that of the Wamirans (Spriggs 1984:129). My ability to gather data on yields from taro gardens was slightly hampered by the Wamirans' need for secrecy about garden activities and by their suspicions about my calculating and revealing information about yields. As a result, my figures are based upon the yields from only one family's taro garden which, however, is representative of Wamiran gardens in general.

Food consumption

Appendix E presents a table of all major foods eaten with their caloric and nutritional values. Appendix F lists average daily food consumption for a male and a female for both the dry and wet seasons. These data are based on records kept for one family over a two-month period. Because figures of food intake are not comfortably revealed by Wamirans, I gathered my data only from the family with which I lived. They may have eaten slightly more than a "typical" family because I supplemented their diet somewhat by receiving garden produce from other Wamirans in exchange for tobacco. According to my calculations of food consumption, the average daily caloric intake for an adult Wamiran male is 3,440 and for an adult female is 2,831. According to established figures (Food and Agriculture Organization of the United Nations 1957; Wilson, Fisher, and Fuqua 1965:14–15), this level of caloric intake is adequate for people of Wamiran stature.[2] The figures exceed suggested caloric allowances for New Guinea populations, which are 2,000–2,500 calories per day for adult men and 1,600–2,600 for adult women (see Hipsley and Clements 1947:134). They are comparable to, or greater than, caloric intake reported from other areas of New Guinea (Clarke 1971:178; Hipsley and Kirk 1965:79, 90; Rappaport 1968:75; and Salisbury 1962:80–1).

The average daily protein intake is 44 grams. This figure is higher than the protein allowance of 33–7 recommended by the Food and Agriculture Organization of the United Nations (1964) or that of 40 grams suggested by Hipsley and Clements (1947:134). It appears average for Papua New Guinea (see Clarke 1971:178 and Rappaport 1968:75).

Nutritional status

The general health of Wamirans seems adequate on the basis of the results of a nutritional survey I conducted with children in 1981 as well as on my daily observation of the adults' physical energy and mental alertness. The survey

[2] In Wamira, average male height is 1.58 meters (5 feet, 2 inches), and average male weight is 49 kilograms (109 pounds). Average female height is 1.53 meters (5 feet), and average female weight is 44 kilograms (98 pounds). These figures are based on a survey of 26 males between the ages of 16 and 74, and 43 females between the ages of 14 and 75.

Table 3. *Nutritional status according to weight for age*

WEIGHT FOR AGE	NUMBER OF CHILDREN	PERCENT OF TOTAL
OVER 100%	2	5.1
90 – 100%	5	12.8
80 – 89%	14	35.9
70 – 79%	17	43.6
60 – 69%	1	2.6
TOTAL	39	100

Table 4. *Nutritional status according to weight for height and height for age*

		WEIGHT FOR HEIGHT	
		ABOVE 80%	BELOW 80%
HEIGHT FOR AGE	ABOVE 90%	NORMAL 31 (79.5%)	WASTED 2 (5.1%)
	BELOW 90%	STUNTED 6 (15.4%)	WASTED AND STUNTED 0 (0%)

was carried out on thirty-nine of the forty Wamiran children (one child failed to attend) under the age of five. The results are presented in Tables 3 and 4.

According to calculations of weight for age, only one child was below the seventy percent weight level and none was below sixty percent, the standard cutoff for defining malnutrition. Thus, there was no extremely low weight or marasmus. On the basis of the Waterlow classification, which takes height into account and is therefore more accurate, two children, both of whom had recently been sick, were wasted (too thin for their height, indicating recent malnutrition) and six were stunted (too short for their weight, indicating nutritional dwarfism), but none was wasted and stunted, which would have been evidence of severe chronic malnutrition. In a letter analyzing the results, Manming Hung, the provincial nutritionist at the time, commented that "the nutritional status of the Wamira village children under five can be said to be relatively fair" (Manming Hung, personal communication, 1981).

The village is not free from diseases common to lowland Papua New Guinea. According to data from St. Barnabas Hospital at Dogura, the most common disease treated is malaria. Following malaria, the other most commonly occurring illnesses are respiratory infections and infected wounds. Of the twelve

medical problems listed, malnourishment was twelfth in order of prevalence
(Dogura Hospital Records 1978).

Drought and famine

Thus far we have seen that the Wamiran environment provides relatively fertile soils, which do not require unusually high labor input, and which produce
sufficient crop yields. The villagers, on the whole, enjoy an adequate and
varied supply of food and a fair nutritional level. As described in Chapter 1,
however, the environment is marked by seasonal extremes and, more significantly, by annual fluctuations.

References to drought and famine are scattered throughout the written records. Newton makes one brief reference to a famine in the Taupota area,
twenty kilometers east of Wamira, which occurred prior to the time when
records were kept (Newton 1914:165). The first recorded account of food
scarcity is found in 1895 when the Resident Magistrate reported that the year
was "an exceptionally dry one" (*British New Guinea Annual Report* 1895/96:
Appendix O) and in 1896 when there was a "dearth of food along the coast
of the mainland" (*British New Guinea Annual Report* 1896/97:49). Three
years later, in 1899, upon visiting Boianai, thirty kilometers west of Wamira,
the Resident Magistrate described that

the people are suffering greatly here from scarcity of food consequent upon a severe
drought. Mr. Buchanan (a new lay missionary) informed me that the old men say
they recollect two such occurrences before, but on these occasions they were able to
eke out a scanty subsistence by eating their neighbors, whereas now they feel the
pinch with increasing severity. (*British New Guinea Annual Report* 1899/1900:16)

The following year, however, it was reported that "the natives had a fairly
plentiful supply of food all along this coast excepting at Taupota village"
(*British New Guinea Annual Report* 1900/1901:71). In 1902, we find that
there was a "very severe" drought during which "the natives were, in many
instances, reduced to semi-starvation owing to the complete failure of the
crops" and that rations of rice were issued in some parts (*British New Guinea
Annual Report* 1902/03:23). Again, in 1911, drought "affected all the Division, but came hardest on the people inhabiting the rather dry belt on the
northeast coast" (*Papua Annual Report* 1911/12:112).

The effect of the drought has been keenly felt by the Mission societies, especially the
Anglican Mission on the northeast coast, and their help and assistance in the distribution of relief rice to the natives is much appreciated. (*Papua Annual Report*
1911/12:118)

The next year, it was once again recorded that the food was "plentiful"
and the health "good" (*Papua Annual Report* 1912/13:103). In 1914/15, the
Resident Magistrate reported that

droughts, which in previous years have proved very trying, have been much less severe. This is more noticeable on the northeast coast where good harvests have been obtained, and where the yield was sufficient to tide over the dry spell experienced at the end of 1914. (*Papua Annual Report* 1914/15:30)

In 1918/19, the Resident Magistrate reported that "with the exception of a small portion of the northeast coast, food has been plentiful throughout the Division . . . ." Half a ton of rice was sent to the Anglican Mission for distribution, but the Reverend P. C. Shaw said it was not really necessary (*Papua Annual Report* 1918/19:35).

Thus, archival references to drought in the Wamira area occur in the years 1895–6 and 1899, and to severe drought and food scarcity in 1902 and 1911. For the period from the 1920s to the recent past, there is no mention in the written record of severe drought. From rainfall figures taken at the weather station at Dogura, we do know, however, that rainfall was extremely low in 1926 (1,020 millimeters), 1930 (1,071 millimeters), 1931 (749 millimeters), 1958 (1,010 millimeters), and 1966 (1,006 millimeters).

The most recent drought occurred in 1980. Upon my return to Wamira the following year, I was greeted by animated renditions of the calamity and its outcome. The normally long dry season had lasted an additional two months, the result of which was that the Uruam River (from the taro gardens at the base of the foothills to the river's mouth) was stone dry. The scarcity of water made irrigation impossible, and crops died. People subsisted on a meager supply of produce; they asked relatives in town for money.

In September 1980, the Provincial Government sent 800 kina (US $912) worth of relief food to Wamira (Department of Provincial Affairs 1980). Wamirans eagerly described the details of the food and its distribution to me.

We received rice, tinned fish, tinned meat, wheatmeal, and biscuits, but *no* sugar! Government officials gave it out according to the number of people in each household. Households with two adults received two tins of meat, two tins of fish, a small bag of rice, a small bag of wheatmeal, and four small packages of biscuits. Families with children got more. The food lasted about a week or two.

By placing the droughts in historical perspective, we can infer that droughts are experienced with decreasing amounts of anxiety. The adaptive responses to drought, both in the past and the present, are short-term mechanisms. In the distant past, prior to contact, drought meant that Wamirans resorted to wild "famine foods," such as the wild yams, licorice root, *Cycas* palm fruit, *mola,* and wild chestnuts, and increased their trade with other villages. As we learn from the 1899 quote, cannibalism was also a strategy that they could employ. Since contact, however, the government and mission have come to the villagers' aid by supplying relief food which, undoubtedly, has altered these traditional responses to drought. Most recently, as increasing amounts of money sent by town dwellers have made trade store food more accessible,

Wamirans have been able to augment their supply of indigenous foods in times of need. As a result, the people of Wamira are much more insulated from climatic fluctuations than they were prior to contact.

Even though Wamirans were, and still are, familiar with drought, at no time did I hear accounts of the devastation and doom we know from the nearby D'Entrecasteaux Islands, where drought, starvation, and death were realities related in chillingly descriptive tones (Fortune 1932:131; Malinowski 1935a:160–4; Young 1971:173–4). In all my personal inquiries, I learned of only one death, many years ago, that was attributed directly to drought and starvation. On the other hand, I was told of numerous instances, the most recent in 1981, in which Wamirans were swept out to sea and killed by the raging current of a flooded river during the wet season.

Wamiran droughts, sandwiched as they are between years of "plentiful" food and "good" health, produce a fickle environment rather than one that is permanently inadequate. The total picture is of an environment that is unreliable and of a people who must survive in the face of insecurity. If, as we have seen in both this chapter and the previous one, their daily definition of "famine" does not have a physical reference, why do they persist in perceiving and describing their environment in terms of scarcity?

"Famine" as a psychological adaptation

In his fine analysis of food, leadership, and social control on nearby Goodenough Island, Young suggests that the precarious environment is the cause of a "collective obsession with the bases of subsistence" (Young 1971:185). In his words, "the ambivalent set of attitudes towards the size and state of bellies and gardens seems inextricably bound up with attitudes towards a fickle environment" (Young 1971:185). More specifically, he interprets abstemious behavior in the realm of food as having practical survival value, viewing an obsession with food and abstinence as a long-term psychological solution to an unpredictable situation.

For Wamira, as well, a preoccupation with food seems to be a long-term psychological coping mechanism to an unreliable and uncontrollable situation. Their physical strategies for dealing with insufficient food supplies are short-term responses. An "obsession" with abstinence and control, however, is a long-term psychological reaction to the need to master the indomitable and conquer the anxiety that enslavement to uncertainty generates. Unreliable surroundings may generate the need for a total, and less immediately visible, cultural ethos of control.

What appears to be an "obsession with food" in Wamira can be interpreted more insightfully as an "obsession with control." An obsession with control suffuses their total cultural orientation. Food is just one arena – and, to be sure, the most overpowering one – in which struggles about control and about the paradoxes of human needs and fears of greed are played out. Wamirans emphasize a strict maintenance of control in their daily confrontation between mercurial resources and what they view as human needs, greeds, and desires. Wamirans' vision of their universe as one that offers perpetual "famine" is, I feel, their psychological technique to keep their passions and desires in check.

Their dependence on unreliable food resources parallels their dependence upon their (equally unreliable) fellow human beings. Insecurity in one sphere may trigger parallel anxieties and behavior in another. Insecurity arouses the need to control both an independently spirited environment and one's more immediate and tangible world of human beings.

In Wamira, the realm of food, the human dependence upon which triggers desire and the uncertain supply of which evokes anxiety, becomes a prime arena for the symbolic expression of ambivalent emotions about desire, fear of greed, and control in social (and, as we shall see, especially sexual) relationships. It is to the symbolic relationship between food and things that are not-food, and the ways in which Wamirans use, manipulate, and "think" food to express and control these that I now turn.

4. Tamodukorokoro: the monster within

To ask Wamirans why they feel there is "no food," or why they observe such tightly governed food-related customs and taboos, immediately yields the standard response: "Because of Tamodukorokoro." They told me that Tamodukorokoro, a hairy, ugly ogre, was "their monster" who would have brought them a life of bountiful food, but they both "desired him" and "feared him" and, as a result, "chased him away." They attribute their present circumstances to their unfriendly actions toward him; they now have to suffer forever after, destined to what they perceive as a life of persistent and unchangeable "famine."

I present the myth of Tamodukorokoro in this chapter. Wamirans narrate the myth as an etiological one which, for them, explains the causes of famine. My perception, however, is that the myth is not etiological, but teleological. Rather than explaining famine, it creates and exaggerates the illusion of famine in order for "famine" to be used euphemistically as a means for controlling desire. The idea of perpetual "famine" becomes a mechanism for social control by rendering desire objectionable and satisfaction unobtainable. By destroying Tamodukorokoro, Wamirans eradicate the potential for accumulating abundance, something which they desire as individuals but which they fear collectively because of its implications for causing envy, jealousy, and social chaos.

Upon detailed analysis of the myth, we see that, although it is ostensibly about food and famine, the myth is actually concerned with a hunger that has little to do with the belly. The myth is about sexual desire and the need to control it if people are to function as social beings. The seemingly contradictory aspects of Tamodukorokoro, who is a harbinger of bounty, yet fiercely ugly, and who is desired but feared, represents the paradox that occurs when biological beings must control their desires and live in a social world.

Food as sexual symbol

The symbolic relationship between eating and sexual intercourse has been described in various cultures and is even suggested to be universal (Leach 1964:42; Lévi-Strauss 1962a:105). A belief in the close relationship between digestive and reproductive processes appears as early as 3000 B.C. among the earliest dynasties of Egypt. The sky goddess Nut, for example, was envisioned as a woman who swallowed the sun each evening. After passing through her body, the sun reappeared from her vagina when she gave birth to it again each morning. More contemporary examples of the association between food and sex come from places as diverse as South America (Chagnon 1968:47; Gregor 1985; Henry 1941:146; Nadelson 1981; Reichel-Dolmatoff 1976:312), South Asia (Appadurai 1981:497), and Australia (McKnight 1973).

In Papua New Guinea, anthropologists have noted incidents where the oral ingestion of semen is thought to be necessary for male growth (Herdt 1981), where women are thought to have a "tube running from mouth to vagina" (Errington 1974:60), where "sexual intercourse is also 'food' " (M. Strathern 1972:167), or where "eating together is eminently a symbol of sexual relationship" (Meigs 1984; Serpenti 1965:138–9; Sillitoe 1979:80; Wagner 1972:35; Young 1977). In particular, sexual intercourse has been equated with the ingestion of "meat" (Kelly 1977:220; Tuzin 1978). The Ilahita Arapesh, for example, make a distinction between "cooked" meat and "raw" meat in their saying: "Cooked meat goes in the mouth and *down* the body; raw meat goes in the vulva and *up* the body" (Tuzin 1978:92).

The connections between food and sex have been treated in numerous ways. Biologists and zoologists have explored the physiological relationship between food and sex (Bates 1958; McClean 1963). Psychologists have linked food symbols and behavior to unconscious sexual desires (Freud 1938; Laing 1970). Anthropologists have also explored the dialectical nature of the relationship between the two realms. Influenced by Freud, who worked in a society where sex was controlled and food abundant, Audrey Richards (1932) conducted a study in a society where the opposite was true, namely, where food was scarce and sex abundant. An inversion of the two human needs with the ability to satisfy them has also been the topic of several humorous literary pieces. One example tells of a future time when eating is obsolete. As a result, food becomes a four-letter word and pictures of food are peddled surreptitiously as pornography (Matheson 1954). Another describes a fictitious people called Erophagi. They are nudists except for an armlet which covers a nipplelike growth that secretes a delicious liquid essential to the well-being of the race. Physical love is carried out in the open, but indulgence in the nipple is entirely surreptitious (Maurois 1934).

Of all the activities in which human beings engage, ingestion and copulation most fundamentally challenge the autonomy of individuals and, thus, their ability to master their appetites and themselves. Gustatory union between eater and eaten, and sexual union between female and male, are the main activities where physical welding between self and other takes place, where one is most dependent on something or someone else beyond one's control. This union of ingestor and food, or of male and female, is effected, according to Lévi-Strauss, because of a "conjunction by complementarity" (Lévi-Strauss 1962a:105–6). The merging of boundaries between self and other, or the lack of one's autonomy, is epitomized both in sexual relations and in the human relationship with food. In the words of Laing, "to eat and to be eaten, to have the outside inside and to be inside the outside" (Laing 1970:83) is unique to these two types of human behaviors. With these themes in mind, we now turn to the Tamodukorokoro myth about "famine."

The Tamodukorokoro myth[1]

Rekuboe and Kawaviro, two sisters from the Wamiran hamlet of Garala, made plans to visit friends in the inland village of Tauaga and to go fishing along the way.[2] Taking their fishnets and fishing baskets, but nothing to eat, they set out from Wamira and proceeded upstream. They continued up the river, catching fish and one eel. Before long they saw bananas floating down the river towards them. Since they were hungry, they tried to discover where the food was coming from.

Soon they came upon an old woman sitting by the side of the stream who was separating bunches of bananas and throwing them into the water. The old woman had no mouth; she placed her food in a hole in the top of her head. They were scared and asked her whether she would kill them. She could not speak but motioned with her hand that the girls would be safe. The two girls went up to the house with the old woman and asked her to set out a wooden bowl. They took their fishing basket and dumped the contents, including the live eel, into the bowl. When the old woman saw the eel squirming around, she was frightened. Suddenly, in fright, a hole burst open in her face, creating a mouth.

The girls stayed with the old woman that night. The following morning, after cooking and eating, they went to the garden to look for food. Upon returning in the evening, the old woman said, "Girls, one of you should go and take food to my 'pet.' "[3] Rekuboe, the older of the two sisters, answered, "All right, if you prepare the food, I'll take it." She took the food, but upon arriving encountered a huge

---

[1] The Tamodukorokoro narrative is known and owned by all Wamirans. Here I present the version that I recorded from Alice Dobunaba, who related the myth to me three separate times. In addition, I recorded the myth twice from an old man, Osborne Kaimou, and once again from Norman Tolewa, a Wamiran living in the neighboring village of Divari. Published versions occur in Ker (1910:103–7), Seligmann (1910:397–8), *The Papuan Villager* (1930:7), and *Baniara Patrol Report* (1955: Appendix A). Minor details vary among the different versions, but the general plot is the same.

[2] Their names, Rekuboe and Kawaviro, have no particular meaning.

[3] Here the word *gamogamo* is used, which can refer to either a child or an animal, and carries the same connotations of domestication and care as does the English word "pet."

snake. Frightened, she threw the dish of food at the snake and ran away. She said, "Old woman, you lied to me, your pet is a snake. I thought you were talking about some other 'pet,'[4] so I went. I am not going back again."

The next day the old woman again went to her garden in search of food. After she came home and cooked, she went to look in on the pet. She groomed the snake until he shed his skin and looked attractive. When she finished, she returned to the two girls and said, "Girls, which of you will go and look after the pet?" This time the younger sister, Kawaviro, replied, "I'll go." When she arrived with the dish of food she discovered a handsome young man instead of a snake. She laughed at him because he flaunted a mouth full of ugly black teeth.[5] She set the food down and groomed the man until he became even more handsome. She grabbed the young man, hugged him and played with him, and stayed and slept with him.[6]

The older sister said to the old woman, "You lied to Kawaviro and she went to the pet. I'm sure the snake killed her so I'll go and see what has happened." When Rekuboe arrived, she saw that Kawaviro was sleeping with a young man and said, "Oh my, I thought this was a snake, but now I see that you have married a nice young man. I made a mistake." Rekuboe tried to lie down next to them, insisting they make room for her, but no matter where she tried to put her head or arm, Kawaviro pushed herself between Rekuboe and the man.

They both stayed there for a long time, and eventually the young man also married the older girl. Before long the younger girl gave birth to a child. One day she said to Rekuboe, "We have been here a long time and have not seen our brothers for quite a while. Let's go back to Wamira and visit them." When they informed the old woman of their intention to go back to Wamira, she said, "All right, go back. But when you come to a fork, do not take the cleared path. Be sure to continue on the overgrown path."

The two girls left, carrying Kawaviro's small child with them. When they came to the fork, the older one said, "Our mother-in-law said that we should take the cleared path." The younger girl insisted that it was the overgrown path upon which they should walk. But the older girl persisted and, contrary to their mother-in-law's warning, they went on the cleared path.

Just as they turned the bend onto the cleared path, a flock of small birds fluttered about and an old ugly monster, called Tamodukorokoro, appeared from the bushes and said, "Who is coming? Oh, my two wives, come here."[7] Although the two girls were scared of his grotesque hairy appearance, he coerced them with his special magical powers to marry him. They sat down, he gave them areca nut, and they all chewed areca nut together.[8] He asked where they were going and said that he would accompany them to Wamira. He said, "Give me the child and I'll carry it while you carry my pouch."[9]

As they rose to walk on, the two girls intentionally left his pouch behind. The

[4] This time the word *tia* is used, which refers to an animal and indicates that it is "edible meat."
[5] Black teeth are usually the result of chewing areca nut. See M. Panoff (1968:293–4) for an analysis of the association between tooth blackening, menstrual blood, and sexual intercourse.
[6] To "sleep together" indicates marriage.
[7] Tamodukorokoro is said to be "the same as the snake-man from the mountain village." For Wamirans, his agility at disappearing as one figure and later reappearing as another does not cause logistical problems. In many Melanesian myths, snakes, in particular, by shedding their skin, transform themselves into other beings.
[8] To give someone of the opposite sex areca nut is a traditional gesture of matrimony.
[9] He had a small pouch of woven coconut leaves in which he carried his areca nut paraphernalia.

child, enveloped in the monster's arms, cried the entire way. When they arrived at Tanopota, an inland village near Pova, he said to the girls, "Give me my pouch so I can chew areca nut. You take the child." They then said, "Oh, we are sorry. We forgot your pouch." He ran back to retrieve his pouch while they waited with the child. As soon as he was gone, the girls hid in the bushes in an attempt to rid themselves of him. When he came back with his pouch and discovered they were gone, he sang out a magical spell:

Kaipokina kivivi,
Tautauvaona kivivi,
Tevera matana gugu ke kani.
Footsteps of the barren woman,
Footsteps of the young nursing mother,
The bees ate out the child's eyes.

When they heard this, they giggled from their hiding spot, "Here we are." He again said, "I'll carry the child and you take my pouch." And once again, they left it behind.

[At this point in the narrative, the same scene of abandoning the pouch and later unintentionally revealing themselves by laughing when they hear his magical spell, is repeated in three more locations as they gradually approach Wamira. These are Idei, a spot in the mountains; Aimutuara, one of the mountains; and Vuvura, a natural spring directly behind Wamira.]

When the monster ran back from Vuvura to Aimutuara to retrieve his pouch, the girls ran all the way to Wamira. They ran up to their brothers, warned them of the ogre, and begged to be hidden. The brothers concealed the girls behind a stack of firewood inside the house. When Tamodukorokoro arrived, he walked directly to the correct house and sang out his spell:

Kaipokina kivivi,
Tautauvaona kivivi,
Tevera matana gugu ke kani.

Once again, beyond their control, they found themselves drawn back to him.

The brothers feared Tamodukorokoro and conspired against him. They beguilingly told their brother-in-law they would help him make a new taro garden. When they cut the grass, they told him to stand in the center and they tried to chop off his legs with their sharpened sticks. But he jumped away as he sang out a spell:

Am gwada ritiriti,
Am gwada monamona.
Your taro pudding with ginger,
Your taro pudding with coconut cream.

No matter how hard they tried, they could not kill him. Instead, they harvested some taro and ate together.

The following day, while burning the scrub, they made Tamodukorokoro remain in the middle and tried to surround him with fire.[10] Again, he sang out his spell and leaped across the fire.

Am gwada ritiriti,
Am gwada monamona.

When the garden work was finished, they again dug up taro and ate communally. The next day, at daybreak, they went to turn the soil in the garden. When they

[10] In the myth, the taro gardening process is condensed. The various stages, which normally span several weeks, occur on successive days.

turned the sod with their sharp digging sticks, they tried to stab his legs. But he sang his spell and escaped.

Am gwada ritiriti,
Am gwada monamona.

They harvested taro and ate with their brother-in-law.

Trying yet another way to rid themselves of him, they told him that, having finished the garden work, they would go diving for clams at the beach near Loimara hamlet. They instructed him to put his arm into the clam's mouth to pull out the meat. It snapped shut with Tamodukorokoro trapped inside. Pleased with their accomplishment, the men returned to eat their taro, only to find that while they were dishing it out, Tamodukorokoro walked up from the beach. The tide had turned, and, as the water rose, the clam opened its mouth, disgorging Tamodukorokoro. The monster's stomach was bloated with water when the waves washed him ashore, but a small bird pricked it open and brought him back to life. As the water gushed forth from his stomach, heavy rain fell upon Wamira.

The men feigned joy at his return, handed him a dish of taro, and invited him to sit and eat with them. They told him of their plans for the next day. They decided to pick *kumika*.[11] They planned to roast the *kumika* on hot stones and eat communally.

The following day they all set out from the Uruam River, collecting stones for their oven and picking *kumika* along the way. When they arrived at the other end of the village near the Wamira River, they made the fire, heated the stones, and set the *kumika* inside to roast.[12] They took the hot *kumika* from the fire, rubbed it in their hands and, calling out *egubeda*,[13] asked Tamodukorokoro to open his mouth so they could throw in the *kumika*. They did this twice, but the third time, instead of picking up *kumika*, they took a red-hot stone from the fire and tossed it into his mouth.

At that point Tamodukorokoro rose in anger. No matter what he tried to do, he could not rid himself of the stone. He snatched up his pouch, grabbed his two wives, and left Wamira. He tried settling in a number of nearby places but was always tormented by the visibility of Wamira. At Vurolagalaga, near Divari, he sat down to sharpen his *irama*.[14] While resting there, he sighted Iriwavo [Fergusson Island] and decided to cross the bay and settle forever on Iriwavo. He sat down with his back to Wamira and one wife on either side of him. They all turned into stone and are now the three peaks one can see across the bay on Iriwavo.

According to Wamirans, this myth explains why there is perpetual "famine" in Wamira in contrast to other places, such as Iriwavo, where they believe there is an abundance of food.[15] They concisely explain that if the monster

---

[11] *Kumika* is a wild pungent fruit that can be eaten raw or cooked.

[12] The method of roasting is called *latana* and consists of piling up heated stones, placing food on top of them, and then covering the food with leaves and more hot stones.

[13] *Egu* is a prefix that, when joined to the name of a food, becomes a term of address indicating close friendship between two people who have shared that particular food. In this case the "food" is *beda*, i.e., areca nut. (See Schieffelin, 1976, and A. Strathern, 1977, for a description of the same phenomenon among other groups in Papua New Guinea.)

[14] This is a stone adz used only to sharpen the digging sticks men utilize for planting and harvesting taro.

[15] This interpretation is unique to Wamira. Although the plot of the myth is constant over a wide geographical area, interestingly, only the Wamirans have given it the "that is why we have no food" twist, and adopt it as the explanation for their "famine."

had stayed in Wamira, food would be plentiful. But they were both attracted to and repelled by him, both desirous and fearful of him and, in their ambivalence, "chased him away." They rejected the possibility of ever having an abundance of food. They say that in the act of throwing a hot stone into his mouth instead of food, they tossed famine out upon their land. They compare the roasted stone to the parched land where it is hard to grow food, calling their land *latana,* like the heated stones of the oven they built. The myth, the exegesis of their destiny, can almost be interpreted as their own "original sin" for which they have to pay forever after, the price being perpetual "famine."

The snake-man Tamodukorokoro

A better understanding of the association between the desire for food and the desire for sex, and how the control of sexual relationships is expressed in the domain of food, can be gained by analyzing the symbolism of Tamodukorokoro. Tamodukorokoro is, in fact, the snake-man. In most versions of the myth, the snake-man from the mountain village and Tamodukorokoro are said to be "the same."

In Wamira, snakes and eels, although distinguished from one another, are given the same name, *mota.* In daily life they are greatly feared by women. Moreover, the consumption of *mota* is taboo to all women who are sexually productive; only men and postmenopausal women may eat snakes or eels. *Mota* play prominent roles in numerous myths. A brief examination of some of these is necessary before proceeding with the analysis of Tamodukorokoro.

In one myth, Wamiran men catch, cut up, and attempt to cook an eel. The eel, however, refuses to die and talks "like a person" from inside the pot of boiling water. The people are frightened and throw the eel away, at which point chaos, darkness, and destruction engulf Wamira. Only upon returning the pieces of eel to the inlet from which it was originally seized does calamity leave the village. The various pieces of the eel become the numerous saltwater varieties presently caught and eaten.

In another myth, while fetching water from an inlet, a woman is tugged into the water by an eel who desires to marry her. She is frightened and manages to escape by deceiving the eel. Later he emerges from the water in search of her and coils himself in a wooden bowl filled with water inside her house. The girl's father tries to kill the eel by hacking him to pieces. Again, the eel will not die, but talks, and begs for his head to be buried in the earth by the side of the house. The buried head of the eel eventually sprouts into a particular variety of coconut palm called *pa waduwadu.*

The Wamiran myth about the origin of taro relates how a male child's father chops him up and plants the pieces in the garden. The pieces of the child later grow into taro. In the nearby village of Boianai, a transformation of this myth exists in which a woman, tempted by the delicious taste of a snake, decides to eat one. Later, to her horror, she gives birth to a snake-son. She tries in vain to rid herself of him and eventually butchers him and plants the pieces in her garden. In the Boianai version, it is a snake, and not a human, who then grows into taro.

From even this brief summation of the above myths, various themes about eels and snakes emerge, among them the following:

1. The attraction between *mota* and women, either for sex or as food
2. Women's ambivalent feelings of desire and fear of *mota,* also in either a sexual or edible manner
3. Men's fear of *mota* and their attempts to destroy them by throwing them away, killing them, chopping them up, and/or cooking them
4. Resistance of *mota* to death, and their vitality, often in human form, as indicated by their speech
5. Asexual regeneration of *mota* (usually in fertile surroundings of water or soil) in the form of food or human offspring

The snake-man Tamodukorokoro clearly possesses the characteristics and qualities of *mota*. Like *mota,* Tamodukorokoro desires women, who are both attracted to and repelled by him. He is controlled by men, who wish to annihilate him. Yet, he refuses to die.

The snake-man first appears when the girls stay with the old woman. In the same way that women react to *mota,* the girls are both intrigued and repelled by the "pet" (to whom they alternatively refer as "pet animal" and "edible meat"). The older girl approaches him with a dish of food but throws it at him in fright. Eventually the younger girl marries him and bears his child. Tamodukorokoro next appears when the girls take the wrong path on their way back to Wamira. In the true *mota* fashion, he desires them. He entices them with areca nut, the Wamiran symbol of sexual union, and with magic against which they have no antidote. Again, in keeping with women's reactions to *mota,* they both desire and fear him. He is hairy and unkempt in appearance, and frightening to the girls. They try to rid themselves of him but, lacking control, they are continually drawn back.

Once back in Wamira, Tamodukorokoro's brothers-in-law attempt to destroy him. They try to slash his legs, surround him by fire, and drown him in the sea. Yet, like a *mota,* he refuses to die.

Moreover, he is able to regenerate himself (or would be able to, had they not chased him away) in the fertile surroundings of soil. The garden land the men cultivate with him lies in the most fertile area of the plain behind Wamira and today bears his name in memory of him. In the myth, during the gardening process, he continually escapes their malice by singing out a spell in his special magical language that refers to the abundance of food. As Tamodukorokoro escapes their attempts to kill him, he dangles the notion of taro pudding, festively prepared with ginger and coconut cream – a symbol of productivity and virility – in front of them.

Am gwada ritiriti,
Am gwada monamona.
Your taro pudding with ginger,
Your taro pudding with coconut cream.[16]

Tamodukorokoro, who would have provided food for the Wamirans, departs when they feed him a stone instead of food. As he rises in anger and flees Wamira, symbolically, he still flaunts his horticultural productivity. According to one version, when the hot stone descends through his digestive tract, smoke rises from his stomach and spirals from his mouth "in the same way that a thin stream of smoke rises from a garden when someone performs fertility magic." When Tamodukorokoro leaves Wamira, his final deed, while eyeing the island of Iriwavo where he decides to settle, consists of sitting down to sharpen his *irama*. As noted, this adz made of especially hard stone is sharpened with potent magic and used only to chisel the digging sticks that men utilize in planting and harvesting taro.

Like *mota,* Tamodukorokoro eventually reappears in the form of a purveyor of abundant food. He sits across the bay on Iriwavo where, according to Wamirans, "food is plentiful." No longer within their reach, he is always visible nonetheless – a constant reminder of the potential for horticultural abundance.

The ambivalence of desire and the attempt to control it

Although the figure of Tamodukorokoro is cloaked in images of horticultural productivity and bountiful food, the snake-man, once divested of outer skin, exposes the dilemma of sexual, not horticultural, desire. This message comes across poignantly in the sexual relationships triggered by Tamodukorokoro's appearance.

As mentioned, the relationship between Tamodukorokoro and women is ambivalent, one of attraction and repulsion, desire and fear. The two sisters, Rekuboe and Kawaviro, represent the two faces of the dilemma of sexual relationships. Clouded by desire and fear, they approach Tamodukorokoro ambiguously. On their journey back to Wamira, they run away from Tamodukorokoro. Yet, they are unable to escape his and their desire. The recurring

---

[16] *Am* means "your." *Gwada* is taro pudding prepared specially for festive occasions. The two main ingredients that make festive *gwada* different from ordinary taro are ginger and copious amounts of coconut cream. *Ritiriti* is a particular type of cane with thorns on the outer bark used for grinding ginger root. *Monamona* is fat or grease and here refers to the cream squeezed from grated coconut.

scenes of approach and avoidance revolve around hiding and finding his pouch of areca nut. The association of areca nut with sexual union and marriage has been noted. It is the pouch that the girls desperately try to abandon. Yet, each time Tamodukorokoro returns carrying it, the girls become prisoners of powers beyond their control and return to him. While trying to rid themselves of Tamodukorokoro, the girls continually reveal themselves by laughing, a strange and ambiguous reaction from girls who also fear him.

The two girls, who are continually juxtaposed as younger/older and fertile/barren, together represent the dual and ambiguous nature of sexual temptation. The younger girl's actions lead to a handsome man, marriage, and offspring, whereas the older girl repeatedly fails to follow advice and opts for the "nonproductive" path. For example, when the older girl takes food to the pet, she is frightened at the sight of the snake, throws the food on the ground, and runs away. The younger girl, however, is not afraid, feeds the snake, and discovers he is a handsome young man. She marries him and soon becomes a young mother. Later in the myth, Tamodukorokoro emphasizes the girls' opposing qualities of fertility and barrenness when he sings out "footsteps of the barren woman, footsteps of the young nursing mother."[17] When the two girls confront the fork in the path, again it is the younger girl who recalls the correct advice, but hesitates and succumbs to the persistent remarks of the older girl. Thus, because of the older girl's blundering, they proceed on the path they had been admonished not to take, which leads them to Tamodukorokoro and eventually leads Wamirans to temptation they cannot control and, hence, to their life of deprivation.

Whereas the feelings Tamodukorokoro prompts from women are the ambivalent ones of desire and fear, the feelings he elicits from men are envy and competitiveness, and the desire to control and destroy. The multiple identities of the snake-man Tamodukorokoro and his relationship to his Wamiran brothers-in-law illustrate these various male tensions. In one version of the myth, the snake-man and Tamodukorokoro appear as two distinct individuals. The narrator of this version explained that it was the snake-man who threw the hot stone into Tamodukorokoro's mouth because "he was jealous of Tamodukorokoro for marrying his two wives." As other Wamiran men explained, "We wanted to kill Tamodukorokoro because we were envious of him." In the myth, men aim their hostility at Tamodukorokoro. Yet he himself represents the epitome of male achievement and success. Thus, their desire to control by destroying can be interpreted as being directed at their fellow men, especially those who, like Tamodukorokoro, exhibit horticultural productivity or sexual success.

---

[17] *Kaipokina kivivi, Tautauvaona kivivi. . . .* This is their magical language (constructed primarily by the prefixing and infixing of *k*s). *Kaipokina* is *aipoina* (literally "dry as wood") which means "barren woman." *Tautauvao* is a fertile woman who has recently given birth (literally, a "person who has planted taro").

The men's attitude of envy and hostility toward Tamodukorokoro is couched in terms of largess and benevolence. They deceitfully tell him that they will "help" him make a new garden, yet during each step in the process they try to destroy him. No sooner do they attempt to rid themselves of him than they sit down and eat together with magnanimous gesture. When the garden work is completed, they bid him dive for meat but again have ulterior motives. The final hostile act occurs when they ask him to open his mouth to feed him *kumika,* calling out *egubeda* as a sign of friendship and trust, but toss a hot stone into his mouth instead.

The men's feelings of envy and anxiety are so strong that, in an attempt to control their passions, they literally destroy. By chasing away Tamodukorokoro, they kill the potential for the collective achievement of abundance, which individually they desire. They drive Tamodukorokoro away and, in their homeland of Wamira, are left with perpetual "famine."

A journey in search of "meat"

In the myth, food that ostensibly is eaten to satisfy physical hunger often represents "food" for sexual consumption. In general, the girls' journey in search of "meat" can be interpreted as a journey in search of a husband and affinal connections.

Wordplays highlight the association between food and sex, or ingestion and reproduction. The myth opens with the girls' plan to go fishing (*lebaga i rauogei*), which can be translated as a "search for meat" and refers to meat that can be consumed either for food or for sex. Moreover, when the older sister returns from taking food to the "pet," she says, "I went because I thought it was some other kind of 'meat.' " She uses the word *tia,* which indicates something she could "eat." When the younger sister goes to "feed the snake" she instead finds a husband, or "sexual meat," and soon thereafter gives birth to a child.

The various sections of the myth both delineate and accentuate the association of edible meat with sexual meat. The events take place in four geographical locales: an upstream journey away from Wamira toward Tauaga; the inland mountain village; an overland journey from the mountain village back to Wamira; and their home of Wamira. These four temporal sequences are characterized by the accompanying absence or presence of food and the absence or presence of marriageable men.[18] Edible food is found together with husbands. Famine occurs where brothers live.

In the first setting, when the two girls leave Wamira, they are "hungry"

[18] See Young (1971:186–7) for a Goodenough Island myth in which temporal sequences are associated with the existence or nonexistence of food and the existence or nonexistence of society.

and "in search of meat." They set out with "nothing to eat," carrying fish-nets and empty fishing baskets. However, as they proceed further from Wamira, they catch an eel, the sexual symbolism of which has been discussed. They continue to move toward food, which literally comes floating down the river at them in the form of bananas, a food Wamirans associate with men.

In the second setting of the mountain village, they receive food from an old woman who lacks the orifice necessary for proper ingestion and communication. (In another version of the myth, she also lacks a vagina, thus making her unable to reproduce as well.) Only after the old woman sees the squirming eel does she, for the first time, burst open a hole which becomes her mouth. From then on, she is able to eat and talk in a normal human fashion. (In the other version, she is now also able to reproduce; she simultaneously acquires nutritional and sexual needs and desires.) The mouthless old woman, who becomes the girls' mother-in-law, not only gives them food to eat, but offers them a marriageable man (sexual food) as well. She grooms the snake-man for them until he sheds his skin and becomes a handsome young man. She then encourages them to "feed the snake." The younger girl, who is not afraid of the snake-man, sleeps with him, marries him, and bears his child. However, after a while, because they long for their brothers, they decide to return to Wamira.

At this point in the myth the events reverse themselves both in physical direction and in the content of the plot. In the third part, the girls move from the inland village of food, snake-man, husband, and child to their home of brothers and no food. Whereas they encountered food on their trip upstream, they now, on their inland journey home, meet the monster Tamodukorokoro who eventually brings famine to Wamira.

In the fourth location, they return to their brothers with their husband, who elicits envy and hostility among Wamiran men. The brothers attempt to kill Tamodukorokoro during various phases of producing food and searching for meat. (Another version of the myth includes a hunting scene during which the men also try to kill the monster.) The brothers' efforts to destroy him are thwarted by magic beyond their control. Unable to kill Tamodukorokoro, they eventually anger him by failing to feed him. They replace food with a hot stone and he departs from Wamira, leaving them at home to a destiny of perpetual "famine."

In sum, "hungry" and empty-handed, the girls leave their brothers. Away from Wamira, haunted by temptation and fear, they find food and a husband. Back in Wamira, ensconced in the safety of home, they encounter "famine." The relationship between sister and brother, which is asexual and safe, is one of "famine." The sexual relationship between wife and husband, on the other hand, although frightening, is productive. The girls' journey to the inland village in search of "meat" is a journey that is socially necessary. Shaken by their conflicting feelings for that which they desire, they must still venture forth in search of a husband, children, and affinal connections.

Marriage as the regulation of sexual desire

Anxiety exists in Wamira over more than just food. Although couched in idioms of food, there is also anxiety over sexual desire and the need to control it.

Sexual desire is controlled primarily by the regulation of marriage. Prohibitions exist against women marrying their lineage members, or "brothers." In addition, men remain geographically stationary and women "marry out." In the symbolic language of the myth, women may not marry their "brothers," but must search for "meat" among potential affines, such as those in the remote mountain village. Thus, the perceived paradox of desiring "food," but being condemned to "famine" at home, echoes the reality of desiring the safety of one's lineage "brothers," but being forced to seek husbands among strangers.

The perpetuation of Wamiran society is rooted in this paradox. For women, who unite with "strangers" in marriage, the dilemma is between the comfort of "brothers" (to whom they can safely run for protection from monsters), and the attraction to, but fear of, potential husbands (who appear as black-fanged snakes or ugly, hairy monsters, and from whom they cannot escape). For men, tensions are present between affines. Moreover, men in general are competitive with one another over their unequal access to women. Men struggle with the contradiction of desiring abundance (in the form of large gardens, festively plump taro, and "two wives") on an individual scale, yet, moved by envy, desiring to destroy abundance on a social scale. The result is "famine" at home for both women and men, while women continue to journey to "remote mountain villages" in search of "meat."

The regulated movement of women in marriage, alone, mediates the food/famine conundrum. Lévi-Strauss aptly described the paramount importance of marriage regulation:

The perpetuation of a group can only be effected by means of women, and although varying degrees of symbolic content can be introduced by the particular way in which a society organizes them or thinks of their operation, marriage exchanges always have real substance, and they are alone in this. The exchange of food is a different matter (Lévi-Strauss 1962a:109)

Tamodukorokoro is a mythical monster. So too is the lack of food, or the fear of too much food, for which he stands. The human dilemmas and paradoxes he represents, however, are real. In the myth, women run away from Tamodukorokoro but cannot escape from him. Men try to kill him, but he will not die. Wamirans finally succeed in chasing him away, but his silhouette still looms across the bay. Try as they may, Wamirans are unable to escape from both Tamodukorokoro and from their human dilemmas. The best they can do is keep their desires under control, as they keep temptation, in the form of their monster, across the sea. Permanently and visibly perched across the bay, immortalized in stone, he appears to be a daily reminder of the monster that lurks within.

5. Pigs and pork: the domestication of affinal tensions

In the previous analysis of the Tamodukorokoro myth, tensions between men, who are dyadically linked through women, are made explicit. The unequal access that men, as brothers or husbands, have to a woman's reproductive and nurturing abilities generates feelings of envy, competition, and resentment among them. Men deceitfully phrase their hostile feelings toward one another in terms of magnanimity. Under the guise of sumptuously feasting together, in fact, they intend to kill. In the myth, conflict between affines is ultimately resolved by the departure of Tamodukorokoro. In daily life, however, the tensions do not vanish as easily.

Men are biologically dependent upon women for the perpetuation of society. Yet, men are unable to represent, manipulate, or control that aspect of a woman upon which they most depend, namely, her sexuality and fertility. This dependence on women's sexuality creates tensions between men as well as between men and women. As brothers and husbands to women, men's relationships to one another are unequal and antagonistic. Men need sisters to continue their lineage; they need wives to bear and nurture their offspring. Moreover, because women generate tensions among men, relationships between the sexes rest on insecure foundations. As sisters, women abandon their brothers for other men, for whom they produce offspring. As wives, they create links between men who are otherwise envious of, and antagonistic toward, one another.

Male solidarity is threatened by men's needs to make alliances elsewhere to secure offspring. In this matrilineal society, in giving up sisters and in marrying wives, men lose their lineal substance to the offspring of their sisters and their brothers-in-law. As Gewertz (1982:315–6) says for the Chambri, men can neither live with nor live without the social relationships established through women. If men refuse to marry, they cannot reproduce. If they marry, they lose their patrilineal substance to matrilateral kin. This dilemma creates

74

a double bind, a situation in which "no matter what a person does he can't win" (Bateson 1972:201). Gewertz discusses a possible solution:

In such an impossible situation, escape can be found by shifting to a metaphorical order of response. Thus one can defend oneself metaphorically by becoming some-one else, or by insisting that one is somewhere else, or by transforming the very nature of the interaction. (Gewertz 1982:315–6)

In Wamira, pigs become the metaphorical medium by which men can escape their double bind. It is in behavior and beliefs about pigs, that Wamiran men symbolically attempt to control female powers of reproduction upon which they depend but can never possess. Unable to master women, men attempt to master pigs which serve as tangible, manipulatable, and composite symbols of the unharnessable characteristics of women.

Pigs, which, like women, are natural sources of fertility and suppliers of food, appear to be female surrogates. Wamiran men symbolically manipulate them in corresponding ways. In Wamira, pigs and women are seen as eco-nomic and social extensions of individual men. The exchanges of both are valuable in linking men and maintaining male relationships; men exchange piglets (for domestication) and pork (for consumption) with the same people with whom they exchange women for marriage. Both pigs and women bind men together in potentially contentious relationships as husbands and brothers to the same woman. In the ritualized exchanges of piglets and pork, as well as in the myth about the origin of domesticating and eating pigs, men usurp control of natural female reproductive powers. Pigs (like taro, as we shall see in Chapter 6) are facile symbols through which men alone can be masters of reproduction and procreation. Through the manipulation of symbols, such as the pig, men become independent of women. In this light, pigs are symbols of *controllable* female sexuality.

Domestication and exchange of piglets

Pigs (*Sus scrofa*) are the largest animals traditionally domesticated, hunted, or eaten in Wamira. Although fish, wallaby, bandicoot, and now also beef and tinned meat (and human flesh until the turn of the century) are consumed, pork remains the flesh food most desired, valued, and passionately ex-changed. It is the main source of protein, as well as a primary economic and symbolic medium for establishing and communicating men's sense of power and reknown.

Living among the roughly four hundred Wamiran villagers is a population of approximately one hundred pigs. In 1977, I conducted a pig survey, which I updated in 1982, in the largest hamlet, Inibuena. I gathered data from each household about the number of pigs owned, the pigs' names, their histories, and information as far back as the residents could recall about former piglets exchanged for raising or grown pigs exchanged at feasts. In 1977, Inibuena hamlet, which consisted of eighty people, had a population of forty-four pigs. The high ratio of pigs to people represented in Inibuena (where eighteen percent of the people cared for forty-four percent of the pigs) is not characteristic of Wamira as a whole. Many Wamirans have no pigs at all in their immediate possession. For instance, none of the residents of the Damaladona ward raise any pigs because, as they explain, "Our taro gardens are too close to our hamlets and the pigs would ruin the taro." Although the two wards are disproportionately represented in terms of pigs present, the difference between them in terms of actual pig wealth diminishes when we consider the fact that residents of Damaladona own pigs that temporarily reside in Rumaruma.

Wamirans distinguish between two types of pigs: bush and house pigs. "Bush pigs" (*poro modu*) are wild and forage on their own, rummaging for food away from the village and, much to everyone's annoyance, also in the taro gardens. Bush pigs are the domain of men, who occasionally hunt them. "House pigs" (*poro numa*) are domesticated and, although loose, usually remain in the vicinity of their owner's house. House pigs, in contrast to bush pigs, are the domain of both women and men who, respectively, feed and exchange them.

The domestication of piglets involves a minimum of ritual. Unlike taro, pigs do not need continual human attention and intervention to ensure their proper growth and reproduction. Pigs feed and breed on their own. Indeed, human care is required solely to control the pigs' rapacious and procreative habits. Such control is of both the nurturing and castrating kind. In the process of domestication, women feed pigs to keep them from going wild and becoming bush pigs. Men castrate male pigs to harness their sexual desires, an operation that is thought necessary to make them grow large. Thus, domesticated sows mate with feral boars and give birth away from the village. After piglets are born, they remain in the wild for several days until the mother appears in the hamlet with a cluster of squealing piglets behind her.

In general, domesticated pigs are owned jointly by husband and wife. In the words of Wamirans, "Husbands give piglets to their wives to feed and raise." As we shall see, this often-quoted phrase could be extended with: "Wives give grown pigs to their husbands to exchange at feasts." Household pigs thus link husband and wife in webs of mutual dependence and cooperation. Women are needed to nurture the animals into exchangeable items of wealth. Men then manipulate and circulate the wealth and, in doing so, form and maintain necessary social networks, primarily with their wife's lineage members.

As soon as piglets are weaned from their mother, the household that owns them usually farms them out to the wife's matrilineal kin for domestication. Only rarely do owners keep a piglet or give it to a child within the family. Kin who receive female piglets reciprocate several years later by giving back an offspring of the pig. This process of reciprocal exchange of live female pigs for domestication between a woman and her lineage members continues at intervals of one pig generation. As Schwimmer describes the situation among the Orokaiva, "One might say that the offspring of the donated pig returns to its 'mother's' village" (Schwimmer 1973:142–3.). It is important that complete equivalence be maintained. For example, if X gives Y a female piglet A, Y later returns a female offspring of pig A to X. Likewise, male pigs are reciprocated with male pigs although, naturally in the case of males, they are not direct offspring of the original pig.

The domestication and ownership of piglets are processes that call for continual personal input. When a young piglet is given to an individual for raising, the new owner washes it in the sea and, by feeding it, encourages it to stay near the house. A bond of familiarity is slowly established between the piglet and its provider. Successful domestication signifies ownership. If the domesticated pig runs away and becomes a bush pig, it simultaneously becomes unowned and anyone may hunt it.

The piglet is earmarked by its owner to distinguish it from feral pigs. As the owner slices small pieces from the pig's ears, he or she calls out the name that has been chosen for the pig. This is done to "put the new name in the pig's mind." The owner ritually tosses the small cuttings taken from the pig's ears onto the roof of the house. This is done to ensure that the piglet stays near the house and does not wander into the bush and become wild.

Names given to pigs refer either to the new owner or to the owner's lineage. About half of the names from my survey refer to distinguishing characteristics of the new owner, such as:

Boroko. The owner went to carpentry school in Boroko.
Tagotago ("one"). The owner was the only female born to her parents.
Toupika ("cries a lot"). The owner cried a lot as a child.
Matagalawa ("naughty boy"). The owner was a naughty child.
Ice Cream. The owner, a young girl, was known for the large quantities of ice cream she consumed while living in town.
Bada ("leader," "elder"). The owner was the hamlet leader.
Kedakeda ("orphan"). The owner was an orphan.

The other half of the names refer to totems, places, stones, animals, or foods associated with the owner's lineage. For example:

Lamogara. A peninsula west of Wamira over which the members of Iriki lineage journeyed on their way to Wamira
Babanai. An inlet east of Wamira past which the members of Manibolanai lineage traveled on their way to Wamira
Kwarara. A large ancestral coral, associated with Ewa lineage, that was displeased with the behavior of its Wamiran descendants and "swam" away to Divari
Abaria. A large boulder associated with Aurana lineage
Bouri. The fish that is taboo for the members of Labolabo lineage

Names that are associated with the lineage may explicitly and strategically recall the foundation of wealth upon which social relationships are based. For example, when I was given a piglet by the family with which I lived, its name was decided for me. I was to shout out "America" as I earmarked it and each time I called it for feeding. Not only was America the locale of my "lineage members," but the name, for Wamirans, conjured up images of the bountiful wealth they believed I possessed and saw as necessary items in my relationships with them.

In general, names allude to the way in which personal identity is established through the exchange of wealth. For example, the name *bada* ("leader"), mentioned above, refers to the owner's possession of resources necessary to create and maintain exchange partners and social networks. Other names, such as "Market," "Miti" (meat), "Rice," and "Ice Cream," indicate not only the association of pigs with edible exchange valuables, but that nowadays wealth appears in many new forms.

Irony is a device used to name pigs. Names may refer to a lack of resources and thus, to an absence of group membership, social networks, and personal identity. *Kedakeda* ("orphan") is an example. Two other pigs names, not mentioned above, *Voladaga* and *Lamolamona*, refer to a person who has neither possessions nor kin. In neither case were the owners of the pigs identified as "beggars." Instead, humility and a touch of humor were seen as the motives in choosing the names.

Pigs as female surrogates

The exchange of piglets for domestication has economic value. The giving of pigs creates an exchange system whereby an individual has more credit owed to him than actual currency. Moreover, everyone involved in the exchanges gains because with each pig pregnancy the wealth expands exponentially. While conducting the pig census, I was occasionally told that individuals had few or no pigs in their care at the moment, but that they had pig offspring in other villages or in other hamlets in Wamira. These pig offspring would be given to them if needed for a feast, or would eventually be returned to them for raising. This method of doling out one's wealth allows individuals to invest their resources in as wide a circle as possible, and thus has the advantage of minimizing economic risks and possible losses while simultaneously maintaining social relationships.

The practice of piglet lending, however, cannot be accounted for in solely practical terms in Wamira.[1] On a social and symbolic level, the lines along which piglets are exchanged for domestication parallel those along which women move in marriage and thus have significance on these levels. Piglets can be viewed as female surrogates, and piglet exchange can be seen as a way of

[1] The custom has been viewed as a practical measure primarily in areas of Melanesia where hundreds of pigs are slaughtered at one time (see Rappaport 1968; Salisbury 1962:91–2, for example).

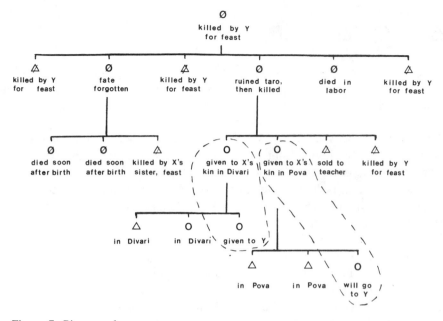

Figure 7. Pig genealogy

maintaining links between affines. As Schwimmer notes concerning the Oro-kaiva, "the institution of pig-lending becomes a simulation, on a minor scale, of the customs of marriage exchange" (Schwimmer 1973;142–3).

Figure 7 is the genealogy of a pig, originally owned by a wife – husband pair (indicated by "X" and "Y"). The genealogy includes two examples of exchanging piglets for raising between Y and his affines. Several of the grown pigs killed by Y for feasts had also been cared for by affines until needed. At the time the pig census was taken, X and Y had only one pig in their house-hold, but had pig offspring in the villages of Divari and Pova. As Figure 7 illustrates, male pigs tend either to be sold to nonkin for cash or kept and butchered by the owners for feasts. Female pigs, however, are valued for their reproductive ability and thus are eagerly exchanged.

If attention is shifted from the pigs to the people exchanging them, the focus changes to the affinal links between men, as illustrated in Figure 8. Although having the appearance of amicable affinal reciprocity (A), the exchange, in fact, reinforces bonds in two social units that are in competition with one another (B and C). The piglet exchange visibly forces men of different lin-eages who are related to one another only through a woman to engage in repetitive and reciprocal exchanges (A). The exchange reiterates two compet-ing relationships, each of which is equally important in the maintenance of social life. One (B) is that of brother and sister. Piglet exchange reinforces

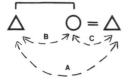

Figure 8. Affinal pig exchange

the connection between a married woman and her own lineage members, including the "brothers" from whom she was taken during marriage. The other (C) is that of husband and wife. Once the piglet is among its new owners, the process of its domestication emphasizes the cooperation between husband and wife that is necessary for the production of food, the reproduction of offspring, and the accumulation of wealth; in short, those things necessary for the perpetuation of social life.

Men appear to be independent and in control during the exchange of piglets. However, the exchange is rooted in the fact that their dependence upon one another is a mirror of their dependence on the women who link them. Exchanges between a man and his wife's matrilineal kin are reciprocally balanced. Yet, these exchanges mask social asymmetry and tension. Although pig exchanges draw a woman back to the lineage from which she was taken during marriage, they also join her to her husband. In simultaneously communicating both messages, the exchanges loosen a man's single-handed control over the woman: over his sister and the perpetuation of his lineage on the one hand, and over his wife and his offspring on the other.

This ambiguity can be seen in beliefs about exchanges. Although a piglet becomes attached to the household of its new owner, its association with its original owner is never completely severed. For instance, a pig's physical condition is read as an indication of the psychological state of its *original* owner. This reflection, in the pig, of its original owner's disposition was reiterated in the words of one woman:

If your "insides are good" [if you have good intentions] when you give a pig to someone, then the pig will live and grow large. But if your "insides are bad," if you ask for payment for the pig, if you talk about the pig after you have given it away, or if you did not really want to give it, then the pig will die.

This statement indicates the ambivalence of piglet exchange. Although always given in a spirit of amity, piglets may serve as an idiom in which feelings of envy, suspicion, ill will, or outright hostility are revealed. As we shall see shortly, the presentation of butchered pork at feasts among men teeters on a thin line between the amicable sharing of food with one's friends and the aggressive killing of one's enemies.

By giving the semblance of equality and social harmony, the exchange of piglets "domesticates" the tensions between a woman's husband and her lineage brothers. A woman's husband and the men of her lineage (who engage in the continual exchange of piglets with one another) stand as unequals to one another through their different relationship to the woman. In marriage, the husband gains sexual access to the woman. However, the children of this sexual union remain members of *her* matrilineage. The ambience of equality, imposed in the piglet exchanges, insures the muting of an otherwise unequal, contentious, and potentially volatile relationship between men over their control of a woman's reproductive powers.

The exchange of pork at *torela*

The main traditional feast at which pork is distributed is the *torela*. Although *torela* may be both intravillage and intervillage affairs, those that are the most lively and colorful occur between different villages. At an intervillage *torela*, more people are involved, more pork is exchanged, and, because the guests have walked greater distances, the feast usually lasts for two days instead of one. During a *torela*, pork meat is exchanged along affinal lines. Affinal tensions and ambiguities are communicated by the presentation of meat; the line between friendly feasting and hostile fighting is thin. The people outside their village with whom Wamirans feast and form marriage alliances are those with whom they fought and, indeed, prior to contact, those whom they ate.[2]

Torela illustrate the close symbolic association between gustatory and sexual appetites, evident in the narrow lines between affinal feasting and fighting, and between the exchange of pigs and women. One woman remarked that "a *torela* looks as though people are fighting with one another, but they are just exchanging food." Someone else explained, "If people don't present enough pigs, it is because they *want* to fight." Indeed, I was persistently dissuaded from going to *torela* on the grounds that "*torela* are bad. . . . They are like fighting. . . . They can be dangerous."

Affinal relationships are established by the movement of women at marriage; they are continually confirmed through the exchanges of piglets for raising and of pork at *torela*. These relationships are rife with tensions and riddled with ambiguity and, as such, beg for control. At feasts, men prominently, even if temporarily, hold positions of authority. In exchanging pork, they desire control over these ambiguous relationships mediated through women and upon which they depend for the reproduction of their society.

I describe *torela* in general and, for unity of focus, take specific examples from a feast I attended in Pova in 1981. My data on *torela* come from local oral accounts as well as from my own observations. Following the descrip-

---

[2] About twenty percent of Wamiran marriages occur with these "enemy" villages.

tion, I analyze the manner in which the exchanges of pork at *torela* are mechanisms for controlling the tensions that exist between men.

Several weeks before a *torela* takes place, men sponsoring the feast go to the houses of the affines who are invited and throw a makeshift spear into the wall of the kin's house. Then the sponsor sits down and chews areca nut and smokes tobacco with his affines. The "speared" guests know that this unspoken message signals an upcoming *torela* at which they must present a pig and bundled taro to the hosts. The *torela* in Pova, for instance, was sponsored by four agnatically related families. Among them, they had "speared" eight houses in the neighboring villages of Wamira, Wedau, Divari, Davudavu (a small inland village), and Magavara.

Prior to the *torela*, hosts gather their pigs, harvest their most impressive taro, and build a special shelter for the temporary storage of the food. An upcoming *torela* is heralded, in the villages of both hosts and guests, by the pained screeching of pigs being strapped onto poles and readied for the feast. Guests who arrive carrying a live pig on a pole must dress in warriors' attire. The men blow conch shells, beat drums, and clutch spears, followed by women who hold warriors' mother-of-pearl breastplates to their chests. Each guest who is ritually invited by a spear must, upon arrival, "retaliate" by throwing a spear at the house of his host.

Hooting, shouting, and dancing wildly, the guests aggressively present their food. Occasionally they engage in destructive behavior. At the feast in Pova, a group from Divari arrived carrying three large poles, two of which had pigs strapped to them. A large bundle of taro was strapped to the third pole, which was repeatedly thrust into the house of their hosts in an attempt to knock it down. They also swung machetes and fiercely chopped at a mango tree. As the house buckled and the tree shook, the guests shouted to their hosts that the hosts were merely "orphans" (*kedakeda*) and "impoverished people with no possessions or kin ties" (*lamolamona*). The owner of the collapsing house had presciently prepared for this by emptying his house of its possessions earlier in the day. The destructive behavior customarily continues until the host "closes the fighting" by throwing a live pig strapped onto a pole at the rampaging guests. This was soon done, and the people from Divari stopped trying to destroy the houses. Many agreed that, had the pig not been thrown in the guests' direction, the house would have been knocked to the ground.

On the day of their arrival, guests receive only boiled taro pudding (the *gwada* to which Tamodukorokoro made reference in his magical spell). All day, hosts stir the *gwada* with long wooden paddles in large earthenware pots whereas the invited guests, who desire the *gwada,* are arranged on the periphery of the cooking area according to village groups. Ritually prepared leaves are put into the bottom of the pudding pot as hunger suppression magic. The

4. Pigs being singed at a *torela* in Pova

guests, who have "come for their taro pudding," are given it only late in the evening, until which time they must sit patiently "like beggars." The giving of *gwada* is a sign that on the following day, pork will be distributed.

After the guests have received and eaten their *gwada,* the all-night dancing, performed in warrior's attire, commences. Any guest who wants to sleep must do so out of doors. In contrast to the usual pattern of visiting among relatives, where visitors are beckoned into the homes, on this day it is taboo for guests to enter their hosts' houses.

The second day, during which it is taboo to light cooking fires, is the grand occasion for the distribution of the raw food, both that brought by the guests and that amassed by the hosts. The counting and measuring of the taro and pigs lasts most of the day. Pigs are carried out from their temporary pens, their sizes are assessed, and their worth is appraised. The men responsible for killing pigs do so by stabbing the pig in the heart with a spear. When the pig ceases squirming, the man plugs the wound and the flow of blood with the regenerative stalk from a taro plant (the significance of which will be discussed in Chapter 6). The pig is thrown onto, or propped over, a large fire, where it is singed until its skin is black and its body stiff (see Plate 4). Still primarily raw, it is retrieved and butchered, the usual division being into eleven sections, as illustrated in Figure 9.

Toward evening, when the food is ready to be distributed, the hosts sit in

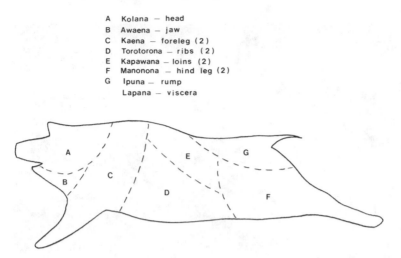

A   Kolana — head
B   Awaena — jaw
C   Kaena — foreleg (2)
D   Torotorona — ribs (2)
E   Kapawana — loins (2)
F   Manonona — hind leg (2)
G   Ipuna — rump
     Lapana — viscera

Figure 9. Method of butchering pig

the center of the feasting grounds behind a fortress of piles of pork and taro.[3] The guests remain on the outskirts in the same spots they have occupied since the previous day. It is taboo for any of the visitors to cross into the center of the circle where the food is amassed. I was told that should they approach the food, they would immediately be killed by the hosts. Several people explained to me that if the visitors came near, they would be able to steal food peelings or the leaves upon which the food is spread, all prime vehicles for the practice of sorcery aimed at the devastation of the hosts' crops. The hosts (*taniwaga*), who are competently organizing the food distribution, are seen as omnipotent. The guests, hungrily watching, are said to be "beggars" (*tabawabawa*).

The host responsible for calling the feast sits in the center and shouts out orders, chews areca nut, rattles his stick loudly in his lime pot, and fasts.[4] As one man explained, "The chief host puts on a show in public, but later, when he is alone, he eats in his house." His public behavior is said to prove the potency of his hunger-assuaging magic. All the food distributed and consumed at a *torela* is infused with potent hunger-suppression magic. This, I was told, explains why people eat only a small portion and feel satisfied.

[3] There are two categories of intervillage *torela*, depending on how the food is distributed. In one (*walaga*), a large platform is built and the food is placed on top of it. In the other (*garakaibadi*), the food is piled on the ground. (See Newton 1914:148–59 and Seligmann 1910:589–606 for detailed descriptions of the *walaga*. Their observations come from feasts that took place as early as 1901. Yet, the great similarity between the description of events then and now, eighty years later, is remarkable.)

[4] See Young (1971:249) for a comparison with Goodenough Island.

Once the distribution begins, the hosts pick up pieces of pork one at a time and literally throw them on the ground, usually aiming the meat at a bundle of taro. As the meat is tossed through the air, one of two phrases is shouted out. Either the host says, "Oh, so-and-so, rotten" (*O, aiai, bova*), which indicates that the pork is a payment for a piece of pork previously received. Or else he says, "Oh, so-and-so, tomorrow at such-and-such a place, I shall look up" (*O, aiai, au maratom mepa a na goutata*). "Looking up" refers to seeing meat being tossed down in the future and indicates that it is not a payment but will have to be reciprocated at a later date. As with the exchange of piglets, the distribution of pork is a strictly reciprocal exchange. For example, if X gave Y one pig's hind leg at a previous *torela*, Y returns one pig's hind leg to X. At the *torela* in Pova, twenty-two pigs were distributed.

A *torela* is also an occasion for people to settle debts and grievances.[5] As the host tosses the pork into the air, he may also call out any complaint he has. One Wamiran man, who arrived at Pova empty-handed, received a piece of pork together with the comment that his in-laws were angry that he did not visit them enough. Thus, the food was tossed down to initiate an exchange. It placed him in an economic and social debt to them, to repay the piece of pork as well as to visit.

When the food distribution is finished, the visitors load their pieces of pork and taro into baskets and return home, where they cook and eat. The hosts, who have put aside some of the pigs presented by the visitors, eat communally after everyone has left.

One man, bemoaning the aftereffect of a *torela*, said:

It is bad to have a *torela* because, when it is over, there is "famine." People have harvested all their taro, and it will take at least six months for it to grow again. The visitors will pay back, but not right away. Maybe two or three years will elapse before the visitors will give food to "their friends."

Many of the ritualized customs at a *torela* allow for the symbolic expression of the ambivalence of the affinal relationship while simultaneously controlling the competing desires to feast or to fight. As noted, on the occasion of a *torela*, the hosts reign supreme. Guests are forbidden entrance into the houses of their affines. Surrounded by their piles of food, the omnipotent hosts clearly communicate to their in-laws that, at least on this day, their lineage and its territory are taboo and sacred. The atmosphere is suffused with the hosts' anxiety over their guests' potential hostility. This anxiety manifests itself in such rituals as the taboos against crossing into the inner circle where the food is held for distribution. Hosts are always in fear of, and thus prepared for, guests' attempts to knock down houses, chop down trees, and ruin taro crops with sorcery (all symbols of their procreative powers). The aim is to keep

---

[5] Again, see Young, 1971, for comparison.

hostility and aggression, which may easily surface, under control. Guests are kept physically separate from hosts, sitting wistfully on the outskirts, and always reminded, ''like beggars,'' of their dependent and subordinate position. Food, that multifaceted pretense for calling the feast, is apportioned in a calculated and reciprocal manner. Most importantly, the food is imbued with hunger-suppression magic. This is to tame the most frightening of uncontrollable behaviors – namely ravenous, rapacious desire, both gustatory and sexual. If these lines defining people and their relationships to one another were not drawn as tightly as they are, conflict between men, and confusion between desires, might erupt.

The pig who gave birth to a boy

The same people with whom Wamirans held *torela* and occasionally intermarried, were those they ate in the days of cannibal warfare. Since contact, cannibalism has been eradicated. All that survives of the taste of human flesh in Wamira today are legends which the villagers relate with mocking gustatory delight.

According to Wamirans, ''before the missionaries arrived, the only meat eaten was human flesh; the missionaries taught villagers not to eat people and to eat pigs instead.'' The explanation for this transition from eating human flesh to pork is said to lie in a myth which I narrate and analyze below. It illustrates how men appropriate female reproductive powers symbolically in the realm of the pig.[6]

An old man lived together with his domesticated pig. After a while the pig gave birth to a human boy who the old man raised as his son. One day while the man and the boy were working in their taro garden, the people in the village killed the boy's mother, the pig, to eat her. At the same moment that the people speared the pig in the village, the boy accidentally stabbed his foot with his garden stick [an omen of misfortune]. ''Father,'' he said, ''what is happening back in the village that I should spear my foot?'' The man responded, ''Sit down while I plant two more taro stalks and then we'll return to the village.'' The boy rested in the shade until the man finished planting.

As they walked into the village, they saw pots resting over the fire. The boy asked, ''What are you cooking?'' An old man answered, ''We killed the pig and are cooking it. The pig always ruins the gardens and steals the taro, so we decided to kill it.'' The boy sat down and cried, for they had killed his mother. He said, ''All right, eat your pork but do exactly as I tell you with the bones.''

They lifted the pots from the fire, and all the people began to eat. The boy fetched a pandanus mat and spread it out. He instructed the people, ''When you have finished eating, place all the bones on this mat. Be sure not to throw any of them away.''

[6] I recorded this particular version from Simon Darita in 1977. It was elaborated upon by Osborne Kaimou in 1978. Another version of the myth was recorded by Seligmann in 1905, indicating that it was in existence already then (Seligmann 1910:415–16).

They did as the boy asked, and, when they had finished, the boy wrapped up the pig's bones inside the mat.

The following day he set out early, carrying the bundle of pig's bones. At Idei, in the hills behind Wamira, he got hungry and sat down to eat. As he ate, the pig's jaw fell out of the mat and turned into a pig that ran over the cliff and down to the water. It became a wild pig. When the boy finished eating, he took his mat and walked on.

As he approached Wanama, an inland village, he heard lots of noise and wondered what was going on. He saw that many people had gathered and were preparing for a feast. They were feasting on human beings. People were strapped onto poles by their arms and legs. The boy walked up to the leader and said, "What is going on here?" The leader responded, "Tomorrow we shall have a big feast and eat meat. You are lucky to have arrived today."

The following day the leader remarked, "There will be many people for us to feast upon. Look, already several days ago villagers brought people on poles. Their arms and legs are rubbed raw from having been carried strapped to the poles. The arms and legs of the people brought yesterday and today are still fine." The boy said, "Unfasten the cane rope from all the people who were brought recently and set them free. Those who were brought several days ago will remain strapped to the poles." The leader untied some of the people as the boy requested. Then the boy said, "Lend me some strong young men who can come down to the river with me."

Together with the young men, the boy carried the empty poles down to the river. He took his bundle of pig's bones. At the river he dug a hollow in the ground to get fresh spring water. When he finished doing this, he said to the men, "Get ready, when I call, run quickly."

He took out a bone and muttered a spell over it as he washed it in the spring water. It turned into a live pig. He called out, "Hurry up!" and the young men ran and grabbed the pig's leg. They tied the pig onto one of the poles. He took out another bone and said, "Get ready!" as he washed it in the water. He shouted, "Run, run!" but they failed to catch it, and it ran into the bush. He said, "Never mind that one. It will become a wild pig." He continued washing all the bones, and they all turned into pigs. He did this until they had as many pigs tied to poles as previously they had people. They carried the pigs back to the leader. When the people in the village saw the pigs, they were astonished.

The boy told the villagers, "This is the proper way to have a feast. This time roast people and distribute them, and then roast pigs and distribute them. Take good care of the offspring of these pigs so that later, when the pigs grow big, you will feast only upon pigs and not on people."

The boy slept in the village. The following day he walked to five other villages and taught them the same thing. Now people in this area feast upon pigs, and they no longer eat people.[7]

What is said to be a myth about "learning to eat pigs," upon closer examination appears to be a myth about men's desire to control reproduction. The myth distinguishes various reproductive categories.

---

[7] It must be noted that Wamirans, in professing their shift from cannibalism to eating pigs, have altered historical facts. Abundant historical and ethnographic evidence indicates the central importance of domesticated pigs to Wamirans in precontact times (King 1899:15; Maclaren 1891a, 1891b; Newton 1914:59; Seligmann 1910:599–606, 635–7). Elsewhere (Kahn 1983) I have discussed the discrepancy between historical fact and Wamirans' interpretation of it in terms of their "episodic" view of the past.

First, it accounts for the differentiation of species between people and pigs. In the beginning of the myth, pigs and people are relatively undifferentiated. The old man lives with his "domesticated pig" in much the same fashion that a man would live with a wife. Indeed, the female pig then gives birth to a boy who, in all respects, seems to be the man's son. In short, sexual union occurs between a human male and a female pig, the result of which is a human boy. Clearly, the exact distinction between pig and human, especially in their reproductive abilities, is not of paramount importance at the onset of the myth.

By the end of the myth, however, the boy has taught the villagers to make the distinction between human beings and pigs. He has also defined the procreative spheres of the two, as well as the proper manner of ingesting/not ingesting them. He teaches the people to "take good care of the offspring" of the pig so that, from then on, the pigs will reproduce on their own. He also teaches them to make the transition from ingesting human flesh to eating pork. He spreads his new dogma to other villages in much the same fashion that missionaries spread theirs. The boy, originally born of the intermingling of pig-mother and human father, now has taught people how to differentiate pig from human, pig reproduction from human reproduction, and cannibalism from feasting on pork.

The myth also accounts for the differentiation between domestic and feral pigs. In the myth, we see a reversal of male and female roles in these two realms. In daily life, it is primarily women who domesticate pigs by feeding them. Feral pigs are the domain of men, who hunt and kill them. In the myth, men alone are accountable for the domestication and regeneration of pigs. Women are conspicuously absent from the myth; the only female to appear is the pig. Although it is the female pig who produces and nurtures by giving birth to the boy, providing food for the people, and regenerating all future pigs with her bones, it is men who assume control of the pig's reproduction. Men are able to regenerate the pig, however, only with the assistance of magic. Through correct magical manipulation of her bones, they create domestic pigs. Through their negligence, by failing to catch pigs, they create the separate category of wild pig. In the myth, wild pigs are a result of men's failure to control (through magic, their main tool of creation), just as in daily life, wild pigs are a result of women's failure to control (through feeding, their main means of domesticating).

The mythical procreation of pigs is achieved by men by means of asexual regeneration. Using magic, the boy causes live pigs to spring from the bones of his mother. Bones play an important part in the creation myth of pigs, in the same way that blood, as we shall see, plays a significant role in the creation myth of taro. Bones, like blood, are regenerative elements, par excellence.[8] The boy gathers the bones from his deceased pig-mother and wraps

---

[8] See Battaglia 1983; Gillison 1983; and Goodale 1985, for analyses of bone symbolism in the context of Melanesian reproduction.

them in a mat in the same way that dead people are wrapped for burial. By washing the bones and uttering magical spells, the boy creates pigs.

In conclusion, pigs symbolically represent female sexuality. Men do not have female reproductive powers, but adopt them through symbol and metaphor in the realm of the pig. In this way men can escape the "double bind" of their male existence: Men are dependent upon women's fertility to reproduce themselves and achieve immortality, yet these children perpetuate their mother's, not their father's, lineage. Thus, men are dependent on women to produce offspring over whom they lose control. The greatest tensions, resulting from this "double bind," exist between affines, asymmetrically linked to one another because of their unequal access to a woman's sexuality.

Pigs appear as symbols of female sexuality in the ritualized exchange of piglets for domestication and of pork for ingestion. The exchange of piglets for domestication is tied into the existing relationship between a woman's husband and her lineage "brothers." The exchange signifies the positive, nurturing aspects of female sexuality. The exchange of pork for consumption, which also occurs between affinally related men, emphasizes the negative feelings of the relationship. Exchange of pork at *torela* expresses and controls tensions among affines. During the exchanges of both piglets for domestication and pork for ingestion, pigs are female surrogates that are separable from physical female sexuality and, as such, can be manipulated and controlled by men to escape their "double bind."

6. Taro: the cultivation of men's "children"

How do Wamiran men resolve the dilemma of the "double bind"? We have seen that through their exchange of pigs and pork, they symbolically express and control tensions that originate in the affinal bond. I now suggest that through the ritual creation of their own "children," they avoid the affinal bond entirely by sidestepping the shortcomings of its ties. Lévi-Strauss addressed this issue of men creating their own "children" symbolically through ritual for the Aranda. Whereas women really bear children, he said, men must

confine themselves to imagining that their rites result in the increase of . . . species. In the former, although it [child bearing] may be described in conventional terms which impose their own limits on it, what is in question is primarily a way of doing something. In the latter it is only a way of saying something. (Lévi-Strauss 1962a: 109–10).

Similarly, in Wamira, a distinction is made between women giving birth and men employing ritual to reproduce themselves symbolically (or between women "doing something" and men "saying something").

It is in the realm of taro that Wamiran men engage in rites that result in their symbolic regeneration and immortality. In the words of Wamirans, "taro are people." To justify their belief, they relate the following myth about the origin of taro.[1]

Long ago a man lived with his wife. The wife gave birth to a son who soon grew big and strong. But they had nothing to eat. One day the man cleared a new garden and dug many hollows in the soil. Upon observing his labors, his wife said to him, "Where is the food that you intend to plant? I see you have made many hollows, but we have nothing to put in them." He told his wife not to worry. Then, when she was not looking, the man killed their son and cut him up into many pieces. He placed a piece in each hollow and poured some of the blood onto each piece. At night the

---

[1] This particular version was narrated to me by Osborne Kaimou in 1978.

90

wife worried because her son was missing. Her husband consoled her by saying that the son would appear later. The next day when she went to the garden, she saw taro growing. She feared what had happened and ran back to the village. Her husband revealed that he had killed and planted their son so that they would have taro to eat.

The myth embodies two prominent themes about sexual relations and roles in the reproduction of society. One is that of competition and destruction among men. (In the myth it is intergenerational, being aimed at the woman's son rather than at her brother.) The other is that of male appropriation and imitation of female powers of reproduction.

First, the myth alludes to competitive aggression among men during male acts of production. Although versions of the myth vary slightly, a man always kills another *man* in order to produce taro. Sometimes he chops his grown son to pieces, sometimes his younger brother. The life that he takes is necessary for the production of taro and is always that of a close male relative, slightly lower in status, but with whom, in daily life, he must cooperate during the cultivation of taro.

The horticultural domain is a microcosm for the realities of male conflict; taro cultivation is the primary area in which daily rivalries among men are expressed. On the one hand, horticultural units of production correspond to patrilocal residential hamlets and, as such, reinforce male group solidarity. However, a man's relationship to the tubers he nurtures is that of self-definition and individuality. Taro, in addition to being a man's main medium of economic and social exchange, is a symbolic indicator of his personal status and virility. Taro, more than any other cultigen, is nurtured with potent magic, a man's private tool for production. Its destruction is believed to be a result of sorcery, a man's secret weapon against other men. As a result, taro plants grow and wither to the pulsating rhythm of cohesion and conflict in their cultivators' patrigroup.

Second, the myth distinguishes separate female and male domains in the processes of reproduction: Women produce children, men produce taro. Moreover, the man, in demonstrating his powers, emulates a woman's reproductive and nurturant abilities. In the beginning of the myth, the woman gives birth to a son. However, "when she is not looking," her husband steals the son, hacks him to pieces which he douses with blood, and produces taro. Thus, we can read one of the themes in the myth as the man's appropriation of the woman's fertility. In the myth, the man confiscates his own offspring, born from a woman, and transforms this human product of sexual reproduction into taro, a vegetable product of asexual regeneration. In doing so, the husband regenerates himself in the same biologically asexual manner in which taro is reproduced.

In daily life, Wamirans draw parallels between human beings and taro, and symbolically equate the female realm of human reproduction with the male realm of taro production. Women are said to supply offspring with blood and milk, the main ingredients embedded in matrilineality. In this way, women are believed to control the procreation, nourishment, and growth of human beings. Men's reproductive success is measured in rituals of taro production and during the ritual manipulation of the harvested tubers.[2]

Taro

Time and again, while accompanying families to their gardens or participating in feasts, I heard variations on the following statement:

Our life is taro. We use taro to pay for our land, for the building of our houses, for our weddings and our funerals. We need taro. We must plant taro so that we can survive.

Although taro (*Colocasia esculenta*) plays such a significant part in Wamirans' social lives, it comprises only about 25 percent of their diet in terms of weight and calories. Both the starchy, grayish corm and the large, heart-shaped leaves are eaten. To harvest taro, Wamirans sever the edible corm and leaves from the regenerative stalk, which they replant. The replanted stalk reproduces by asexual vegetative propagation, or cloning. The cultivation of taro is a cyclical process whereby small-scale harvesting and replanting are continually undertaken. One replanted stalk regenerates one new corm, although additional smaller shoots occasionally sprout from the tuber's sides. In Wamira, the taro is ready to harvest in six to eight months. The regenerative stalk, defoliated and severed from the corm, must be replanted within two or three days, lest it rot. The tuber and leaves, likewise, must be cooked and eaten within a few days.

Wamirans distinguish more than sixty varieties of taro, which they classify according to the color of the regenerative stalk. These named taro groups are said to belong to different *dam* (the same word used to refer to matrilineal groups of people). Wamirans value taro according to its consistency. The denser the corm, the more it is relished. Taro is the most preferred *lam* (vegetable food). It is believed that only taro makes Wamirans' stomachs "full, heavy, and happy," and their bodies "strong and healthy." As mentioned, they say that taro, in contrast to other vegetable foods, fills their stomachs and sits solidly inside them "like stone," thus giving them "energy and life."

Garden groups: male units of production

Taro gardens are located in isolated pockets that mirror patrilocal residential units. They can be approached only by secret networks of paths known solely

[2] The conceptual separation of what are perceived as sexually antagonistic realms of production is widespread in Melanesia (Gillison 1980; Herdt 1981, 1982; A. Strathern 1979; Weiner 1977, 1979) and has been discussed in the Introduction.

by those people to whose plots the paths lead. Most garden areas lie at the base of the foothills and are separated from one another by the undulating terrain. Should a garden lie close to a communal area, high wattles of sago or coconut branches are built to protect the growing taro from the eyes of passers-by. Once within the garden, cultivators work quietly amid rectangular patches at various stages of cultivation: plots of freshly turned sod, of newly planted stalks bereft of leaves, and of older taro with large, heart-shaped leaves. Small thatched garden huts, used by the cultivators when they rest in the heat of the noonday sun, or take shelter from sudden rain, dot each garden area.

During some cultivation stages, such as breaking the sod, communal help is necessary and men work cooperatively. Otherwise, individual men or women, and occasionally married couples, go off to their garden alone. Teenagers sometimes accompany their parents to the garden, where they begin to learn the many customs and "laws" that pertain to the cultivation of taro.

The physical layout of the taro gardens and of the irrigation canals that feed them mirrors male-oriented social and political organization. Units of horticultural production correspond to patrilocal hamlet groups.[3] As described in Chapter 1 (see Map 3), Wamira is divided into two residential wards: Damaladona and Rumaruma. Each of the two wards irrigates its taro gardens from a different river. Damaladona utilizes water from the Wamira River. Rumaruma uses that from the Uruam River. Within each ward, the taro gardens of one residential hamlet are separated from those of another. Within each hamlet, households of one hamlet division work in gardens that are adjacent to one another, and yet are separated from the gardens of the other divisions within the hamlet.

Taboos surrounding the irrigation canals further reiterate the residential structure of Wamira. Because of the prevailing atmosphere of suspicion and the intense fear of sorcery (to be discussed shortly), it is taboo for people from one ward to cross over the canals or to look into the taro gardens of the other ward. Likewise, within one ward, people must not cross over the canals that lead to the gardens of other hamlets within the ward. As the wards, hamlets, and hamlet divisions become more narrowly defined, so, too, do the demarcating lines of canals over which people must not cross. Only members of a hamlet division, most likely brothers, sons of brothers, or fathers and sons, have adjacent gardens and share one irrigation canal (the same men who, in the myth, kill one another in order to produce taro).

The manner in which the location of taro gardens, and the irrigation canals that delineate and separate them, parallel male-oriented residential groups, is illustrated in Maps 4 and 5, and in Figure 10. In Map 4, the letters A (of which there are two for easier reference to Map 5), B, and C refer to hamlet

---

[3] Only four percent of Wamiran men do not cultivate taro gardens together with their hamlet members.

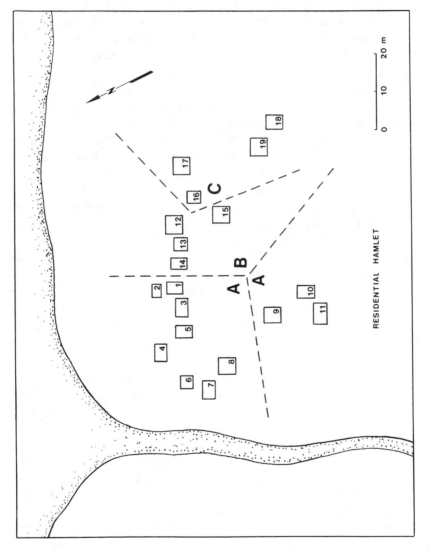

Map 4. Residential hamlet

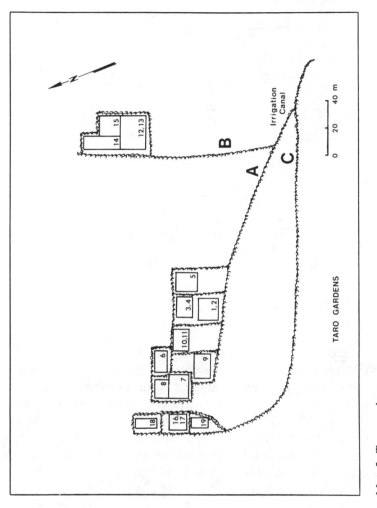

Map 5. Taro gardens

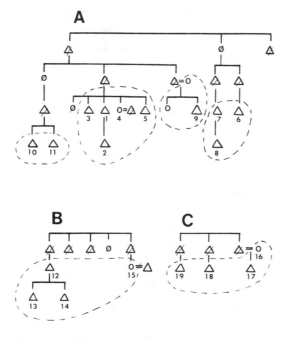

Figure 10. Hamlet genealogy

divisions, and the numbers to households. In Map 5, the letters A, B, and C refer to the corresponding irrigation canals which define that division's gardening area. People irrigating from canal A must neither trespass across the canals leading to, nor peek into, the gardens of those irrigating from B or C, and vice versa. The numbers indicate the garden plots that coincide with household numbers in Map 4. In Figure 10, the letters on the genealogical chart correspond to the hamlet divisions and irrigation groups; the numbers correspond to the households and their garden plots.

Magic: men's tools of production

In the Wamiran universe, acts of creation and manipulation are believed to be brought about by magical incantation.[4] Magic is said to be a person's "power," and its secrecy is closely guarded. The most private of personal property and the most valued form of traditional wealth, magic is strictly kept within the nuclear family, and is passed on by fathers to sons and by mothers to daugh-

---

[4] Here we recall two such occasions from myths. For instance, Tamodukorokoro, a symbol of productivity, repeatedly chanted his magical spell to escape situations in which his existence was threatened. Or, to create pigs, the boy in the pig myth muttered a spell over his mother's bones while washing them in water.

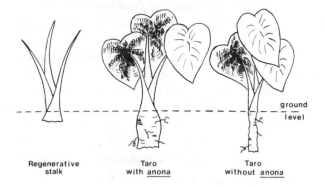

Figure 11. Taro with and without *anona*

ters. Magic always consists of incantations (*pari*) chanted in a special magical tongue, and the manipulation of natural substances (*muramura*) such as particular leaves, plants, tree barks, or pieces of food.[5] Each type of magical power encompasses its own food proscriptions and prescriptions, which are followed by the owner in order to render the spells most potent.

The primary arena for the use of magic is the taro garden, where the cultivation of the tubers offers numerous opportunities for men to exhibit their powers of production. "Magic," Wamirans say, "is what makes taro grow." Failure of a taro crop is attributed primarily to the ritual incompetence of the cultivator or to the sorcery of his enemy. Each step in the process of cultivation is accompanied by magic. During the initial stages of preparing the plot for planting, the leader of the garden group (discussed in Chapter 1) performs magic on behalf of the entire group. During the latter stages, only individuals perform rituals and spells. At harvest, magic is abandoned. Taro magic is allocated according to sex: Men possess magic for planting taro; women own magic for weeding and tending the growing tubers.

The aim of magic is to insure the presence of *anona*, a term that refers to inner substance in general, and here specifically to the essence of the tuber. *Anona* is what makes a taro corm heavy and swollen and thus, according to Wamiran thought, nutritious.[6] Its presence or absence is revealed entirely by the appearance of the tuber and is observable only when a person unearths his taro. As illustrated in Figure 11, taro with *anona* appear healthy and robust. Taro without *anona* are simply empty, shriveled skins (which when eaten, even in large quantities, do not provide a sense of nourishment or satiation).

[5] In deference to the Wamirans and the importance of the privacy of magic, I do not include any details of individually owned magical spells or knowledge.

[6] This concept is similar to that discussed for the Maenge, where "food is nutritious only because it possesses a soul" (F. Panoff 1969:28).

When men harvest their crops, the appearance of their taro informs them of all they need to know: their horticultural potency, the accuracy of their magical knowledge, and the intentions of their friends and enemies. Thus, during the entire process of cultivation, a gardener lives in constant doubt of the efficacy of the magic used and in fear of evil sorcery that might devastate his crop. This concept – that only harvested taro will reveal his and others' inner qualities and intentions – was explained to me by a man who used the following Christian analogy. The quote conveys both the idea of living in a continual state of anxiety that one's fellow human beings may wish one ill, and the importance of appearance as a proof of human intentions and desires.[7]

God's magic is different from Wamirans' magic. God wrote his knowledge down in the Bible for everyone to see. In Wamira, magic is private. We never reveal to anyone what is most important to us. No one knows the magic of another person. No one knows whether the magic someone else uses is good or bad. Only later, when a man harvests his taro and sees the tubers, will he know. If the taro are small and rotten, someone "lied" [sorcerized them]. In Wamira, our religion is good because after six or eight months when we harvest our taro, we can see whether people told the truth or lied. If one is a Christian and believes in the Bible, it is no good. Christians will never know whether God is telling the truth or lying because they have to wait until they die to find out.

The power of magic is a double-edged sword. When not used properly (if, for example, the spells are chanted incorrectly or if food proscriptions and prescriptions are not obeyed), magic may backfire on an individual. One way in which such calamity occurs is when a man greedily eats some of his own first-harvested taro (or other food). It is customary for the cultivator to give such produce to someone else, even to his wife, rather than eat it himself. Wamirans readily point to individuals whose teeth have fallen out, whose heads have turned prematurely bald, or whose limbs are deformed, saying these are the result of eating from their own first-harvested taro. A more severe outcome of eating one's own bespelled tubers is that one can never again produce decent taro. As a result, for the remainder of one's life one is condemned to "theft" (both stealing food from another's garden and stealing the essence of another's food by means of sorcery).

The strong taboo against being the first to eat one's own food is due to the belief in the creative and transformative qualities of magic. A man strongly identifies with his tubers. The process of creating and generating one's physical offshoots entails infusing them with one's magic and, thus, with one's personal essence and power. In doing so, one endows them with life substance of their own.[8]

[7] See Kahn 1983 for a discussion of this latter point.
[8] This belief is also seen linguistically. The word for magic is *kaua*. The verb *kauei*, derived from the noun *kaua*, means to "make," "do," "create," or "construct." *Kaua* also refers to the character or quality of a person, animal, plant, or an object created with magic.

Just as taro magic serves as a man's main productive tool, so does sorcery, or evil magic, serve as his most destructive weapon. Suspicion of other men is a daily anxiety with which every Wamiran man lives. Taro sorcery is practiced by men against other men only, and is done because a man either is jealous of another man's adulterous liaisons with his wife, or is envious of another man's flourishing taro crop (both situations in which the sorcerer's sexual or horticultural potency has been challenged). When such evil magic (*gagala*) is used to destroy taro, magically charged substances either can be slipped into the soil at the edge of the garden or can be wrapped into a small parcel which is then placed in the irrigation water and directed to flow toward the garden of one's foe. The threat of sorcery accounts for the strong prohibitions against crossing the canals that separate one man's taro garden from another's and for the taboos against trespassing onto another's garden. An individual discovered in someone else's taro garden is considered guilty of committing sorcery. The taboos against crossing the canals are suggestive of the strong taboo against *torela* guests crossing into the inner food-circle discussed in Chapter 5. In both instances, physical space and distance are communicators of social relationships and the control needed to keep superficial amity from revealing hidden enmity.

Sorcery is most common immediately after planting. If, for example, a man steals young taro shoots that were recently planted with nourishing magic, the thief acquires the effectiveness of the spells, together with the stolen taro. When he later plants his plunder in his own garden, his taro will prosper and the taro remaining in the original owner's plot will wither. When sorcery is practiced against a man's taro, not only does it completely ruin his crop, it also destroys his image as a producer in the eyes of other men. Thus, his status decreases as his tubers shrivel. Taro sorcery practiced among men is relatively common. As one man pointed out, "The nature of taro is that people place evil magic on it." Countersorcery also exists, and the most powerful and respected men are those possessing forceful antisorcery magic.

The cultivation of taro, an activity that offers numerous opportunities for the use of magic and sorcery, is replete with possibilities for men to express their competitiveness in symbolically potent ways. The harvested tubers, whether plump and erect or withered and wizened, bristle with significant messages about the virility and status of their cultivator, and about the nature of his relationships to other men.

Women's powers of production

For Wamiran women, powers of reproduction are located in the realm of human being; they are embedded in child bearing and the reproduction of the matrilineage. It is felt that women are naturally able to produce and nourish children because of their biological substances of blood (*tara*) and breast milk (*gugu*), which are seen as the main ingredients necessary in the creation and nurturing of life.

Wamirans believe that a woman's main substantive contribution in the reproduction of human beings is blood (*tara*). The main substance contributed by men, but not viewed with as much import as blood, is bone (*gelamina*). Human beings are believed to consist of an outer skin (*opi* or *ini*) which encases the two elements of blood and bones. Blood is seen as responsible for the existence of life. It is said to be "bad" or "poison" because it (or its loss) can cause sickness and death. Most physical states are expressed in terms of a person's blood, which is viewed as the essential factor determining any human biological condition. For example, when a person's "blood runs around" (*tara e rubaruba*), one is healthy; but when the "blood unites" (*tara e vitagogiei*) and forms clusters "like stones," one is sick. "To be strong" is phrased as having "big blood" (*tara i rata*), and "to be dead" is to have "no blood left" (*tara i kwa*).

Conception is said to occur when a man's semen (*moro*) mixes with a woman's blood, at which time the blood coagulates in her "stomach" and her menstrual flow ceases. (Wamirans are vague when describing the man's role in making the blood coagulate.) Thus, when a woman is pregnant, her "blood is closed" or "stopped up" (*tara i gudui*). Magic aimed at bringing about an abortion is said to make the "blood separate" again (*tara i vilamoni*). Wamirans believe that during the first few months of pregnancy, the fetus is not yet formed, but consists of lumps of blood only.

A belief in the transference of a woman's blood to her offspring underlies the idea of her unassisted role in transferring matrilineal substance to her children. Wamirans feel that each time a woman gives birth, she loses more of her blood, which has gone into forming the baby. This gradual loss of blood over her lifetime, necessary for the reproduction of children and the perpetuation of society, is said to cause her withering and death.[9] For example, the fact that a woman has only one child and fails to produce another is explained by her "not having enough blood" and that her blood was already "finished" early in her life. Or, the fact that a woman gives birth to several children and then dies is said to occur because in giving birth so often, she "used up her blood."[10] This notion of giving birth to the limit of one's blood is expressed in the same manner as the notion of dying. For a woman to have "no blood left" (*tara i kwa*) may indicate either that she cannot produce any more children or that she is dead. We might interpret the dual use of this

[9] This concept of limited and unreplenishable biological substance seems similar to that discussed for males in the New Guinea Highlands. Herdt (1981, 1982), Kelly (1976:44), and Schieffelin (1976:124), for example, note that male vitality is embodied in semen which must be acquired at puberty. The gradual depletion of semen over a lifetime is believed to account for the withering and eventual death of men.

[10] The average number of children born to a Wamiran woman is four.

linguistic idiom as an indication that the purpose of a woman's "blood-running" life is the creation of new human beings.

Once the baby is born, the mother, more than the father, continues to play the significant role in its nourishment and growth. It is the mother's breast milk that is seen as responsible for making the baby grow. Moreover, a mother, in feeding her child, is seen as continuing to transfer matrilineal substance, this time in the form of milk, to her child. For example, the word for breast or breast feeding (*gugu*) is interchangeable with that for matrilineal group (*dam*).

As is the case in her powers of reproduction, a woman's powers of destruction are aimed directly at people and, specifically, at her lineage members. This occurs as witchcraft, an activity that is often associated with women in Melanesia (Fortune 1932; Malinowski 1922). Wamiran witches (*parauma*) are old (i.e., nonreproductive) women of a haggard countenance, stingy nature, and nasty disposition. Such women are believed capable of bodily transformation. Wamirans say they observe the witches going about their evil activities at night, visible in the form of fireflies. A witch conjures over special black stones topped with silver speckles by tapping on the stone as she sings out her spell. In performing her duties, she (her empty body) lies in the house at night while her *arua,* or shadow double, flies about. A witch may receive her special powers by engaging in sexual liaisons with elflike beings (*bariawa*) or by inheriting the magic from her mother. A witch's husband is usually ignorant of his wife's special powers.

Witches aim their evil magic at members of their own matrilineage, usually siblings or children. One illustration that witchcraft is often aimed at one's siblings occurred when I was joking with an old woman about my fear of her being a witch. Her response was, "But I cannot be a witch because I am an only child. I have no brothers or sisters!"

"Taro are people": male emulation of female reproductive powers

In contrast to women, who reproduce society naturally by producing human beings, men reproduce society metaphorically by producing taro. Men's powers of reproduction find their locus in taro cultivation and associated ritual. As will be demonstrated in Chapter 8, men further control and communicate their powers during the exchange of harvested taro during feasts. The parallels between human beings and taro, and between the female role in producing human beings and the male role in producing taro, are many.

Wamirans say "taro are people"; they attribute human qualities to the tubers. For example, they believe taro possesses the capacity to speak, hear, smell, and see. One woman offered evidence of taro speech in saying, "When a person hears a crackling noise in the garden, it is the taro talking." The tubers have ''ears,'' which allow them to hear spells that nurture them. They also possess ''noses,'' which they use to smell the substances, such as coconut cream on the cultivator's skin or meat on his breath, that threaten their existence.

Taro *anona,* or inner substance, discussed previously in connection with magic, is related to the anthropomorphic qualities of taro. *Anona,* also a human attribute, is dependent upon two entities: the shadow-reflected *arua* and the ancestral *konaga.*

Like a person, a taro tuber possesses an *arua,* an immaterial, two-dimensional shadow, reflection, or double self, which replicates the physical container but lacks inner corporeal substance. It adheres to the skin of the taro but can detach itself, as happens when the *arua* is captured by a drawing or a photograph. (The word for photograph or drawing is also *arua.*) In human beings, the *arua* is the aspect of the self capable of independent journeys during dreams, the skittish nighttime activities of witches, permanent departure at death, or even departure at "temporary death."[11]

Taro are also the main dwelling places of *konaga,* spirits of the cultivator's deceased ancestors. *Konaga* are formless beings that reside next to one's house, alongside one's taro garden, and within one's taro plants. When hovering near the individual, they adhere to the inside of the elbow. The patrilocal attachments of the *konaga* account for the patrimonial preference to garden land and house sites. The presence of one's *konaga* is continually felt. *Konaga* instruct one on all matters of social behavior. They appear in dreams, advising the dreamer about his or her actions. An individual's strength and success depend largely on that person's relationship with the *konaga.* For example, if the *konaga* are pleased with an individual's proper observance of "custom," he or she will enjoy a healthy and productive life; if not, illness and death will result.

Responses of the *konaga* are directly observable in one's taro. They answer to the beneficent magical spells properly chanted by a cultivator in the garden, as well as respond to the sorcery practiced by envious foes. If the *konaga* are pleased, the taro grows strong and heavy. Should the ancestral spirits be disgruntled as a result of improper observance of custom and taboo, the taro leaves will appear deceptively healthy and lush; however, when the owner uproots his taro, he will discover that the tuber is puny, shriveled, and rotten because of the absence of *anona.*

Moreover, taro, like people, are said to possess "blood." The importance of blood in stimulating the growth of taro was noted in the taro origin myth. There the father doused the pieces of his son with blood to make them grow.

---

[11] The notion of "temporary death" being likened to permanent death, and the belief that both are due to the departure of the *arua,* is illustrated in the following statement by an elderly man. He said, "I have died three times in my life. The first time I died was in Wamira. The second time I died was when I was sick in the hospital in Samarai. The third time has not occurred yet."

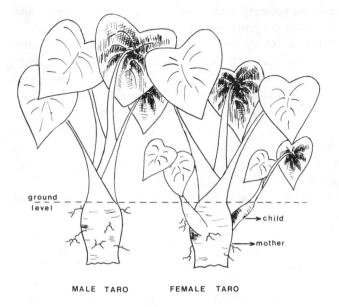

ground level

child

mother

MALE TARO   FEMALE TARO

Figure 12. Male and female taro

In a different version of the myth, the narrator insisted that it was not the entire son who was cut up and placed in the ground but only his liver which, when mixed with the blood, grew into a red-tinged taro (*nakwaria tarana*). This type of taro is said to be the first one in existence, and is viewed as the most delicious. Its name refers to the large quantity of "blood" (*tara*) in its corm.

As illustrated in Figure 12, taro, like people, appear in male and female forms. Those tubers that simply regenerate themselves are said to be male. Those that, in addition to reproducing themselves, produce small "children" that cling to the parent corm, are designated as female. In the latter case, the corm is said to be the "mother" who "gives birth to children."[12]

The role of *anona,* or essence, in taro reproduction is likened to that of a woman's blood in human reproduction. In talking about human reproduction, Wamirans say that "as a mother produces children and loses blood, she becomes progressively weaker." The mother, in giving birth, transfers her substance (her blood) to her offspring. Likewise, for taro, "mothers" transfer their *anona* to their "children." Regenerative stalks of "mother" taro are not replanted once the tuber is harvested and eaten. Only those of the "children" are returned to the soil. Wamirans believe that the "mother" taro, if re-

---

[12] Among the Maenge, Panoff also notes that taro are both male ("taro without cormlets") and female ("taro that produce cormlets"). Moreover, "the taro itself copulates" (F. Panoff 1970:248).

planted, would be weak and withered because she transferred her strength and substances to her offspring in the process of producing them.

The part of the taro with which men are most closely associated is the replantable stalk. Wamirans express this identification of men with the regenerative aspect of taro in their saying: "Men are *diwara* [bundled taro with stalks], and women are garden baskets [used for presenting taro corms]." The stalk is called *vegavega,* the same word used for the umbilical cord of a newborn baby. When a taro plant is flourishing in the garden with the stalk, leaves, and corm attached to one another, the animate attributes discussed earlier, permeate the total plant. After the corm and leaves have been removed from the stalk, the animate attributes reside only in the regenerative stalk.[13] As mentioned earlier, the stalk is also that part of the taro by which men distinguish one type of taro from another.

This distinction, between the reproductive value of the regenerative stalk and the nutritional value of the edible corm and leaves, is carried through in exchange at harvest time, and is of great significance symbolically. As we shall see in Chapter 8, a crucial difference exists between a presentation of taro with the stalk attached (made only by men) and one without the stalk (made by men or women). Moreover, only "male" taro are amassed into *diwara,* the festive bundles of harvested taro prepared for a feast. During the exchanges, the regenerative stalks, although initially presented with the corms, are *always* retrieved by the male cultivator.[14]

The parallels between female reproduction of people and male production of taro do not end after acts of creation are completed. Similarities continue during processes of nourishment and growth. As one young mother explained to me, "Just as a woman breast-feeds her baby to nourish it and make it grow, men lead water to the taro plants to make them thrive." Parallels are also present during acts of destruction. We recall that women, by means of witchcraft, are able to destroy what they create, namely lineage members. By means of sorcery, a male activity only, a man is able to destroy another man's taro, the tangible symbol of his reproductive powers.

Sexual dependency and autonomy during cultivation

An analysis of the stages of taro cultivation, from planting to harvesting, reveals ways in which the two major Wamiran tensions in sexual relations are expressed and resolved symbolically. Tensions between men are expressed in

[13] Among the Orokaiva, Schwimmer notes a related but slightly different concept where the "spirit life" of the taro is lodged in the leafy top and the taro "dies" when the stalk is severed from the corm (Schwimmer 1973:114).

[14] Schwimmer notes that the Orokaiva distinguish between raw taro with the tops attached, given by men, and cooked taro corms without tops, given by women. According to Schwimmer (1973:121), taro presented with the leafy tops attached still contain the spirit of the plant and are "alive." Men give these gifts (which contain part of the cultivator's essence) to initiate relationships. Cooked taro are given to maintain relationships.

5. Men turning soil in taro garden

the shift from male group solidarity to individual autonomy; tensions between men and women are communicated in the alternation of male and female participation in the gardening process. A brief outline of the stages of cultivation illustrates the symbolic expression of these tensions.

The process of cultivation is divided into several stages, each of which is preceded by magic and accompanied by strict custom and taboo. Male group solidarity, which rests on a shaky foundation, is continually threatened and strictly enforced. For example, when the members of a garden group make new taro gardens, it is of the utmost importance that all members follow through the stages in unison. No man can begin a stage before the leader of the garden group has initiated it, and no stage can be initiated by the leader until everyone in the group has completed the previous one.

The initial step in preparing a new taro garden is the cutting of the grass by the men (*petoi*). On the first day of work, the men in the garden group clear only the garden leader's plot. The following day, they continue with the remaining plots, working uninterruptedly from one tract to the next. In a day or two, all the plots are completed. A few days after the cutting, when the remaining grass stubble has dried, men again work together to burn them off (*arai*).

The soil is then turned (*uata*) by groups of five or six men, each wielding a digging stick (*ipa*) that is three or four meters long (see Plate 5). The term used to designate the five or six men working together is *ipa tagogi*, or "one digging stick,'' which gives an indication of the technological importance of male cooperation in this labor-intensive task. During this cooperative stage, after completing the leader's plot, the workers proceed from one man's plot to the next. The work is strenuous, and it usually takes an entire day to turn the sod in one garden. The garden leader performs group magic, yet each man also performs his own magic before the work is done in his garden. This stage is especially riddled with suspicion of one another and fear of sorcery.

After this task is finished, the emphasis shifts from communal male efforts to individuals working alone. After the garden soil has sat in large clods for about two weeks, each man reworks the soil in his garden into grains of a finer texture, a process called *dabara*. Using an even longer digging stick, he swings its sharpened end parallel to the ground as he knocks it into the large clumps to break them apart. Each man prepares only his own plot and uses his magic.

Once the group leader has performed planting magic in his garden, each man secretly begins to plant, quietly beginning before dawn. This is the sacred occasion for a man to imbue and nurture the planted stalks with his magic. Only taro is planted in a newly prepared garden, and only men may plant taro. To plant, a man places his long digging stick into the ground and rotates it in a circular fashion to widen a hollow. After preparing all the necessary hollows, he places taro stalks into each one. He then proceeds from hollow to hollow as he straightens the stalk and mounds up the earth around its base, firmly packing the soil into place with his hands. When planting taro, a man starts at the inland end of the plot and gradually proceeds toward the sea as he fills the entire area.

Once the taro is planted, the process of cultivation is ''passed from men to women.'' When the taro is about two months old (gauged by the fact that the stalk has put out two or three leaves), all the women of the garden group communally perform the task called *garai*. They awake long before the sun rises and sedately walk to the gardens, pausing along the way to bathe ritually in the river. In the gardens, they silently bend over the taro and, with a sense of ceremony, dig hollows around the bases of the young plants with short, flattened digging sticks (*pawana*). This is done so that later, when the men let the irrigation water into the garden, the water seeps deeply into the soil and reaches the growing tubers (see Plate 6). As the women move together from one plot to the next, proceeding from inland toward the sea within each garden, they pluck out the weeds and grass which, since planting, have sprouted up among the taro. The women complete up to ten gardens in a day, working steadily, neither talking nor eating until all the work is finished.

The next stage in the tending of the taro (*guruvi*) takes place about two months after the women have weeded and dug the hollows, and is also done communally. With the *pawana,* they now mound up the earth around the base of the taro plant, which by this time has produced several more leaves.

6. Women weeding taro garden

The women perform their final task (*goru*) of cutting away the dried and shriveled leaves from the sides of the taro, which are carefully disposed of far away from the garden. When the women finish tending the taro, they "pass the work back to their husbands" for harvest. During harvest, a man no longer performs any magic because the plants are fully grown and magic is no longer necessary.

If taro are to be for a harvest display (*viega*), they must be unearthed by a man. Using his long digging stick, he probes the ground just below the taro corm and carefully loosens the soil around it. Using his stick as a lever, he slowly pushes up the taro plant. Once the taro are presented to the receivers, and the stalks are retrieved by the cultivator, the process described above begins again.

Figure 13 summarizes the way in which the cultivation stages articulate with the shifts in male and female involvement in production and, within the male phases, from group solidarity and cooperation to individual autonomy. In this way, the ritual of taro cultivation symbolically and concisely reiterates daily concerns: tensions between the sexes, struggles for sexual autonomy in productive and reproductive activities, and male rivalries and suspicions which result in the continual threat of group disruption.

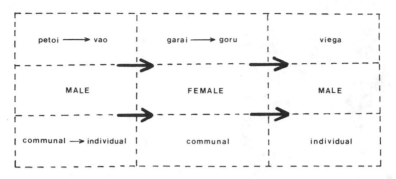

Figure 13. Stages of taro cultivation

Displaying virility

The condition of the harvested taro reveals the potency of the magic and the virility of the cultivator, as well as the cohesiveness of the garden work group. Although the Wamiran ideal boasts of male solidarity and cooperation, the reality is one of rivalry, antagonism, suspicion, and sorcery which continually threaten to tear the group apart. Garden leaders, envied for their horticultural knowledge and expertise, are primarily evaluated on their ability to hold the group together. Thus, at harvest, men symbolically expose their, and their garden leader's, virility. While intending to impress, they must display modesty. Leaders and cultivators desire to be productive, yet fear being seen as *too* productive because this would elicit envy and, hence, sorcery from others.[15]

When the men of a garden group harvest their first taro, they unearth only a few tubers and display and share these solely within their group. This is done to check the quality of the taro, and hence the effectiveness of the magic and the presence or absence of sorcery.

Soon thereafter, couched in the occasion of a general, village-wide feast for a different purpose (such as a feast that marks the end of a village dance, the saint's day of the village church, or the farewell festivities of the anthropologist), they reveal their taro to everyone else in Wamira. At this time, a mixed atmosphere of self-importance and muted envy prevails. Only the garden group members, with great pomp and pride, acknowledge and plan for the impending display. All others, however, who quietly have been calculating the passage of time since planting began, greet the displayed taro with feigned surprise. Onlookers exhibit great indifference toward the bundles of tubers while, out of the corners of their eyes, they gauge and appraise the height and plumpness of each corm and the size and crispness of the leaves. The condition of the group's taro reveals the strength of the group's magic. If the harvested taro are large, everyone knows that the garden leader and the

---

[15] The word used to indicate a harvest display is *viega*, which literally means "to negate" or "to nullify."

individual owners used powerful magic. If, on the other hand, a group displays puny and premature taro, the other men laugh and taunt the members of the garden group, ridiculing them as merely "small boys" who are "playing."

The manner in which taro are presented is of great significance. The ideal of group solidarity, cohesion, and cooperation is outwardly displayed; so, too, is the ideal of egalitarianism among men who are engaged in exchanges with one another. Bundled taro given at a feast must, at a future date, be paid back measure-for-measure down to the precise number of taro in the bundle. There are only three ways Wamirans may bundle taro for feasts. Thus, the recipient, without having to count the corms, immediately knows the exact value of the transaction. The three methods are as follows:

1. *Ewa* is a small bundle, consisting of five or six taro, and is presented by only one man.
2. *Diwara* consists of nineteen taro gathered by two or three men who garden adjacent plots. The tubers are bundled in three concentric circles of 1-6-12.
3. *Diwara gaegaena* are twenty-five taro amassed by the men of an entire small hamlet or a division of a large hamlet. The bundle holds nine taro at the center and sixteen around the outside.

Once the taro have been presented, the receivers remove the edible leaves and corms from the stalks with a pearl oyster shell (a metal utensil, such as a knife, is believed to displease the taro stalk which would "smell the rust and refuse to grow"). The regenerative stalks are then rebundled. Surprising to me is that each man who presents taro is able to distinguish the stalks belonging to his corms, and retrieves them. As discussed, it is extremely important for a man to retain his replantable stalks. The prevalence of this custom has been noted in Melanesia, where it is common for men to "exchange women but to refuse to exchange seeds" (Lévi-Strauss 1962a:110). Perhaps, it is precisely because men are "saying something" in the rituals of taro cultivation and exchange (as opposed to women, who are "doing something" in giving birth and breast-feeding children) that men retain that part of the plant which represents their reproductive ability. After all, keeping the taro's regenerative stalk is the main way a man can control his regenerative abilities.

In the analysis of the Tamodukorokoro myth, conflicts among Wamiran men over sexual competition, as well as between men and women, were expressed. Feelings among men are those of controlled envy, competition, and aggression. Those between men and women are ambivalent, oscillating between the need for mutual dependence and the desire for individual autonomy in realms of reproduction. As we have seen, the themes expressed in the myth ring true in daily preoccupations during the domestication of pigs and the cultivation of taro. I now turn to a more analytic unraveling of these gender-based relationships, which sometimes in concert, sometimes in conflict, are always necessary in the perpetuation of society.

7. Digestion and reproduction: parallel acts of regeneration

We can best understand the more subtle aspects of gender-based relationships by examining how food and gender categories fit into a larger framework of beliefs about the creation, destruction, and regeneration of life. Creative acts usually entail dissolving boundaries and fusing categories. In this way, substances that are otherwise separate become synergistically transformed. Digestion is a process that creates new substances and, in doing so, regenerates life. Sexual intercourse is another act that may create new forms through the mingling of discrete substances. Both processes challenge the autonomy of categories and energies. Yet, precisely because they merge during creative processes, it is important that they also remain independently defined. In this chapter, I analyze how Wamirans conceptually merge categories during creation and regeneration, while simultaneously defining them as autonomous entities.

Wamirans view digestion and reproduction as parallel acts of creation. Energy spent on the production of food is seen as having the same source, and symbolically parallel results, as that spent on the reproduction of human beings. As a result, taboos are necessary to keep competing energies separate. In Wamira, the categories that are most clearly defined and separated are those of male and female. Those of food and sex, however, are viewed as interrelated. In keeping with the Wamiran world view, categories of food and human being, or digestion and reproduction, are no longer opposed to one another. Rather, they are complementary and reciprocally transmutable aspects of a larger life cycle.

Cycles of regeneration: an exchange between human beings and food

Wamiran ideas about food and sex constitute part of a larger belief that the universe has a fixed and finite amount of life-creating energies and resources.

110

Both food and human beings are integral parts of a total system of energy exchange. As such, these elements do not stand apart from their universe, but interact with it. The relationship between people and their cultivated and domesticated foods is one of mutual dependence. Each nurtures and gives life to the other. In the process, each is dependent upon, and is controlled by, the other.

Inherent in the notion of a circular and bounded system is the idea that accretion at one node necessitates depletion at another, and vice versa (Kelly 1976:43–5). Because energy resources are seen as restricted, they may be removed from the system only if they are converted back into the total life circuit. For example, when taro is harvested, the crop's energy is depleted. But, during the process of digestion, taro gets converted into human life-giving energy. In turn, human energy is spent on the cultivation of taro. Thus, the taro a person eats, the creation of a person's vitality and substance (*anona*), the energy an individual expends in cultivating taro, and the taro's *anona* are all interactive and mutually dependent.

As will be seen shortly, laws and taboos that regulate behavior are aimed at maintaining equilibrium within this system of finite resources. Breaking a taboo is believed to cause vulnerability; if individuals fail to follow the proper prescriptions and proscriptions, they believe they will become ill or even die. This belief about the detrimental effects of disrupting the system's balance pertains to the realms both of food and of sex. As noted in Chapter 2, eating too much is thought to bring on sickness. Gluttony, improvidence, and unbridled greed all upset the flow of energy. Adultery is also thought to cause similar disaster. This is related to a belief, widespread in Melanesia, that overindulgence in sexual relations is thought to bring on the slow drying up and withering of men.

Digestion, like reproduction, is seen as a form of regeneration. Sexual energy is conceptualized in the same fashion as is food energy. This belief is evident in Melanesian mythology, where it is common to find myths in which women give birth to edible plants and animals, or where animals give birth to people (Jones 1980; Jorgensen 1985:220). I have discussed one such myth in Chapter 5, where a pig gives birth to a human boy.

Death and ingestion are the processes by which energy is exchanged between people and food. Death within one form is the necessary precursor of life within the other. This is evident within the human cycle and the food cycle, but is most prominent in the relationships between the two. The two categories of human being and food are seen as related during the processes of creation, destruction, and recreation. A cyclical relationship exists between the two, where the substance of each category, when destroyed, is thought to be creatively transformed into that of the other. Specific examples will demonstrate how ideas about death and ingestion, or destruction and regeneration, are all intimately interrelated in Wamiran thought.

Taro and human beings are seen as especially interrelated in the processes of creating and perpetuating life. Wamirans believe that people's growth, health, and vitality depend directly on their ingestion of taro. Conversely, they believe that the production of taro is related to, and dependent on, the death of human beings. This reciprocation between human death and the growth of taro is evident in beliefs, myth, and behavior.

Wamirans believe that as they expend energy, especially in the cultivation of taro, which they view as their most arduous and life-threatening activity, they deplete their human strength and vitality. As I noted in Chapter 2, they feel that they must immediately replenish their weakened bodies with food, preferably taro, after working strenuously. Indeed, the process of making a new taro garden is called *rauirage,* which can be translated as "to cause death." The human death referred to is both that resulting from the depletion of human strength as people expend their energy in cultivating the crop, and that which may be induced by the sorcery of one's envious foes.

This transference of energy from people to taro is further illustrated in beliefs about spirits that mediate between human corpses and regenerative taro stalks. Wamirans believe that there is a mutually dependent relationship between elflike spirits (*bariawa*) and witches (*parauma*). *Bariawa* are believed to dwell inside all animals, trees, and plants, and to inhabit every mountain, ocean, stream, and stone. Some *bariawa* protect the taro in the gardens and ensure their growth. Those that guard the taro survive by ingesting human flesh. Witches keep the taro *bariawa* content by killing people and carrying the corpses to a cave on the far shore of the Uruam River where these *bariawa* dwell. In exchange for the human flesh, the witch receives taro stalks to plant in the gardens. One man described the transaction in the following way:

The chief of the taro *bariawa* waits at the opening of the cave. When the witch arrives, she gives the human body to the *bariawa* and gets taro stalks in return. If the witch had previously received taro from the *bariawa* without having repaid him with human flesh, he would be angry and would eat the witch instead.

The idea that human death precipitates taro growth also occurs in the myth recounted at the beginning of Chapter 6. The mythical origin of taro is a direct consequence of the death of a human being.[1] The man kills his son, who will "appear later." When he does, it is in the form of taro. The slain and dismembered boy is transformed into taro which, when eaten, is transformed into human energy and life. Because taro is the transformation of a human son, in effect, parents are eating their children. A human being (the son) is killed and transformed into food (taro), which is then ingested and trans-

---

[1] Jones notes themes of vegetable life springing from human death among the Faiwol in the Telefomin area of New Guinea. There a mythical ancestress, Karigan, kills her brother and uses his bones to produce taro (Jones 1980:138).

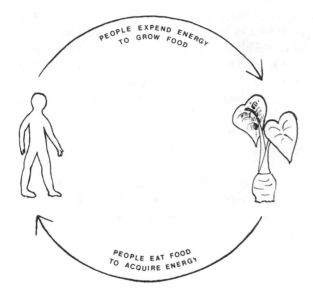

PEOPLE EXPEND ENERGY
TO GROW FOOD

PEOPLE EAT FOOD
TO ACQUIRE ENERGY

Figure 14. Energy exchange between people and taro

formed into human energy. Thus, through the cyclical processes of death and ingestion, both human beings and food are able to regenerate themselves by first being transformed into the other.

Taro is not the only food that constitutes part of a larger interactive cycle with human beings. The regeneration of pigs, like that of taro, is also a result of death and ingestion. In the myth of the origin of domesticating and eating pigs, the villagers slay and eat the pig. Then, through the magical manipulation of his pig-mother's bones, the boy is able to regenerate all future pigs. Thus, the boy and all the villagers, from then on, eat his mother. In the taro myth, parents kill and eat their child to produce food and replenish their energy. In the pig myth, a child eats his parent to produce food and replenish energy for the entire population.

Figure 14 illustrates how the processes of destruction and regeneration are interactive across boundaries of human beings and food, in this particular case, taro. Human beings must ''kill'' and eat taro in order to grow and survive; yet in cultivating a taro garden, human beings must die.

This notion of the cyclically interactive forces of death and regeneration – between the two categories of human being and food – is common throughout Melanesia. For example, Lindenbaum discusses the Fore's ''cycle of birth and return as it applies to gardens and people'' (Lindenbaum 1976:55), and Panoff assesses the same idea in the Maenge horticultural cycle (F. Panoff 1970). About the Morehead region in western Papua New Guinea, Ayres reports, "Just as people 'grow' in life from food produced from the land, their grave sites and the memories of them are eventually transformed into gardens, the ultimate return of the place of the living" (Mary Ayres, unpublished data, 1983). DeCoppet says of the 'Are 'Are on Malaita that "it must be noted that the chain followed by 'bodies' after natural death leads to gardening, which produces taros and coconuts. This vegetable food will 'replace' the 'bodies' . . . of persons . . ." (DeCoppet 1981:197). The central premise throughout is that one form of life must be depleted in order to create new life. Thus, one life-creating or -sustaining action is seen as a natural consequence of another.

A belief in the cyclical flow of energy between human beings and food, especially taro, lies at the heart of Wamiran ideas about the continuation of life. As noted, it is of the utmost importance to regulate these flows of what are seen as finite energy sources. Only by means of control can equilibrium be maintained; only then is regeneration a creative, rather than a chaotic, process.

Taboo and the struggle to keep sexual categories separate

Because women create children and men produce taro, the categories of female and male are the main ones that Wamirans keep separate in order to ensure the proper flow of energy between human beings and food. I now turn to their conceptual struggle to maintain the distinction between sexual categories, while still accounting for creative and transforming processes between human beings and food.

Returning to the diagram of the transformations of human beings and taro, I now include the associated categories of female and male. Women perpetuate society biologically by creating human beings. Men, by adhering to parallel beliefs and customs, reproduce society metaphorically by producing taro. Figure 15 illustrates cycles of energy exchange between people and food correlated with female and male categories.

During creation, whether of children or taro, the separation of sexual categories is emphasized to ensure that each gender properly channels its energies into its own creative realm. The separate channeling of sexual energies is expressed ritually in the cultivation and exchange of taro. I have noted in Chapter 6 that during taro cultivation, women and men symbolically communicate their conflicts about dependence and autonomy – both among men, as well as between women and men – to one another.

Further indications of the opposing relationship between the male realm of *lam* (taro) and the female one of *tia* (human beings and pigs)[2] occur in the pig

---

[2] In precontact days when cannibalism was practiced, human beings were flesh food (*tia*) par excellence.

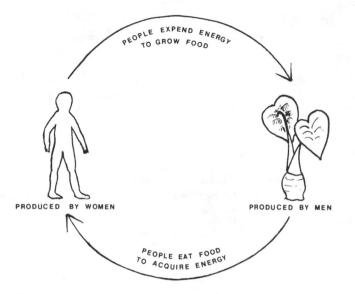

PEOPLE EXPEND ENERGY TO GROW FOOD

PRODUCED   BY   WOMEN   PRODUCED   BY   MEN

PEOPLE EAT FOOD TO ACQUIRE ENERGY

Figure 15. Energy exchange between people and taro correlated with female and male categories

myth recounted above. In the myth, the pig, capable of regenerating both human and pig offspring, exists in opposition to taro, a man's product of creation. While the man and boy are *planting* taro in their garden, the pig-mother is *killed* in the village. In other words, the creation of taro (symbol of male virility) is juxtaposed against the death of the pig (symbol of female sexuality). Even after the boy stabs his foot and wants to return to the village, the man steadfastly continues to plant his taro. When the man and boy return to the village, they learn that the pig was killed because it "ruins the gardens" and "steals the taro," thus indicating the conflicting energies between female sexuality and male virility.[3]

Taboos, listed in Table 5, intervene to separate the respective female and male spheres to human reproduction and taro production. The nourishment and growth of both children and taro are held firmly in the grip of unwritten laws. Any defect in the growth of a child or taro is immediately attributed to a failure on the part of either parent or cultivator in following the customs. As one woman said,

[3] The act of cannibalism, in which Wamiran men killed and consumed other men, could be seen as the epitome of men's control of regenerative processes through ingestion and, in fact, has been viewed in such terms for the Gimi by Gillison (1983). However, I do not take this interpretive approach here.

Table 5. *List of taboos*

Taboos for pregnant or nursing women
Sexual intercourse
Eating greasy foods such as meat or food cooked with coconut cream
Using greasy substances, such as coconut cream or soap, on one's nipples
Eating salty foods such as fish from the sea or seaweed
Going near coral in the sea

Taboos for men cultivating taro
Sexual intercourse
Eating greasy foods such as meat or food cooked with coconut cream
Using greasy substances, such as coconut cream or soap, on one's body
Eating salty foods such as fish from the sea or seaweed
Going near coral in the sea (no sea fishing)

General taboos during taro cultivation
Menstruating women
Women who are shredding a leaf skirt, knotting a fishnet, or making a string bag
Coconut palm on the land

A child is like taro. If we do not adhere carefully to the customs surrounding the growth of children, our children will get sick and die. If we do not follow the customs of the taro garden properly, our taro will not grow well.

Taboos are used to maintain the discreteness between categories. According to Leach (1961, 1964, 1976), whose ideas are based on Lévi-Strauss (1962a), reality exists along a continuum. The human mind then segments the world into categories by ascribing names to things and ideas. In this fashion, the mind interprets the continuum as though it were composed of discontinuous segments. With the world thus categorized, human beings are able to perceive, assimilate, and mentally exercise some control over their world. Whereas the process of punctuating reality by naming artificial categories is believed to be universal, the variety of ways in which cultures internalize versions of reality seems virtually unrestricted (Leach 1976:36). In his attempt to clarify Lévi-Strauss's ideas on how human beings perceive reality, Leach presents a useful diagram, illustrated in Figure 16 (Leach 1964:35).

It is by means of taboos that overlapping conceptions and energies are kept apart in order for individuals to define them more clearly and to control them. Again, Leach's diagram, illustrated in Figure 17, helps clarify the ideas (Leach 1964:35). According to Leach, "it is the nature of such markers of boundaries [taboos] that they are ambiguous in implication and a source of conflict and anxiety" (Leach 1976:34). Were these markers absent, the categories people carefully separate would blend together. The tabooed areas become sacred, unmentionable, intriguing, dangerous, and powerful, precisely because they can mediate between categories.

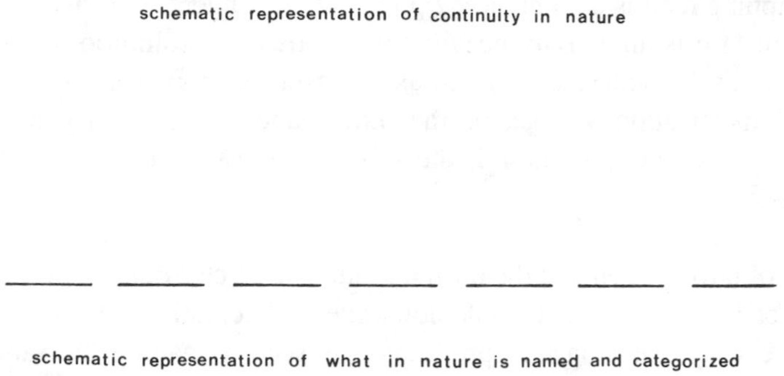

schematic representation of continuity in nature

schematic representation of what in nature is named and categorized

Figure 16. Schematic representation of continuity in nature and of what is named and categorized

named categories

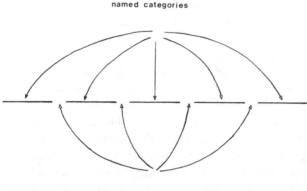

tabooed areas

Figure 17. Relationship of named categories to tabooed areas

Barth's concept of taboo provides a useful elaboration on Leach's approach. Barth, in writing about the complexity of various categories of taboos among the Baktaman of New Guinea, states that although taboo is "a binary idiom par excellence," the concept of taboo does not construct a simple dualistic universe, but one portraying a "chemistry of essences" (Barth 1975:170). He recognizes "the fundamental character of Baktaman taboos as injunctions against the *associations* or *combinations* of things, states, and persons" (Barth 1975:169).

Barth also makes a distinction between what he calls dangers and powers. Taboo keeps dangers (in the form of substances) apart from powers (in the form of activities). The dangerous substances and their sacredness vary according to context and individuals. At critical moments, contaminating individuals or substances must be segregated from those activities endowed with power. In their taboo-laden world, Wamirans punctuate the continuum of their reality at overlapping realms of contending powers and dangers. For instance, the cultivation of taro is an activity heavily surrounded by prohibitions concerning greasy and salty substances. Taro, as a substance, however, is never tabooed. The domestication of pigs, on the other hand, is an activity completely devoid of taboo. Yet pork flesh is the substance most frequently hedged with restrictions.

The cultivation of taro by men and the birth and nurture of children by women are occasions for men and women to demonstrate their creative powers. As we have seen, energy spent on taro production is seen as having the same source, and symbolically parallel results, as that spent on the reproduction of children. From the Wamiran point of view, energy spent by one sex must be strictly separated from energy spent by the other. Taboos are created and maintained to regulate and minimize conflict between female and male domains of creation. Thus, throughout regenerative cycles, the categories that remain most adamantly opposed to and separate from one another are those of female and male spheres of production. Taboos ensure that neither women nor men engage in the productive activities of the other. In short, women do not plant or irrigate taro, any more than men bear or breast-feed children.

Creative acts are thought to be most effective when directed toward one area only. Thus, neither women nor men may invest their life substance into two opposing reproductive categories simultaneously. For example, a menstruating woman must avoid the taro garden, lest the tubers smell her blood, her main substance of creation, and cease to grow. (A pregnant woman, on the other hand, may enter a taro garden because her "blood is stopped up," and the taro would not be able to smell it.) Similarly, a woman must neither shred a leaf skirt, knot a fishnet, nor make a string bag (all women's productive activities) while working in the taro garden.

Although female and male realms of creation are kept separate most of the time, Wamirans also realize that, at other times, sexual union and cooperation are mandatory. *Both* women and men are needed to produce children; children are made of both "blood" and "bones." And, as seen in Chapter 6, the labors of *both* men and women are needed to produce taro. In short, the relationship between women and men is antagonistic and autonomous, as well as cooperative and interdependent. Totally creative acts, such as the production of taro or the reproduction of children, incorporate a rhythmic alternation between sexual autonomy *and* sexual dependency.

I suggest that several substances symbolically represent sexual union, and therefore are embraced or tabooed accordingly. Among these are greasy and salty substances. Greasy, oily substances, such as meat, coconut, and soap, are associated with semen. The identification of grease with semen and the understanding of it as an agent in fertility (especially where grease is contrasted with dryness and decay) is also reported from other areas in Melanesia (Barth 1975; A. Strathern 1977:504; A. and M. Strathern 1971:162–3). Indeed, in Melanesian pidgin, "gris" is the word for semen. In Wamira, substances that retain a pungent, salty odor, such as fish from the sea, seaweed, and coral, are associated with menstrual blood, the female agent in fertility.

Greasy (semen-associated) substances, salty (blood-associated) substances, and sexual intercourse are all tabooed to Wamiran men and women while engaged in using their creative energies. For instance, sexual intercourse is forbidden to women who are pregnant or breast-feeding, as well as to men who are planting taro. Furthermore, women who are breast-feeding children are not allowed to eat meat or foods from the sea. Similarly, they are not allowed to anoint their breasts or nipples with grease, coconut cream, or soap, lest the baby dies while coming into contact with these oleaginous substances. A man who is planting taro is not allowed to eat meat or foods from the sea. Nor may he use any grease, coconut cream, or soap on his body because it is believed that the taro will not grow properly if it smells any of these. Also, one cannot plant taro if there is a coconut palm in the garden plot. All of these taboos concerning the unfavorable effects of greasy substances on taro apply equally to the male-associated digging stick (*ipa*). For example, a person who has used soap on his hand, or a person who has eaten fish from the sea, must not touch a digging stick, even if it is standing inside a house or resting against a tree in a residential hamlet.

These taboos are schematically diagramed in Figure 18. Substances and activities associated with sexual union, such as blood and semen, or their symbolic equivalents, are taboo while the energy of a man or woman is being channeled into one or another area of production.

When men and women are *not* engaged in creative activities, such as during the junctures between the various gardening stages, men and women may engage in sexual activity, fish in the sea, and eat meat. In the previous chapter, we saw that taro cultivation alternated between separate male and female involvement. A more accurate and detailed picture of taro cultivation consists of a rhythmic sequence of events, alternating between sexual autonomy and sexual dependency, as illustrated in Figure 19. Activities in which male and female channel reproductive energies into one area only, are followed by activities that emphasize sexual union. Once the various powers of production and reproduction have been displayed and the dangers of sexual contamination avoided, sexual union, both physical and symbolic, occurs. During the cultivation of taro, as well as during various stages in the human life cycle, when each stage is successfully completed, men and women communally hold feasts. At such feasts, they *must* consume taro together with pork.

We have seen that Wamirans categorize their world very differently from the way Westerners do. Only by rethinking Western categories, such as those of food and human being, production and reproduction, or digestion and regen-

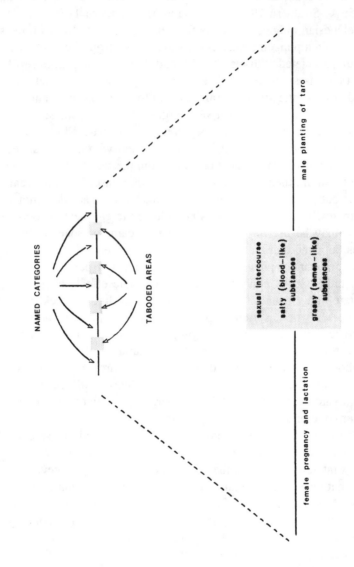

Figure 18. Taboos in female and male areas of creation

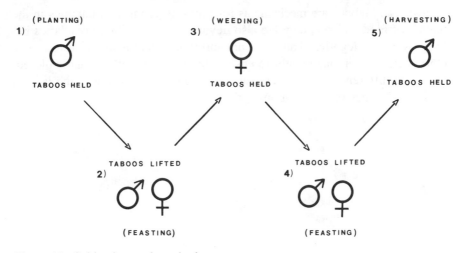

Figure 19. Cultivation cycle and taboos

eration, can we understand the Wamiran perception of their universe, their roles in regenerating it, and their world of "laws" and taboos. Both digestion and sexual intercourse are viewed as parallel and necessary acts in regenerating life; categories of food and sex are seen as interrelated rather than as separate categories of "production" and "reproduction." In this light, categories such as food and human being, or digestion and reproduction, are not necessarily opposed to one another. Categories of female and male, however, are opposed and distinct. They are always interlocked in an asymmetrical, but ultimately balanced, continuum of life.

In Melanesia – and one might wonder whether in other cultures as well – it appears that the realms of food and sex are infused with taboo, surrounded with anxiety, and riddled with symbolic measures of control precisely because Melanesians, at one level, understand that the boundaries between these cultural categories are easily blurred. We recall Leach's comment that "it is the nature of such markers of boundaries [taboos] that they are ambiguous in implications and a source of conflict and anxiety" (Leach 1976:34).

Surprisingly, Wamirans complain about the innumerable prohibitions that restrict them, the very "laws" that, according to them, ensure the proper growth of their taro and children. One man, while bemoaning the proscriptions, exclaimed, "That is why we have no food!" Spontaneously, with a touch of remorse, he then added:

I wish we could be like white people. I want to be rich and have many possessions. I want to dress up in fancy clothes and go out. I want to eat lots of food in restaurants. But I never will. We have too many laws governing our taro garden. That is why we shall always be hungry!

"Laws" and taboos are mechanisms for properly channeling energies in the realms of food and sex; they are also devices for controlling boundaries between sexual categories. Thus, it is not surprising that the many customs and taboos are said, in one breath, to ensure the prosperity of taro and children. Yet, in a different sigh, they are said to account for "hunger" (the lack of fulfillment of personal aspirations and desires).

8. The language of feasts

Up to this point, I have discussed pork and taro, and their symbolic meanings, separately. I now bring the two foods together in the context of a sequence of feasts. During festive exchanges, these two foods are sent on their social way, both to communicate and to resolve rivalries among men. Although the messages communicated at feasts do assuage temporarily, they are rarely permanent solutions. As a result, feasting is a recurring and progressive activity. In the sequence of feasts described and analyzed here, two related conflicts are played out. First, rivalries among competing male leaders are expressed and temporarily resolved. Second, the tension between male solidarity and autonomy, which implies leadership abilities, is communicated.

The ritualized exchanges of pork and taro are occasions during which individual male statuses, political tensions, and powers of control are defined and manipulated. During these exchanges, pork and taro become more than items of sustenance or media for celebration. They are material representations of a man's knowledge, skill, and personal power. As such, they intimately reflect his identity. When men exchange food, they are symbolically manipulating their social selves. In the Trobriands, Weiner aptly phrased what occurs during exchanges in saying, "Trobrianders regularly use the particulars of specific exchanges to read and send messages about each other's states of mind" (Weiner 1976:211). In Wamira, food exchanges allow people to send and receive messages about their "insides" (*orana*), the word used to refer to their feelings and states of mind. Hosts' "insides" are perceived as "good" or "bad," and guests' "insides" can "rise" or "fall," depending on the manipulation of pork and taro at a feast.

Symbolic statements made by the presentation of food, like a grammar, are strictly coded; little leeway exists for misinterpretation. Who is invited to a feast, who comes, who gives food, who refrains from giving, who presents and receives what and how, whether food is distributed raw or cooked, whether

123

raw taro is presented with the stalks attached or detached, along what lines the distribution is made (those of gender, age, ward, hamlet, hamlet division, or household), whether food is eaten communally or separately, who eats with whom, and so on, are all specific actions full of import and instantly meaningful to every Wamiran. The transaction of the food speaks louder than words. As one elder explained to me, "Taro and pork, not people, are the chiefs at feasts."

Whereas taro and pork are the "chiefs" in the symbolic discourse, it is men who are in charge of organizing feasts, and of accumulating, displaying, and distributing the food. In Wamira I have noted that, whereas women are natural creators of society, men create society symbolically. The maintenance of society by women, as manifest in the reproduction and growth of children, is inevitable. Orderly social relations, however, are not. It is during ritual exchanges of food that social relations are controlled by men. In exchanges of pork and taro, men rise to the forefront and define, negotiate, and manipulate their identitites and statuses, primarily in opposition to other men. Women remain relatively passive. On the whole, competitiveness exists between men, but is absent between women. I suggest that this is not simply because men have relegated them to a more demure, submissive status. Rather, as child-bearers, women's reproductive identities and statuses are more substantive and tangible, and thus less vulnerable, than those of men, which rest precariously on extrinsic powers and factors. (Recall that only postmenopausal, nonreproductive women have a means of expressing antagonism, or venting jealousies, namely witchcraft.) Secure in the knowledge of their naturally endowed reproductive powers, women, unlike men, do not need to shout out their abilities in symbolic ways. What appears as passivity, can be interpreted as confidence.

Types of feasts

Wamiran feasts fall into what I perceive as two categories. These correspond to the two major modalities of exchange, namely incorporation and transaction, identified by Barth (1966) and discussed in detail by Paine (1976). I refer to each as the I mode or the T mode in the discussion that follows. An I-mode exchange signifies a relationship of solidarity and incorporation. In such an exchange, individual interests are identical. Independent of the notion of competition, I-mode strategies strive for coidentity and are directed toward maximizing the sum of the individuals' assets. A T-mode exchange, on the other hand, is an exchange generated by conflict and emphasizes the differences between individuals. Social control is maintained by individuals. Whereas an I-mode exchange emphasizes loss of personal autonomy in return for a heightened sense of social identity, a T-mode exchange negates a sense of social identity and allows for more personal autonomy. In view of the Wamirans' concern with balancing individual interests with those of the social group, it is evident that both types of exchanges are equally necessary.

Each type of exchange has its specific grammar. As Paine states, "It may be expected that the T and I modes of exchange, as ideal propositions about relationships, will each have its typical code, and this will be an instrument of the mode of social control prevailing in the relationship" (Paine 1976:73). In Wamira, an incorporation type of feast does not include pork. Taro, the main food presented, is destalked, and only corms are given. After the vegetable food is amassed, everyone unites to prepare and cook the food, which is distributed according to gender or age groups and is eaten in public. In a transaction type of feast, both pigs and taro are presented. Moreover, the taro must be given with the regenerative stalks and leaves attached to the corms. After the taro is presented, the pigs are killed, singed, and butchered, and the taro corms are severed from their stalks. The food is divided and distributed while still raw, and is done so according to male-oriented residential groups of ward, hamlet, hamlet division, or household. The recipients either carry their portions of food home or remain at the feast site while cooking and eating in separate, male-oriented groups. Table 6 summarizes the two different types and gives examples of each.

Within the I mode of exchange are feasts to restore strength following communal labor, to welcome an individual who is returning to the village after a long absence, and now also to celebrate events observed by Westerners such as church activities, birthdays, and Christmas.

Within the T mode of exchange, all feasts celebrate accomplishments in the regenerative activities of women or men; they mark stages of either female reproduction of human beings or male production of taro. For instance, several mark stages in the human life cycle. At such feasts, women's regenerative powers, in the form of lineage affiliation, are activated and confirmed. These include marriage feasts, *kepokepo* feasts for the completion of a house (the outer sign of nuclear family unity), *matarapoteana* feasts held prior to death,[1] and funeral and mourning feasts. At feasts that celebrate women's powers of reproduction, people in each exchange group are united through matrilineal affiliation.

Other feasts within the T mode of exchange accompany the most important stages of men's cultivation of taro, such as turning the sod and harvesting the tubers. As we have seen, these are activities where male rivalries abound, sorcery accusations are rife, and the general atmosphere is one of anxiety. The turning of the sod is the stage at which male cooperation is most needed. Harvest is the time when men's powers and statuses are on display. These T-

---

[1] *Matarapoteana* ("to close the blood") is a feast held when a person is on the verge of death. Through it, an individual's economic and social obligations to his or her *dam* members are settled. This particular feast may be held numerous times in anticipation of the person's death. Each time the feast is sponsored because the individual "may not be there the next time."

Table 6. *Incorporation and transaction modes of feasts*

Incorporation mode	
Characteristics	*Examples are feasts for:*
No pork	Restoration of strength following
Destalked taro corms	communal labor
Cooked food distributed	Return of an individual to the village after
Food eaten communally	a long absence
Food distributed to groups along lines of	Western festivities such as church activi-
gender or age	ties, birthday parties, and Christmas

Transaction mode	
Characteristics	*Examples are feasts:*
Pork	Where people are organized in matri-
Taro with stalks	lineages:
Raw food distributed	Marriage
Food eaten separately	Completion of house
Food distributed to groups along lines of	Prior to death
patrifiliation	Death
	End of mourning
	Where people are organized in patrifiliated
	groups:
	Major stages during taro cultivation,
	such as turning the sod or harvest
	Resolving major sorcery accusations
	among men

mode feasts occur when male competition and suspicion mount, and when it is of the utmost importance to define and control social order. At these times, leadership, as an acknowledged form of social control, is easily threatened and must be commandingly reasserted. This is done through the exchange of food among men.

In this chapter, I examine the feasts that mark the stages in the cultivation of taro by men. I have chosen this focal point for several reasons. First, a sequence of feasts that revolves around male activities highlights what tran-spires at feasts in general. Such feasts more easily allow us to unravel the symbolic dialogue because all food exchanges, regardless of type, are orga-nized, disputed, and reflected upon by men. Second, I was involved in this particular succession of feasts, and my personal immersion provided me with more insight than I might have gained otherwise. I unabashedly use my ex-periences as data because, even though I was definitely the catalyst for the events that developed, I did not alter the underlying conflicts. The leadership tensions were Wamiran and had little to do with me. Indeed, what I learned during my farewell feast, which coincided with their harvest feast, deepened my insights into Wamiran culture.

The setting and the characters

The sequence of feasts I describe and analyze took place in Inibuena, the largest Wamiran hamlet. It is located within the Rumaruma ward of the village.[2] As I described in Chapter 1, Wamira is divided into two geographical wards, Damaladona and Rumaruma. They exhibit great antagonism toward each other and resist unification. The tendency toward fission exists at several structural levels; it is evident between the two wards, among hamlets within each ward, and among divisions within each hamlet.

Map 6 illustrates the structural relationship between Inibuena and the rest of Wamira. At this time Inibuena contained seventeen households divided into four divisions: Diguma, Iriki, Tutuvuna, and Akirani. Residence is principally patrilocal or patrifilial. In addition, as discussed in Chapter 6, these residential patterns and social relationships are mirrored in the network of taro gardens and irrigation canals.

As discussed previously, each hamlet has one leader. In terms of wealth (affinally acquired pigs and patrilineally inherited taro magic), the leader only slightly surpasses other hamlet men. Yet, relationships between men are not immutable. Thus, the leader's primary power, which rests in, but is not guaranteed by, his genealogical status must be continually reaffirmed and strengthened. He maintains his respect through his ability to organize and unify his group, and expresses his leadership through the manipulation of food or feasts. His hamlet consists of smaller, antagonistic divisions, each of which has its own genealogically ascribed leader of slightly lesser status. The presence of these competitors, who aspire to his role, is a constant burden, which challenges his powers and renders arduous his task of unifying the group. Rivalries and conflicts among these minor leaders usually threaten to erupt during the process of taro cultivation, an activity in which male powers are especially vulnerable. Male solidarity is necessary not only for technological reasons, but also as a symbolic statement of hamlet amity and the dispelling of fears of sorcery. In short, group cooperation and harmony are seen as direct reflections of the powers of the leader and of his ability to manipulate human relationships through the use of food. In Wamiran terminology, if the leader is "weak," the group "falls"; if he is "strong," the group "unites and works."

---

[2] Although Inibuena is the largest Wamiran hamlet, and thus atypical, the conflicts and the symbolic expressions of them during feasts are typical of Wamiran culture as a whole.

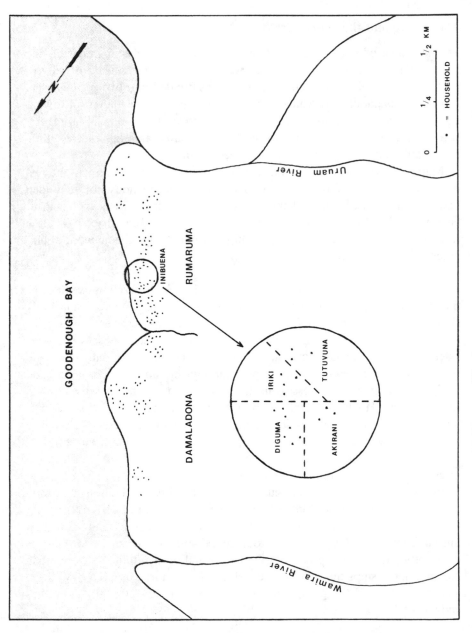

Map 6. Structural relationship of Inibuena to Wamira

7. Jeremiah and Malcolm

8. Osborne

Within Inibuena, Jeremiah was the acknowledged leader. He had two rivals, Malcolm and Osborne (see Plates 7 and 8). A fourth man, Simon (see Plate 9), was less threatening to Jeremiah than were Malcom and Osborne, but nonetheless played a prominent role in the scenes that follow. Jeremiah, a man in his sixties who lived in the Diguma division, was self-possessed and authoritative, and the firstborn son in a line of firstborn sons for several generations. Together with his wife and children, he had spent about twenty years

9. Simon

in Samarai, where he worked at the warehouse of a large department store. Because of this experience, which had given him much contact with white people, he claimed to be more attuned to Western customs than most Wamirans. For example, he occasionally modeled the feasts he sponsored after Western affairs. It was not uncommon for him to give "birthday parties," where he distributed such Western delicacies as tinned smoked oysters.

As a traditional leader, he was superb. However, despite his familiarity with Western business customs (aspects of which increasingly enter into traditional leadership roles), he was a poor businessman. Jeremiah himself once articulated the discrepancy between his success at hamlet leadership and his lack of business acumen when he said, "Money does not grow like taro." When he returned to Wamira from Samarai in 1976, he opened the only trade store in the hamlet. Each time he filled the shelves with goods, the items were gone within a few days because, rather then selling them, he distributed them at feasts. On the one hand, his generous distribution of the goods was a sign of his leadership skill. On the other hand, because he relied on financial help from the hamlet members to replenish his stock, the predominantly barren shelves indicated his failure to muster his group in an effort to earn money. The store itself, to many of the hamlet members, became a symbol for the political strength or weakness of the hamlet. At hamlet meetings, references to the store were used euphemistically to indicate the state of the hamlet's unity. If Jeremiah said, "The shelves of the store are bare. Simon does not want to have sugar in his tea next week," he indicated that the group was not working together harmoniously and that Simon was the cause of the strained and unsupportive atmosphere.

Malcolm was a secondary leader who lived on his father's land in the Iriki division. He was older than Jeremiah, kind and courteous, with thin wisps of white hair, a friendly smile, and soft, somewhat muffled speech due to a complete absence of teeth. His house was surrounded by those of his married sons, who were respected for their willingness to work on village-wide projects, such as the building of the church or school.

Osborne, another rival, lived on his father's mother's land in the Diguma division. He was a man of sinewy build, with a particularly deep and sonorous voice, shifty eyes, and a crafty look. He was a feared sorcerer, who was held responsible for the sickly appearance of numerous taro gardens in recent years. For several months during my time in Wamira, he and his wife resided in their banana garden because he had been ostracized by several hamlet men who believed he had ruined their taro gardens.

Simon, although not really threatening to any of the others, unwittingly managed to interfere with leadership matters by not heeding customs and respecting positions of authority. Simon resided in the Akirani division on his father's mother's land. The fact that he was not living on patrimonial land, together with his young age (about forty), made others consider him a mere "dinghy" who should follow rather than try to lead. His natural, unpretentious manner, however, often put him in the role of an innocent troublemaker.

The events

The feasts that accompanied the taro cultivation cycle began in July, 1977, when the Inibuena men made plans to make new taro gardens. Two weeks after clearing the plots, they discussed the strenuous process of turning the sod, a stage riddled with competition, distrust, and sorcery. Preceding their work, the hamlet members held séancelike meetings for several nights, where they tried to allay their anxieties about producing an abundance and the envy, rivalry, and sorcery that prosperity elicits. Their discussion at one such meeting was as follows:

Jeremiah: Tomorrow before we begin our work, we'll eat together. Bring your "sweet potatoes" [taro]. After we eat, we'll discuss the work.

Copland King (Jeremiah's younger brother): I was sleeping and I dreamed that everything will be "all right" [harmonious and sorcery-free] among us. Men will not "fall" [die from sorcery].

Jeremiah: I, too, dreamed everything will be all right. But to have three leaders [himself, Malcolm, and Osborne] is no good. One is good. If you get sick or "get the feeling" [that you have been sorcerized] put your work aside. Magical substance is in our presence. Tomorrow we'll eat together and then we'll begin our work. We won't become prosperous [so rich that it will cause jealousy and sorcery]. Later we'll have a big feast [indicating successful, trouble-free completion of the gardening process].

Copland King: If your digging stick stabs you [an omen of misfortune], put down your work.

Jeremiah: The women should talk.

Vicky (Jeremiah's sister): You are the leaders. We are just "passengers." What else should we say?

Three days before the men began to turn the sod, the hamlet members held the feast. Fourteen separate households contributed food (in three instances, two closely related households united, thus bringing the total to fourteen rather than seventeen). Malcolm, Osborne, and Simon, those individuals most threatening to Jeremiah, and of whose support Jeremiah needed to be reassured, each proudly arrived with a bundle (*diwara*) of taro. Other households contributed stalks of plantains, a few yams, and sweet potatoes. Three of the households were headed by women (widows or women separated from their husbands) who brought their food, either destalked taro corms or yams, in a garden basket. The various contributions were as follows:

Households headed by leaders and rivals:
1. Jeremiah – one pig, one fifty-kilogram bag of rice
2. Malcolm – one chicken, bundled taro, plantains
3. Osborne – bundled taro, plantains
4. Simon – bundled taro

Other male-headed households:
5. plantains
6. plantains
7. plantains
8. plantains
9. plantains
10. yams
11. sweet potatoes

Female-headed households
12. basket of destalked taro, yams, sweet potatoes
13. basket of destalked taro, yams, sweet potatoes
14. basket of large, festive yams

In addition hamlet members collected five kina (about $5.70 US) from the money they earned at market and bought a second chicken, four small tins of fish and meat, and a package of sugar. The two chickens were presented to Jeremiah because it was taboo for him to eat any of the pig he contributed.

Malcolm, Osborne, and Simon organized the food distribution. First they filled a garden basket with some of the raw vegetables and carried it, together with the two chickens, to Jeremiah, because the leader is not allowed to handle food at a distribution. His abstemious behavior is said to indicate his self-control and lack of greed and, thus, his extraordinary powers. Next they divided the raw foods into equal portions that were presented to the hamlet members according to residential divisions (Diguma, Iriki, Tutuvuna, and Akirani). Within each residential group, the food was further divided into equal portions for each household. Everyone assembled in groups according to hamlet divisions and households within them, prepared the vegetables, and cooked them together with the pork.

The feast described above conveys symbolic messages about social dynamics within this hamlet. Two food exchanges took place simultaneously, each confirming a different aspect of the social order. First, there was an exchange between the leader and the hamlet members. Jeremiah gave the people a pig. In return, they supplied him with vegetable foods, especially taro and plantains (plus two chickens because he could not eat the pork). In this exchange, support of and obedience to one leader were symbolically confirmed. Second, there was an exchange among the households within the hamlet. Each household gave a share, although unequal in quality and quantity. Yet, each household received an equal share in return. Thus, hamlet harmony and cohesion were also established. Moreover, individual men had a chance to express status differences. For example, the three rivals presented bundled taro, whereas the others provided plantains. Lines between gender were drawn as well. Women supplied destalked taro corms in garden baskets, whereas men presented bundled taro. This feast permitted the communication of complete order and control – between the acknowledged leader and his hamlet members, among the households of the hamlet, and between men and women.

After they finished eating, hamlet members talked about their plans for turning the sod. Again, the discussion centered on fears of sorcery.

Sarah (Malcolm's wife): Work slowly. Look with your eyes. Don't make any noise. Don't laugh. Your "insides" will remain silent. Work well. We won't get injured. Where shall we go? [The strong ties to patrimonial garden and hamlet land leave little room for physical escape from rivals.]

Jeremiah: Women, if you are "sick" [menstruating], stay in the village. Anyone, if you "get the feeling" in the morning, if your skin hurts, stay in the hamlet. White people do the same. They make an apology to their friend. If they are tired or sick, they don't work.

Every few days during the next two weeks, the men worked at turning the sod. Several incidents of male rivalry occurred. The first of these erupted when Malcolm ignored customs of land allocation. While turning the sod, he made his garden in such a way as to cut off the garden area of the person whose plot was adjacent to his. In response, everyone ceased work and waited

134   *Always hungry, never greedy*

several days until Malcolm's "insides would be made good again." During this period, everyone threatened to abandon the new project and return to their old gardens. Jeremiah called a meeting to discuss the bonds that held them together. He said, "Diguma [where he lived] is Imara [the original settlement of Wamira]. Iriki [where Malcolm lived] is also Imara. We are all one. We must stay together. The irrigation canals are the dictators." In saying this, he reminded the men that they must remain united. If this did not occur, it would reflect poorly on his leadership abilities.

At the meeting, Jeremiah announced that he would give a "birthday party" for his younger daughter the following day, explaining that he alone would provide all the food (demonstrating his incontestable power and his authority over Malcolm). On the day of the party, however, every household in the hamlet brought vegetable food which they cooked, distributed, and ate together (indicating their support of Jeremiah). When the people finished eating, Malcolm addressed the group and told them that he had decided to cooperate. Jeremiah thanked everyone for coming, saying, "I had just wanted to feed the children, but you helped me and brought food." Thus, under the guise of a "birthday party," hamlet solidarity and acknowledgment of Jeremiah as the leader were once more established.

Another hamlet meeting was held in the middle of August after the sod was turned. The members discussed the feast they would hold to mark the successful completion of this important stage.

Copland King: Next week we shall eat meat. Everyone was afraid of death, but now we have finished seventeen gardens and no one has died. There will be seventeen pots of food for our feast.
Jeremiah: We were scared of death, but now we have triumphed ["triumph" is *vaiuba*, literally meaning "to become cold," which brings to mind its antithesis, magic and sorcery, which are said to be "hot"]. Now we must look for meat. Next week we shall eat well. We'll joke and laugh and be happy. We won't eat rice. We shall eat *gwada* [the festive taro pudding mentioned in the Tamodukorokoro myth, and also that fed to guests at *torela*]. We'll eat together and then we'll separate.

The act of eating "together" or eating "separately" is highly symbolic and deserves further discussion. Behaviorally, "to eat together" indicates openness and trust of one's fellow human beings. Linguistically, it suggests a sense of production and accomplishment. ("To eat together" is called *am gogona,* which is derived from the word *am,* meaning "to eat," and *gogona* which is the adverbial form of the verb *gogo* which means "to sprout" or "to grow.") Conversely, "to eat separately" indicates distrust and antagonism. ("To separate" is *vilamonei,* the verb formed from the noun *lamolamona,* meaning a poverty-stricken, humble being with neither possessions nor kin, such as a beggar.) Thus, whereas eating together indicates trust, cooperation, synergy, and productiveness, not doing so implies unsociability, antagonism, unproductiveness, and poverty.

Late in August, the feast that marked the completion of the turning of the sod took place. The following food was contributed:

three pigs – one from Malcolm, one from Vicki (Jeremiah's sister), and a wild pig caught by various hamlet men
twelve fish – from nearly every household (closely related households joined as one unit)
three taro bundles – one from Osborne, one from Malcolm's son, and one from Aidan (my "mother's" brother)
twelve stalks of plantains – one from each male-headed household
twenty garden baskets of miscellaneous vegetable food (destalked taro, breadfruit, yams, sweet potatoes) – one or more from each household

Jeremiah made the decisions about the food distribution, and Osborne carried these out by dividing the food into seventeen equal portions. One portion was allotted to each household. Outdoors, each household peeled its food, built its fires, readied its pots, cooked, and ate, while remaining separate from the others. Jeremiah announced, "Today we shall cook and eat in Inibuena. We shall not take the food away and eat privately in our houses. Later, we'll plant our taro." He thanked everyone for coming and for bringing food. He asked whether they were happy, and they responded that they were. Copland King said, "Today we have food from our land. We worked together and brought food."

Several differences are apparent when this feast is compared to the one that took place prior to the turning of the sod. First of all, at the previous feast, only Jeremiah contributed a pig. This time, three pigs were contributed, none of which was from him. Thus, the statement about Jeremiah's paramount position within the hamlet, which was stated earlier by his contribution of a pig, was now relaxed. In this feast, Jeremiah contributed only vegetable food. Second, at the earlier feast, gender differences and male statuses were marked by food contributions. Now no gender or status differences were expressed. This time each household supplied plantains as well as garden baskets of destalked taro and vegetables. Almost everyone contributed fish. Of the three men who contributed bundled taro, two were of low status. Of those who provided pork, one was a rival leader, and another a woman. The third pig was given by the whole group.

Each feast makes a different statement about tensions within the group, about the psychological state of the leader, and about the need for social control. At the first feast, which took place in an atmosphere of anxiety prior to the turning of the sod, leadership roles were marked, gender and status were clearly defined, and male rivalry and hamlet fissioning were controlled. The second, which took place after the work was completed and the atmosphere was more relaxed, stressed a lack of defined leadership, as well as equality of gender and status among hamlet members.

The differences in the exchanges can be understood within the context of each feast. The first feast was held prior to the precarious stage of turning the sod. The second took place directly following its successful completion. The tone of the first was fear (''Men will not fall.'' ''To have three leaders is no good.'' ''Magical substance is in our presence.'' etc.). The food exchange communicated a rigid definition of leadership and social control in anticipation of possible rifts, rivalries, and evil intentions. The second, where the tone was elation (''We were scared of death, but now we have triumphed.'' ''We shall joke and laugh and be happy.'' etc.), loosened the controls in retrospective relief. In sum, control of food at feasts is tightened and loosened with the need for control of the social order.

At this point in the cultivation cycle, group cooperation was no longer needed and those activities involving individual privacy and secrecy began. Each man worked the soil in his garden into finer grains to prepare it for planting. Several days later, in September, Jeremiah began planting his taro. Gradually, one by one, all the hamlet members followed, and within three weeks the last person, Osborne, planted his. Throughout the process, the people slept in their garden houses because they were worried about ''pigs eating the new taro shoots.'' As I discussed in Chapter 6, this refers to their suspicion that during this critical stage in the planting, ''people'' (euphemized by ''pigs'') might attempt to steal the young shoots imbued with fertility magic.

In December, after the women had collectively weeded and dug hollows around the base of the taro, many of the hamlet members went fishing upstream along the Wamira River. Upon their return, they held another feast and discussed various conflicts that had arisen among hamlet members. Of principal importance was the fact that the hamlet was not united. The men had not performed the communal task of keeping the irrigation canals free from grass and weeds. As a result, the water, which they said was ''dirty'' and ''poisonous'' (sorcerized), was thought to be ruining the taro. Moreover, Simon was surpassing the others in planting his taro. The discussion of the problems was animated.

Jeremiah: I set an example today. I moved the wall of my house and created a space between my house and my brother's [I dissolved the group]. We are worried about our taro. We have to wait too long for water to come to our garden [the men are not cleaning the canals]. We shall have Christmas in our separate houses [there will be no group cooperation and celebration]. Each of us will look for his own sugar [we'll not share the food brought by our children when they come from town]. Our ''insides have fallen,'' and I don't know who did it. We are finished as a hamlet group. From now on we'll eat tasteless food with no sugar, no rice. There will be no meat.

Sarah: The sun is strong [the taro is not growing properly]. We went to fish. Instead, we should have stayed here and worked on the canals and led the water to the gardens. I am afraid of the dirty [sorcerized] water. It is poison.

Copland King: All right, the discussion is finished. Tomorrow I'll begin work on the canals.

Simon (who was accused of not contributing any fish at the feast): I didn't keep the fish for myself. Ask Alice who was fishing next to me. I didn't catch any.

Jeremiah: I'm not talking about your fish.

Simon: Someone mentioned fish. I fished together with Alice. We shared a fishing basket. Others caught many fish, but I caught none. My wife got sick, and we didn't catch any.

Fanny: Never mind the fish. Women breast-feed their children to make them grow. Men have to give water to the taro to make them grow. The men must clean the canals.

Vicky: Let's talk about the water. Tomorrow the men should clean the canals. We won't talk about fish anymore.

Jeremiah: I wasn't talking about fish. The subject is finished.

Sarah: The whole hamlet should catch fish. Fish are not only for some people.

Jeremiah: We'll separate. Yesterday our "insides fell." Our boys didn't work. We'll have Christmas alone. You [singular] eat your rice. I made a space between my house and my brother's today. We'll go to our individual houses.

Copland King: One person [Simon] has "tapioca" [taro] that comes up to his elbow [indicating an extremely large tuber]. He is a real person. He is a rich man. He did something well. [This was said with irony and hostility because Simon should not have surpassed the leader.] Tomorrow we'll have a problem. Where will we get our food? [What will happen if people exceed the leader and things get out of control?]

Although, on the surface, they were talking about the cleaning of canals and the sharing of fish, they were discussing the dangerous effects of suspicion, fragmentation, and sorcery on group cohesion, leadership, and social order. Throughout the discussion, we note use of linguistic euphemism. The oratorical use of figurative speech – inverted euphemism, double entendre, and metaphorical allusion – is common in Melanesia.[3] In Wamira, speech that is laden with emotional overtones and personal accusations is often softened by the use of euphemism.

This type of metaphorical allusion is employed when the size and scheduling of food exchanges are discussed. For example, the phrases "sweet potatoes," "tapioca," and "rice," are used to indicate "taro." Wamirans know that when the leader tells them to bring "sweet potatoes," they will proudly carry out their prized taro, bundled festively. This use of metaphorical allusion outwardly conveys modesty. Yet, in reality, pride is the intended message. It is employed precisely because it masks the hidden resources and

[3] Strathern, using the term "veiled speech," discusses its function in the Mount Hagen area (A. Strathern 1975). He views it as a form of social control whereby the speaker, by putting the point obliquely, masks the harsh message of his dissatisfaction while preserving social relations.

plentiful caches that a Wamiran, while quietly coveting and cultivating, must never admit to possessing. When a Wamiran displays his taro on the proper occasion, the action is always accompanied by whispers from the guests and onlookers of, "He was lying. He said he had 'only tapioca' but now we see that he really has a lot of taro."

Discussions of group unity or fragmentation are also occasions when euphemisms are used. Earlier I described the example of Jeremiah's "store," where the presence or absence of goods on the shelf is a statement about the hamlet's willingness to unite and help him. Jeremiah's "house" is another allusion to the hamlet's cohesiveness. When Jeremiah arrived in Inibuena in 1976, he mustered the hamlet members to build a house for him. Their work and his daily reimbursement with large quantities of food were statements about his leadership abilities. The house became a symbol of hamlet unity. When he moved the wall of his house to "make a space," he was informing everyone that because they were not working together harmoniously, he was dissolving the group.

A week after the discussion about cleaning the canals took place, a vicious clash arose. It was the most direct sorcery accusation since the cultivation process had begun. Osborne was seen sitting in Simon's garden early one morning. Simon suspected that Osborne had performed sorcery on his taro because, as Simon explained to me, "Osborne is jealous. I have a lot of taro. I have filled four plots. He has filled only one." Next Jeremiah, while working in his garden, noticed that his taro was withering and developing brown leaves. He, too, accused Osborne of sorcerizing the taro. The two men aggressively shouted accusations at each other for several days.

Jeremiah: Osborne, go back where you belong. Go back to Irere. [The hamlet of Irere was Osborne's father's father's place, whereas Inibuena was his father's mother's place.]

Osborne: It is all lies. It's beginning again. Come on, we'll go up to the garden, we'll look at every taro [to check for sorcery]. We'll pull them all out. Not one will remain. Come on. If you want me to move to Irere, come and take the things out of my house. I'm waiting for you. It's not our [inclusive] place, it's your [plural] place. Come on, come up here, I'm waiting for you at my door. Take the things out. You mentioned my things. Come on. We won't go to church today, we'll stay right here, and you can remove my things.

Two weeks later, Jeremiah's piglet was found dying from a knife wound at his doorstep. The crime was generally assumed to be Osborne's doing.

After these events, Osborne was distrusted, denounced, and chastised within the hamlet. In January, he reluctantly gave a small feast at which he killed one of his pigs and distributed pork and a bundle of taro (as indications of his contrition). Everyone else contributed breadfruit only (indicating their disapproval of his behavior). He divided the food quickly and aggressively to everyone in the hamlet according to the four divisions within it. He gave the head and jaw of the pig, the most valued of all pieces, to Jeremiah. In doing so, he appeased their suspicious and hostile feelings and symbolically begged forgiveness for his wrongs. For the next two months, until it was time for harvest, tensions were subdued and the atmosphere in Inibuena remained relatively calm and quiet.

Farewell feast for the anthropologist

Because the harvest of the taro, in March 1978, coincided with my departure from Wamira, the Inibuena men told me they would combine their harvest display with my farewell feast. My plans were to distribute food to everyone in the village, both Damaladona and Rumaruma, in order to show my appreciation for the generous help and kindness demonstrated by all. I discussed these plans with the family with which I lived and with Jeremiah. They decided I should present the Wamirans with beef instead of pork because it was more practical for me to buy one cow rather than several pigs. Everyone seemed amenable to the idea. I proceeded with the plans, assuming that my feast would be a genial and joyous occasion. However, as I describe below, it turned out to be a fiasco.

Three months before my departure (when I first mentioned that I would buy a cow), the people of Inibuena, and especially Jeremiah, suddenly took an active and exaggerated interest in my farewell feast. They told me that by combining my farewell feast with their harvest display, I would bring a neat closure to the events I had witnessed. Jeremiah was especially pleased that my work would be properly concluded. As he said:

You will have seen everything about our lives. You have seen how we make new taro gardens, how men plant taro, and how women tend it. Now you will see the harvest display. You will have seen everything from beginning to end. When you go home, you will know everything about us.

The man who owned one of the cattle projects agreed to sell me a large cow. The only advice people gave me was not to let him bring the cow to me in precut pieces. They feared that if that were the case, he would steal some along the way, and I (and they) would never know. Instead, the Inibuena people suggested that he give the cow directly to them, and they be responsible for transporting the cow and butchering the meat.

From then on, the Inibuena people held daily meetings at which they discussed *their* plans for *my* feast: the location and timing of the feast, what food I was to buy, who would distribute it, how much should go to whom, and so on. The discussion about where the feast would be held was especially intense. The choice of location would determine what kind of feast would be given. If, as I suggested, I held the feast at Werau, one of the two ceremonial grounds of Wamira (not to be confused with the hamlet of Werau), all the Wamira people would come to the site of the feast and observe the food distribution. Everyone would sit down, cook, and eat together (an I-mode feast). On the other hand, if the feast were held in Inibuena, as the hamlet members desired, other Wamirans would not be allowed to come. The members of Inibuena, alone, would distribute the food and send various shares to the respective hamlets throughout Wamira (a T-mode feast). As I was to learn, this second plan would enable them to retain most of the food, and especially the meat, for themselves. My main interest, in contrast to theirs, was that the food be distributed evenly to every Wamiran – an outcome that I later learned was culturally impossible under the circumstances.

The bickering and arguing about my feast continued daily, not only within my hamlet, but among all the people in Wamira. Each time I walked along the path, someone pulled me aside and offered advice. Everyone, except those in Inibuena, agreed with me that the meat should be divided equally, and, for that reason, the feast should be held at Werau. Those in my hamlet argued that because I had lived in Inibuena, and because they had given me land and built my house, the feast should be held in Inibuena and the food should go mainly to them. Because the Inibuena harvest display was enmeshed in my feast, I tried to compromise. I assented to their choice of location, while still clinging to my own ideas about sharing the food evenly.

A month before my departure, another discussion of my farewell feast took place.

Osborne: You arrived here a pitiable person, a pauper, an orphan. The people of Inibuena took care of you and helped you with your work. You enjoyed it here. Now it is time for you to go. You say that the meat should be for everyone in Wamira. But because we in Inibuena helped you, we alone should be in charge of its distribution.
Jeremiah: We in Inibuena gave you land and built your house. Now if you turn against us and "spear" us by having the feast at Werau, we will "spear" you and charge you rent as white people would have done.
Alice: Mimi already paid her rent by buying and distributing a pig when the house was completed. The land is hers now. The transaction is finished.
Sarah: There are too many leaders and too many voices. You are thinking only about food and your stomachs. Aren't you ashamed?
Jeremiah: Mimi, you should give two feasts, one for Wamira and one for Inibuena. People have mouths and have to eat.

At this point three individuals (two of whom were women) interrupted to say that because it was my feast and I was supplying the food, I should make the decisions. I suggested that the feast be held in Inibuena and that they control the distribution, as they wanted, but insisted that the food be divided equally among *all* the residents of Wamira.

As the momentous day approached, I went to Dogura to purchase the food that was to accompany the cow: three large bags (fifty kilograms each) of rice, fifteen packages (one kilogram each) of sugar, six boxes of tea leaves, and twenty loaves of bread. In addition, I bought another large bag of rice, ten tins of meat and fish, five more packages of sugar, and a box of tea leaves for a separate feast that was to be held only for Inibuena a few days after the feast that was to be "for all Wamira."

As soon as I arrived with the boatload of food, and had unpacked and stored the purchases in my house, Jeremiah held another meeting at which the hamlet members discussed the details of my feast one more time. Jeremiah carried a small notebook with him and announced that, "in European style," he would make a list of who was to get what. As I scribbled in my notebook, he did the same in his, continually admonishing me not to copy everything down because it was not an official meeting, but an informal one "to discuss things."

Jeremiah: There are lots of people. They should not come here to see the food. Instead they should stay at home and we'll take the food to them. We are Papuans. We are greedy people. We are not like white people who just eat a small amount and feel satisfied. After the food distribution, there will be a dance at Werau to which everyone is invited. You can give everyone tea and bread at Werau in the evening.

Alice: Forget about the tea and bread in the evening. People are greedy. They will take one piece for their mouth and one for their string bag. We'll divide the tea and bread with the rest of the food in the afternoon.

Jeremiah: If other Wamirans want to help you by contributing food for the feast, they can. We'll keep it in Inibuena and use it for our feast the following week. The food will be divided as follows [and he wrote in his notebook]:

Damaladona – one share
Rumaruma – two shares [I agreed to this because the population of Rumaruma was about twice that of Damaladona.]
Within Rumaruma – thirteen hamlet shares as follows:

> Gomira – one
> Loimara – one
> Agamora – one
> Werau – one
> Garala – two [a large hamlet, about twice the size of the others]
> Inibuena – seven [also a large hamlet, but only three, not seven, times the size of the others!]

When I heard that seven shares were to go to Inibuena, I felt angry and defeated; I decided to let Jeremiah do as he pleased. Later that day, in total exasperation, I even agreed to Jeremiah's revised list: one-quarter of the cow would go to Damaladona (population, 143), one-quarter to Rumaruma other than Inibuena (population, 156), and one-half to Inibuena (population, 80)!

The day before the feast, the Damaladona people told Jeremiah that they gathered food for me and would come to Inibuena to present it. More they would bring their firewood, cooking pots, and water. Jeremiah warned them to stay at home; he would send the meat to them. (The people of Damaladona felt they should receive one-half, not one-quarter, of the cow, and wanted to be assured of this by their presence.)

Jeremiah tried to explain to me that although I had learned many things, I apparently did not understand their main custom. He said, "Our custom dictates that we give food to everyone who *sees* it. If people see that we have food and we don't give it to them, they will be jealous and angry." As he continued to elucidate, the Inibuena people knew how much food there was, but the others did not. By heeding the people of Damaladona, I was "following the path of jealousy about food." If they came and saw the food, and the Inibuena people did not give them a fair share, the Damaladona people would be jealous, and the people of Inibuena would be ashamed. I began to comprehend, but perhaps not in the way Jeremiah had hoped. Until that moment I had naively assumed that there would be no harm in letting others witness the distribution because the Inibuena people would share the food evenly. Suddenly, for the first time, I understood that the underlying motive for the custom of sharing was not magnanimity but greed and fear of greed. It dawned on me that the constant concern with dividing food into equal portions was to ensure that each individual received his or her share without someone else usurping it.

On the day of the feast, everyone in the hamlet rose earlier than usual. I awoke to find fifteen young men at my door, eager to fetch and butcher the cow, and equally eager for me to feed them before they did so. After being fed, they went off to do their work. By noon, they returned (wanting to be fed again) with the cow divided into eight pieces: four legs, two side pieces, the head, and the viscera. In the meantime, the people of Damaladona persisted in threatening to arrive with their food contribution, while Jeremiah kept imploring them to stay at home. The Rumaruma people, other than those of Inibuena, decided not to attend the feast or to contribute food because they were angry with Jeremiah for also banning them from the scene.

Because the Damaladona people had gathered food and insisted on bringing it, I saw no way I could forbid them from arriving. They insisted that I come to Damaladona and accompany them to Inibuena, because it was a Wamiran custom to be led to a feast (if invited) in this fashion. Thus, against Jeremiah's wishes, I went with Alice (from whom I begged moral support) to get the Damaladona people. They were waiting for me with their piles of food under a tree. After I arrived, they bundled together the various taro stalks which they, as individual households, had gathered (the significance of which be clear shortly). The taro was in two separate bundles, which they slung les to transport to Inibuena. As they did this, Alice explained to them he Inibuena people were behaving inhospitably because they had no "food" (taro) to give, not because they disliked them. She tried to assure them that it was for this reason alone that the Inibuena people did not want them to arrive. (Only later did the Inibuena people explain to me that they had not harvested their taro. They had left it in the ground because they feared that, because of sorcery, it would be too puny, and they were ashamed to let others see it.) In response, the people of Damaladona told Alice not to worry, that the taro they were bundling was a "present" for me, and that Inibuena did not have to repay it.

As I arrived in Inibuena with the Damaladona people, I immediately sensed an atmosphere of extreme anger and hostility. All the people had scattered to the far corners of the hamlet and were sitting motionless, in small groups, with their backs to the central area. Only one woman, a close friend of mine who had been adamant that the feast be held according to my wishes, sat alone in the center, nonchalantly knotting a fishnet. The people of Damaladona paraded triumphantly in and threw down their food. After several minutes elapsed, Simon shouted out, "Oh, our friends have arrived!" The response was unanimous silence.

After still more time passed, Copland King got up and shouted out that everyone should bring their food contributions. The rice, bread, etc., that I contributed had been set out in advance next to the pieces of cow. One woman brought out a basket of vegetables and added it to my contribution. A few minutes later another woman added a second, smaller basket of vegetables. The men remained immobile. Finally, Osborne stepped forward angrily and threw aside the coconut fronds that were shading the pieces of meat. Five men quickly and aggressively slapped food into piles. They threw together one leg and one side section from the cow, one bag of rice, five bags of sugar, two boxes of tea, six loaves of bread, and the two garden baskets of food the two Inibuena woman had contributed. They flung these in the direction of the Damaladona people and told them to take it and leave. They said they would divide the rest for Rumaruma and Inibuena later, but first the Damaladona people had to depart. As they were leaving, Osborne shouted out after them that the evening party would be canceled "because it was Lent."

As soon as the Damaladona people were gone, the Inibuena people separated the remaining food into two piles that were roughly equal, except that one had twice as much meat in it as the other. They kept the pile with the larger share of meat for themselves (80 people). They added the vegetable food and two bundles of taro, contributed by the Damaladona people, to the smaller pile. They carried this to Werau, and called out to the rest of the people of Rumaruma (156 people) that their food was waiting for them. The food sat untouched for almost two hours before the Rumaruma people reluctantly and resentfully came to collect and divide their share.

Back in Inibuena, all the men butchered the meat with gusto and distributed it with the rest of their food. Only Jeremiah sat alone and idle, far from the food. He refused to touch it because, as he later explained, he was "very ashamed." The food was distributed according to the four divisions within Inibuena. Each household received an even, and very sizable, share.

Everyone sat around their pots, waiting for the food to cook. I sat inside my house,[4] alternately sobbing about the failure of my farewell feast and fuming about Inibuena's shameless display of greed. As they ate, I could hear them excitedly discussing the next feast that I was to give for Inibuena before I left the following week. After they finished eating, I joined them as they held another meeting.

Jeremiah: I am very ashamed. Today the people from Damaladona came and brought two bundles of taro and what did we give them? They stabbed us with their taro. Today our "insides have fallen." They arrived in the middle of our hamlet with two bundles of taro. Now we have to pay them back with two bundles of taro. If they had put the taro in a basket it would be all right, but they bundled it. The taro stood upright.

Alice: We don't know whether what we did today was right or wrong, but it is done. Mimi did what she had to do, she fed four hundred people. Could any of you do that? I was in Damaladona with her. They bundled the taro in front of us. It wasn't a *diwara*. It was the taro they had gathered as separate households, and they bundled it in front of us. They said it was a "present" for her and that we don't have to repay it.

Jeremiah: When I saw them come into the hamlet today, my "insides fell." I was very ashamed when they arrived. I didn't even go and divide the food. Did you see? I stayed on the beach with my back to it all. I was very ashamed. Today they pierced us. They pierced us with their taro. Plantains must be paid back with plantains . . . money with money . . . and taro with taro. They brought two bundles of taro, and they were tied together. We must follow our customs and repay. Our taro will not lie down. It will stand. Mimi made a mistake. She followed her customs. She didn't follow ours. I thought she had learned everything about us. But today she showed us that she has learned nothing at all. We men have been stabbed.

Sarah: We women made the mistake. We let our men be shamed. We are the ones who behaved poorly. We are only women. You are the men. [This refers to the fact that the women, on the whole, had agreed with me. Moreover, two women, and no men, had contributed food, thus indicating that they had supported the Damaladona people's arrival in Inibuena.]

Jeremiah: I am at the base of the tree and you [talking to Alice] are at the tip. [This is a direct reference to their genealogical relationship. His father was the eldest of two brothers. Hers was the youngest. Moreover, he himself was a first born son.] You took control and changed things around and you shamed me. Men are taro, women are only garden baskets. [Here, in general, he is talking about the reasons for his shame. Alice, who went with me to Damaladona, was not only a woman, but was also genealogically lower in status. The resentment at the loss of his power goes deeper still because I, a status symbol for the village in their eyes, had resided with Alice and not with Jeremiah, as he had wanted.]

Richard: It's a good thing they brought that *diwara*. I was away all day and just came back. Do you know what I found in my house? Squash and sweet potatoes!

---

[4] Because I had presented the food, I was not allowed to eat any of it.

Where is my share of the meat? You should be ashamed. You ate all the meat. I have none.

Henry: I am ashamed, but I am ashamed because of our behavior towards Mimi. She spent a lot of money and gave us a nice feast. She did the right thing, and we ruined it here in Inibuena because we are greedy.

In the evening many of the hamlet members came to me to apologize. They reassured me that the problems were not my fault, but that it was their "custom" to argue about food, to be suspicious, greedy, and jealous. As one man commented, "We are not fighting about you. We are arguing about our customs, our food distribution. Indeed, you should pay close attention to the details and write them all down!"

The day after the feast, people still sat with their backs to one another in Inibuena. Some Damaladona people arrived to explain to Jeremiah that the taro they gave me was a "present" and need not be repaid. One man explained the concept of a "present" to Jeremiah, using the following example:

I once met an Englishman who gave me a box of tobacco. I was very worried about how I would repay it. He explained to me that it was called a "present," which meant that when he went away, he would no longer think about it. He would forget the box of tobacco and would not expect a box in return.

But the explanation was in vain, and the Inibuena people continued to feel shamed and angry. The message conveyed by the exchange of food was stronger than any verbal rationalization of it. The Damaladona people decided to give me a separate farewell party, as did those in Rumaruma outside of Inibuena. Ostensibly, this was because the feast had caused so many people's "insides to fall." In reality, I suspect it was aimed at the people of Inibuena rather than at me, and was a retaliation for their behavior on the day of my feast. Both of these farewell feasts were resented by the people of Inibuena, who warned me not to go, and who, once I returned, diffidently tried to find out exactly what I had been given to eat.

In Inibuena, people continued to eat their meat which, by the third day, was rotting and crawling with worms. Eventually much of it had to be thrown out.

The following week, the Inibuena men harvested their taro and displayed it among themselves on the occasion of my separate farewell feast for them. The tubers were large, yet the feeling prevailed that things had not gone well because, as a group, they had argued and occasionally threatened to disband. At the feast, one man turned to me and astutely said:

You came here to do a study and learn about our life. You should include your farewell feast in your book. Be sure to write down that "just at the end when I was about to go . . . such and such happened . . ." You must put it all in your book because this is what our life is really about.

Of feasts and men

Fortunately, the advantages of geographical distance, emotional detachment, and reflective analysis enabled me to perceive and learn from my mistakes. When I returned three years later, in 1981 (according to Wamiran perceptions, "to feed them properly"), I sponsored an extremely successful welcome feast. When I left again in 1982, I hosted an equally accomplished farewell feast. At both feasts, Wamiran leaders sang my praises and bestowed the ultimate accolade upon me by saying, "You have given an excellent feast. Your feast has shown that you understand our customs. Now you are really one of us." The difference between these feasts and the disastrous farewell feast I thrust upon them in 1978 was simply that in the feasts I gave in 1981 and 1982, I allowed Wamiran leaders to have complete control of the food distribution.

My ignorance about male political tensions had been at the heart of the problem in 1978. I had exacerbated problems of leadership and male rivalries on various levels. First of all, I unwittingly stripped Jeremiah of his authority. By insisting that I organize the feast, rather than letting Jeremiah do it, I, a woman, usurped his power and shamed him in front of his hamlet and the entire village. By escorting the Damaladona people, triumphantly carrying their bundle of taro, into Inibuena, I allowed them to witness Inibuena's lack of taro. Only later did I recall what I had been warned about before I settled in Wamira. Advice, given to me two years earlier by a Wamiran man living in Port Moresby, came to mind.

Don't take sides with different men. They cannot agree on who is the leader among them. This is a matter for men only. You are a woman. It is best for you to keep quiet.

Although I had kept relatively quiet verbally, symbolically I had shouted in thundering tones with food. In bringing the men from Damaladona into Inibuena, I, a foreign woman, had clumsily and threateningly taken command of the main Wamiran means for communicating male powers and statuses and ordering rivalries.

Second, not only was I symbolically acting as a leader in my own hamlet, I was also creating and then usurping the nonexistent position of leader for the *entire village*. As mentioned, there is no authoritative structure within which the two wards can be united. By insisting on dividing the food equally among all Wamirans, from both Damaladona and Rumaruma, I was trying to amicably join the two wards, a feat that had never been accomplished. Thus, not only was I ignorantly acting as a male leader within my own hamlet, but I was creating an even more powerful, and unrealistic, position for myself within the entire village.

Third, the fact that I was unskilled as a leader, yet continued to assert myself in that role, necessarily caused great anxiety among Wamirans. They feared chaos, the very thing their feasts are constructed to control. If they left the food distribution up to me, as I insisted, they had excellent reason to fear that it would get out of hand and that social order, otherwise carefully controlled at feasts, would collapse. My actions undermined traditional leadership, the only authority upon which they could count for restoring order. Their greatest fear, namely of greed running amuck, in fact materialized.

The problems that occurred can best be appreciated by recalling the earlier discussion of exchange modes, namely, those of incorporation and transaction. In allowing the feast to be in Inibuena (as the hamlet members wished), but simultaneously escorting the Damaladona people to the site of the feast (as I wanted), I was combining characteristics of an I-mode and a T-mode feast. The hamlet setting was the site of an I-mode feast. Yet, the arrival of the guests from Damaladona, who carried a bundle of taro, was an action appropriate only in a T-mode feast. In short, I mixed two different modes, thereby communicating mixed messages. My actions were as disjointed and damaging as insisting that the President of the United States give a State dinner for the Soviet Premier at the White House when all that was available in its kitchen was a bag of potato chips.

On Goodenough Island, Young (1971) also notes distinctions in various types of food exchanges. I have followed Barth's, rather than Young's, typology because analytically it comes closest to what I observed in Wamira. Yet, I would like to end with a quote from Young. His description, especially of "political" feasts, is helpful for the light it sheds on the emotional tone of different types of feasts. In contrast to Barth, who differentiates two antithetical categories, Young proposes a three-part classification which corresponds to dimensions of social proximity.

Stated crudely, there are distinctions to be made between food given and received in a kinship context, in an affinal context, and in a context external to these, which may be labeled "political." The last is the realm of "enemies." Food is welcomed as nurturing in the first context, accepted as satisfying in the second, and feared as shaming in the last. The first is given informally and received willingly, the second is given modestly and received diffidently, and the last is given aggressively and received with reluctance which is dissimulated by a show of indifference. (Young 1971:195)

Young's third category, which he labels "political," corresponds to the T mode and to the type of feast I have discussed in this chapter.

The major features of each type of feast convey symbolic messages, and a grammar guides their correct articulation. The incorrect or inappropriate articulation of these features, such as location or type of food presented, results in a breakdown of communication and a feeling of despair and anger such as I described above. In the I-mode feast, which signifies group solidarity, equal distribution is guaranteed by the presence of all who are to receive food. This makes it an amicable and sociable occasion. People cook and eat together. As noted earlier, "eating together" indicates cooperation, openness, trust, and productivity. Because competition among men is absent, food is divided along relatively tension-free lines of gender or age group. Taro is contributed in the form of corms only. Regenerative stalks, symbols of men's virility which hold the power to shame, are absent. Likewise, there is no meat, a tangible symbol of female sexuality which men can appropriate and manipulate.

In the T-mode feast, on the other hand, which allows for the expression of individual dominance, there is no guarantee that food will be divided equally because not everyone receiving food gets to see it. People eat in separate groups, an indication of distrust, antagonism, enmity, and nonproductivity. As we have seen, there is a possibility of men's shaming one another with the food. Taro is displayed with its regenerative stalks. Pork is also distributed. The food is "shared" along lines of male-oriented groups to ensure tight control of competing social units.

During the nine-month period discussed in this chapter, there were four T-mode or, in Young's terminology, "political" feasts. These took place (1) preceding the turning of the sod, when men were suspicious of one another; (2) following the turning of the sod, when men had "triumphed"; (3) when Osborne was accused of sorcerizing his competitors' taro, and feelings of hostility were rife; and (4) at my farewell feast, which was supposed to have been combined with the harvest feast. On these four occasions, rivalries among men were greatest and social control was most in need of being established. This control was expressed by men's use of taro and pork, "the chiefs at feasts."

Conclusion

Food for Wamirans, as for most people, serves purposes other than providing nutritional sustenance. Food furnishes Wamirans with a rich and versatile symbolic vehicle. With it they define themselves, objectify their emotions, express gender qualities, balance relationships between the sexes, communicate tensions among men, and, ultimately, control the ambivalent desires they fear would otherwise control them.

In analyzing Wamiran perceptions and uses of food, we have gained especially deep insight into the ambivalent nature of relations between the sexes, a theme that is common in Melanesia (Gillison 1980; Herdt 1981, 1982; A. Strathern 1979; Weiner 1977, 1979, to name only a few). Interpretations of sexual antagonism and separation in Melanesia indicate that, whereas women are seen as producing offspring naturally, men need to create and control their reproductive powers through cultural means. In Herdt's terms, "femininity unfolds naturally, whereas masculinity must be achieved" (Herdt 1982:55) and is done through rituals of masculinization (Meigs 1976; Newman 1965; Poole 1982; Read 1965 among others). The conceptual separation of what are perceived as sexually antagonistic realms of regeneration, and the achievement of masculinity through ritual are particularly common in the New Guinea Highlands and the Sepik River area, where endemic warfare, big-man politics, male initiation, menstrual huts, and ideas about female pollution are found.

Analyzing food-related behavior and beliefs as expressions of sexual politics, as I have done, suggests that Wamirans hold similar beliefs to those held in the New Guinea Highlands and the Sepik River area.[1] Thus, my use of food as a framework with which to analyze gender qualities and relationships, considerably extends the geographical region where beliefs about sexual con-

---

[1] Forge 1965; Kaberry 1942, 1965; Lea 1964; Scaglion 1978, 1981; Tuzin 1972 and Young 1971 do, indeed, discuss yams in terms of symbols of male virility.

149

flict and antagonism have been found. More importantly, these data indicate that relations between men and women, and among men over conflicts that are rooted in their dependence on women, are more complex, more ambivalent, and in greater need of continual balancing, than a focus on separation or antagonism suggests. Furthermore, this highly charged and delicately balanced relationship between men and women may be expressed in ways that are less obvious than the presence of menstrual huts or initiation rituals.

In Wamira, ambivalence exists between the sexes; competition prevails among men. In this matrilineal society, men find themselves in a "double bind." They depend on wives to produce children for them; yet in giving up sisters and acquiring wives, they lose their lineage substance to their matrilateral kin. Customs of piglet domestication and pork exchange allow men to manipulate symbols of female fertility. In the contexts of piglet and pork exchanges, men are able to control women's sexuality and productivity. Symbolically, they lessen their dependence on women, while simultaneously expressing the competition that exists between them over their dependence on women.

During horticultural rituals, men avoid their dependence on women entirely by imitating female sexuality and producing "children" of their own in the form of taro. Throughout the cultivation cycle, tensions between male solidarity and individuality, as well as between sexual dependence and autonomy, are expressed. Ultimately, through the male cultivation of taro, a balance of creative powers between women and men is achieved.

Men display and exchange the products of their horticultural labor (their "children") at feasts. At these times, they negotiate their statuses to one another and continue to settle competitive disputes among themselves. The feasts they hold fall into two categories: incorporation and transaction. Whereas feasts of incorporation emphasize group solidarity and social harmony, feasts of transaction allow individual men to make personal and political statements about their identity.

In their food-oriented universe, Wamirans define categories and their boundaries very differently from Westerners. On the one hand, Wamirans perceive an interdependent relationship between several domains that Westerners hold in opposition to one another. These are the categories of food and human being, of production and reproduction, and of digestion and regeneration. Conversely, although Wamirans perceive an interconnection between food and sex, they maintain well-defined boundaries between the categories of female and male. Curiously, the boundary between sexual domains, which Wamirans carefully define and continually balance, is one that Westerners presently are consciously trying to erode in various economic, social, and political ways (most notably in the philosophy of women's liberation).

"Famine" is the backdrop for the Wamiran universe. The Tamodukorokoro myth explains the origin of "famine" – a self-inflicted fate that is the result of their mixed feelings about abundance, and that sustains and supports their emphasis on control. Although control is displayed in the realm of food, their "hunger" has little to do with the belly. The Wamiran state of "famine" does not refer to scarce resources, a mismanagement of production, or nutritional deprivation. Rather, it is a qualitative and moralistic evaluation of human behavior. Wamirans utilize their idiom of "famine" to indicate that they have "no food" to exchange or share. Understanding what we do now about the relationship between food and social relations, we can read the concept of "famine" as a statement about their willingness to invest in social relationships. They invest, but cautiously and sparingly.

In a more general sense, "famine" is a comment on the relationship between pursuing individual desires and collective needs. Social life depends on individual effort; individual effort depends on social rewards. The mixture of desire and fear that surrounds such activities as the exchange of piglets and pork, the cultivation of taro by men, and the public display and exchange of their tubers, all ultimately collapse into statements about the ambivalence between behavior motivated by individual needs and that motivated by social concerns. Existing betwixt and between the opposing worlds of individual autonomy and social collectivity, Wamirans rely on their environment of "famine" to restrain their conflict of desires.

Mouths and the struggle to be human

Idioms concerning the production, exchange, and ingestion of food are expressive metaphors for Wamirans' images of human beings. Wamirans refer to people, in general, as "having mouths." A comment I often heard when they wanted to emphasize our mutual human qualities was that I, too, "had a mouth and an anus." Or, Jeremiah, in trying to persuade me to hold the feast he wanted, informed me that "people have mouths and have to eat." In keeping with this view that people's identities are inextricably connected with their mouths, we recall the way in which male leaders are elevated above the status of purely biological being. At feasts, they are not allowed to eat or excrete, nor may they handle food. Their adherence to these rules serves to raise them symbolically above the needy, greedy masses. It portrays them as civilized, not animalistic.

Wamiran notions about human beings are representative of widespread Melanesian ideas where, in mythology, digestive tracts usually mark the differentiation between functional, socialized beings and those who are undeveloped or primeval. It is common in Melanesia for prehumans to be seen as asocial, amoral beings who do not plant food, eat, excrete, copulate, or die. The human state emerges when stony, stationary forms blossom into life, when mouths and genital orifices burst open for the first time, and when digestive and reproductive systems are created and set into motion.

In particular, the possession of a mouth is a common sign of a civilized being. As Young has stated for Kalauna, the mouth is a vehicle rich in cultural expression.

The mouth, from which issues the magic that controls the world and into which goes the food the world is manipulated to produce, is the principal organ of man's social being, the supremely instrumental orifice and channel for the communication codes of language and food. (Young 1983:172)

The distinguishing mark of presocial beings is their lack of mouths and proper digestive systems. Characteristically, prehumans place food in a hole in the top of their head (Gillison 1983; F. Panoff 1970:244). The Maenge of Eastern New Britain relate a myth about the neighboring Vagakusime who, according to the Maenge, live in a primeval condition.

They do not have any digestive system but merely throw whole taro or coconut into a hole, opened at the summit of their skull and reject this food undigested so that their excrement consists of large taro tubers, coconuts, etc. (F. Panoff 1970:244)

In the beginning of time, the Maenge creator "made man just as the Vaga-kusime are: he made a hole in his skull and man threw stones into it" (F. Panoff 1970:244). Only later, when they acquired mouths and learned to digest their food properly, did the Maenge become civilized, moral beings.

The origin of mouths and digestive tracts usually coincides with the origin of genital orifices and the ability to reproduce sexually. In Kalauna, people narrate a myth about Vineuma who is stationary like a rock, and has no mouth, eyes, anus, or vagina. One day her grandson places a snake wrapped in taro leaves at her feet. "The snake stirs slowly. Vineuma feels it. She tries to see and her eyes pop open in fright; she tries to scream and her mouth bursts apart. All her orifices burst open" (Young 1983:181). As with Vineuma, the origin of orifices is often brought about by the person's fright at the sight of a snake or eel. This was the case in the Tamodukorokoro myth and is also the case in other areas of Melanesia (Jane Goodale, personal communication, 1984).

When mouths and genital orifices burst open, physical need and dependence emerge; mouths need food, genitals need sexual gratification. Need evokes greed. With the human ability to ingest comes the capacity to devour; with the ability to reproduce, the capacity to covet. Thus, mouths and genitals produce ambivalent emotions, such as desire, greed, lust, jealousy, anger, hostility, and fear, and call for mechanisms to control these emotions.

Origin myths, such as those referred to above, account not only for how life is set into motion, but how the perpetuation of life, with all its greeds and lusts, is harnessed. Thus, the truly "civilized" state comes when biological human impulses and ambivalent emotions are socially controlled. Errington discusses the presocial *momboto*, or "those who went first," among the Karavarans, in the Duke of York Islands, as lacking social restraint.

In the *momboto,* the Karavarans say, men looked and behaved like wild animals. They did not shave or cut their hair; they had red eyes "like wild pigs"; they were cannibals and ate even those now considered to be their kinsmen as though their kinsmen were animals. There was no kinship; there was no regulation of sex. Men had sexual relations with women who would now be considered their sisters or sister's daughters; men did not purchase brides nor did they pay adultery fines. In the absence of regulation, men simply fought each other to get women. (Errington 1974:21)

As Errington says, the Karavaran image of the *momboto* is a statement of their view of basic human nature, "a nature of greed and violence, characterized by untrammeled exercise of individual interest. The expression of unrestrained human nature is seen as a chaos of conflicting desires and activities" (Errington 1974:21).

If unbridled passions, whether Wamirans' or others', are left unattended, these would destroy life in the same way, and for the same reasons, that Wamirans destroyed Tamodukorokoro. As Young states, "It is almost predictable that the most unmitigated evil of which Goodenough Islanders can conceive is a voracious and insatiable hunger" (Young 1971:182). In myths, at the same time that mouths and genital orifices burst open, people usually gain "cultural" knowledge of a regulatory nature. They simultaneously learn to marry, reproduce children, cultivate plants, cook, share food, and ingest and digest in the proper human fashion (John Waiko, personal communication, 1981; Young 1971:186–7).

Douglas hypothesizes that bodily control is an expression of social control (Douglas 1970:99). Bates, more specifically, proposes reading the language of food as an indicator of social control. According to him, "one can understand . . . control over sexual and food behavior in terms of man's efforts to master his appetites, and thus to master himself" (Bates 1958:28). Wamirans, who consciously integrate their ideas about biological needs with their social values, emphasize control rather than chaos, restraint rather than excess. To paraphrase Bates, Wamirans' control of food is an effort to master their appetites and, thus, to master themselves.

Wamirans brought a mythical plague of "famine" to their land, as we have seen, in an attempt to control their ambivalent instincts. Their belief in "famine," alone, is able to keep their otherwise rapacious and, if unleashed, self-destructive and self-devouring impulses under control. As previously quoted, in a less guarded moment, one man explained,

We say that we are afraid of famine. But we are really afraid of too much food! Were we to have even a little more, there would be no controlling the desire and greed that would set in among us and rip us apart!

Desire, which borders on greed, is felt on an individual level and feared on a social scale. It is kept in check by adhering to ideas and behavior about the production, distribution, and digestion of food.

"Where you come from, people are money people"

Wamirans constantly reminded me that they define their world, themselves, and their relationships in terms of food. To bring their beliefs into a framework that I could more easily grasp, they often explained, "We are taro people, but where you come from, people are money people." Time and again I was told, "In your place people are different. They work for money. That is their life. That is who they are." Comparing the Wamirans' use of food to the Western use of money reveals the accuracy and perceptiveness of this statement.

In Western societies, one notable way in which people define themselves, communicate their statuses, and express and manipulate relationships is with money. People work for money, accumulate money, distribute money, consume with money and, in turn, are consumed by their need and passion for money. In their search for identity, Westerners purchase a Cadillac, a Porsche, or a Mercedes-Benz, not necessarily because of the automobile's superior quality, but to flaunt their affluence and, hence, their status. Expensive jewels are worn for similar reasons. Diamonds are not intrinsically more beautiful, and certainly no more useful, than garnets. Yet, diamonds are the desired gems, worn on occasions when one aims to impress, and bestowed by men upon women to win their admiration. Designer clothes, where the conspicuously placed label is no less than a poorly disguised price tag, provide many people with a sense of identity.

Westerners also control relationships, especially those that are asymmetrical, with money. Children's dependence on adults, women's dependence on men, poor people's dependence on rich people, and, on a more global scale, Third World countries' dependence on industrial nations can be reduced to a relationship between financial haves and have-nots. Power is based on the fact that one group holds the wealth and, by controlling its distribution, can influence the other. The 1981 North–South Survival Summit, held in Cancún, to discuss the redistribution of wealth from the richer industrial nations to the poorer agricultural nations, is an outstanding example of the role that money plays in balancing powers. Keeping in mind the role of taro as a Wamiran indicator of manhood, it is interesting to note that one of President Reagan's aides referred to the Cancún meeting as a scheme "to strip us of our economic manhood" (*Newsweek:*1981). In short, in the same way that taro provides Wamiran men with a sense of manhood, money, on the whole, provides Western men with a sense of manhood.

The ambivalence of mixed emotions, such as dreading that for which one yearns, is equally applicable to Wamirans' conflicts over an abundance of taro and to Westerners' feelings about wealth. We have seen that Wamirans yearn for abundance on an individual level, yet dread its consequence on a social scale. Similarly, Westerners display mixed feelings toward money and items that connote wealth. On the one hand, they see wealth as a road to human liberation from the chains of biological necessity. A pipedream belief prevails that if everyone would be rich, poverty, hunger, crime, and disease would disappear. On the other hand, wealth (''the root of all evil'') is seen as capable of unleashing appetites and, consequently, the degradation of morals (to which anyone who has fought with siblings over an inheritance can attest).

An understanding of Wamiran food-related behavior, and a brief comparison of it with Western money-related behavior, underscores the universality of Wamiran symbolic behavior. Westerners would undoubtedly describe Wamirans, as I have done, as overly preoccupied with food, with questions of who eats what, who gives to whom, and so on. Wamirans describe Westerners as overly concerned with money and possessions. As my Wamiran friend said, ''Where you come from, people are different; they are money people.'' But, in fact, where I come from, people are the same. Whether people are overly concerned with food or with money, whether they feed and master their appetites with taro or with coins and bills, they are engaged in the same activity. They are using symbolic objects outside of themselves to define themselves to one another and to order and control their social relationships.

Toward a more balanced future

What I have presented about the importance of food for Wamirans as an object with which ''to think,'' has great practical significance for international development and global communication. In newly emerging nations, such as Papua New Guinea, food is an area particularly affected by change. Foreign advisers are often in a position to suggest new agricultural technologies, mandate different methods of land allocation, and introduce cash crops. In Papua New Guinea, for example, rural development is now a major concern of the government, which calls in ''technical experts'' for consultation. The complex questions of agricultural change, however, cannot be understood solely from the point of view of economic efficiency, where ideas of ''progress'' and ''profit'' are seen in terms of surplus alone. If levels of subsistence are to be raised successfully, and if villagers are to enter the wider economic market without development destroying their cultural base, a far more comprehensive understanding of their subsistence must be taken into account. Questions about development must consider indigenous conceptions of the environment, cultural meanings attached to foods, as well as ideas concerning control and human intervention in effecting production, distribution, and growth. This is especially important in view of the present concern with the world's food supply and with growing malnutrition in developing nations which, at least in the Pacific, is primarily due to Western intervention (Coyne 1981).

Although the causes of malnutrition are extremely complex, one contributing factor to malnutrition in new nations is the presence of large multinational corporations that increasingly control the production and distribution of food. As agribusiness giants try to dominate the economics and politics of poorer countries, local subsistence farmers and landowners suffer. Landowners are encouraged either to leave their land and move to towns to earn money, or else to use their land to produce crops for export. In either case, they abandon their land and livelihood in order to acquire cash, which is then used to purchase imported foods, often of poorer nutritional quality. Central America has been a case in point where agricultural land, which is under the control of large landowners and corporations, is used to produce cash crops that are consumed by wealthier nations. Mexico, for example, uses scarce foreign-exchange credits to import corn, the main staple of the Mexican diet, while thousands of fertile acres produce a "luxury" variety of corn for North American tables (Keen 1978:79). In Papua New Guinea, increasingly more land is used for purposes of small-scale cash cropping. Fortunately, agribusiness, although growing, has not yet engulfed the country.

If we understand the complexities of nutritional levels and environmental factors, as well as the important social and symbolic roles that food plays in Papua New Guinea, perhaps it is not too late to act responsibly. We should encourage true independence, as well as equally weighted interdependence, for new nations rather than making them dependent on cash, imported food, and outsiders' often exploitative ideas of development. Moreover, forced dependency on cash and imported foods may entail more than a shift from economic self-reliance to economic dependency. In Wamira, replacing taro with cash crops and money would also strip Wamirans of their main symbol of identity and vehicle for communication. The replacement of taro with money would force them to define themselves and their relationships in terms of a symbol that Westerners have devised and control. Thus, if a shift from "taro people" to "money people" were to take place, as some developers are attempting to accomplish, dependency and greater imbalance would result in two realms: economic and symbolic. We must remember that what appears, in Wamira, to be an overly controlled and inflexible preoccupation with food and "hunger," is, in fact, the key to the stability, perpetuation, and meaning of their social order.

Appendixes

Appendix A: Language

For the benefit of readers interested in following linguistic analysis more precisely, I supply a brief description of the language. Copland King, who compiled a grammar and dictionary of Wedau in 1901, communicated the following about his efforts, which were not without hardship, at learning Wedau.

Then we had our troubles about the language. . . . One may readily get a large number of native words and their equivalents by pointing and gesture. But when sometimes the words ended with one syllable and at other times with another syllable, it was puzzling. Of course these terminations meant something, but they were certainly not either the sign of the singular or the plural or of gender. . . . It was the same with the verbs, only there were both ends of the word to puzzle us there. (King 1899:18)

The grammatical complexities Copland King refers to occur with nouns, adjectives, and verbs. In Wedau there are two main classes of nouns. One consists of kin, close friends, and parts of the body (including blood, skin, sores on the skin, a person's name, a person's shadow, a person's photograph, etc.). This class forms the possessive by suffixing the personal possessive pronoun. The second category consists of all other nouns, and forms the possessive by adding the possessive pronoun separately before the noun. For example, "my father" is *amau*, "his father" is *amana*, but "my house" is *au numa*, and "his house" is *ana numa*.[1] Attributive adjectives are formed by suffixing *na* to the adjectival root. *Numa i aburu* means "the house is small," whereas *numa aburuna* means "the small house." Adjectives agree in number and person with the noun they follow. Thus, "you [plural] little ones" becomes *taumi aburumi* and "we [inclusive] little ones" becomes *tauta aburuta*.

[1] The orthography used here for transcribing Wedau words is that established by the missionaries.

Wedau verbs fall into various classes, depending on whether there is partial or complete reduplication of the root in forming the present tense. All verbs can be conjugated according to past, present, future, and "weak obligatory" tense.[2] All can likewise be negated in each tense. For example, "I walked" is *a babara*, and "I am walking" is *a bababara*. Furthermore, transitive verbs take objectival suffixes. For example, "he sees" is *i inanai*, and "he sees me" is *i inanaiu*. Many verbs attach prefixes for various reasons. As examples, *vi* can either indicate causative action or can make an intransitive verb transitive ("to learn" is *aramanei*, "to teach" is *viaramanei*, "I taught" is *a viaramanei*, "I am teaching" is *a viararamanei*, and "I am teaching you [plural]" is *a viararamanimi*). The prefix *vo* indicates action with the hands ("to dig" is *garai*, "to dig with the hands" is *vogarai*). *Tu* indicates action with the foot ("to squash" is *gwadai*, "to trample" is *tugwadai*). *Rau* is a denominative prefix ("broom" is *girigiri* and "to sweep" is *raugirigiri*), and so on.

Wedau is a very adaptable language. English words are easily incorporated with minor phonetic shifts. Thus, "baptism" becomes "bapataito," and "martyr" becomes "maritura." Other incorporations are made by applying Wedau affixes to the English root. For example, "to be prepared" becomes *vi-redi*, and "to pass up a nomination," as for village or church councillor, is to *vi-decline*. The affixes apply not only to create the new word, but to integrate it into Wedau syntax. Thus, *vi-stori* means "to tell stories"; "to continue telling stories" is phrased *vi-stostori*, with partial reduplication of the borrowed element to indicate the verbal aspect.

---

[2] What I call the "weak obligatory" tense corresponds roughly to modal "should" or "ought" in English. On grounds of morphological and syntactic parallelism, it is clearly a "tense" in Wedau.

Appendix B. *Animal foods (3% of total diet)*

Name or description	Local name	Local varieties	Comments
Freshwater fish	*Iana wairei*		Seasonal year round (except where noted), best in dry season
Small fish with suckers		*Ovia*	December–April
Small stinging fish		*Neia*	Eaten only by old women
Unidentified		*Bouri*	
Unidentified		*Moga*	
Unidentified		*Lakeima*	
Unidentified		*Botiri*	
Unidentified		*Waigama*	
Unidentified		*Gadodaba*	Eaten only by old people
Unidentified		*Navakwara*	Found in lagoon
Unidentified		*Waikererei*	
Unidentified		*Touria*	Eaten only by old women
Unidentified		*Gadagadari*	
Unidentified		*Doaraoraoa*	
Unidentified		*Awaria*	
Unidentified		*Tuakala*	
Unidentified		*Takunumaigora*	
Unidentified		*Wapoira*	
Unidentified		*Reureu*	
Unidentified		*Motovi*	
Saltwater fish	*Iana bogei*		Seasonal year round (except where noted)
Tusk fish		*Araraua*	
Sardine		*Oari*	
Flying fish		*Wago*	
Unidentified		*Matamera*	December–April
Unidentified		*Vagewa*	

Appendix B. Animal foods (3% of total diet) (cont.)

Name or description	Local name	Local varieties	Comments
Unidentified		Walapia	
Unidentified		Ore	
Unidentified		Bumoro	
Unidentified		Ipi	
Unidentified		Kieta	
Unidentified		Bumoropia	
Unidentified		Ateava	
Unidentified		Bobo	
Unidentified		Monava	
Unidentified		Vala	
Unidentified		Kaduna	
Black-finned long tom		Wadumo	
Sunfish		Vari	
Fish with black meat		Inapuru	
Unidentified		Topoi	
Mangrove jack		Magara	
Perch		Potumanai	
Sweetlips		Gamokala	
Whitebait		Piramatu	December–April
Small whitebait		Tekwatekwa	December–April
Small stinging fish		Neipiapia	
Unidentified		Kaidobi	
Shark		Botabota	
Unidentified		Kingfish	
Unidentified		Waitarana	
Unidentified		Wewe	
Unidentified		Lago	
Unidentified		Uviuvi	

English name	Native name	Notes
Unidentified	*Mataupaupa*	
Unidentified	*Autana*	
Unidentified	*Tiroitiro*	
Unidentified	*Rearea*	
Unidentified	*Pepei*	
Unidentified	*Obara*	
Unidentified	*Remata*	
Cod (*Gadus*)	*Gavola*	
Unidentified	*Kaidurum*	
Striped butterfish	*Geragera*	
Dart	*Dogi*	
Whiting	*Ipaoi*	
Turtle	*Vonu*	
Freshwater eel	*Tuna wairei*	Seasonal year round
Eel	*Tuna uviuvi*	Eaten only by men and old women
	Tuna gwagwari	Eaten only by men and old women
	Diburuirui	Taboo
	Ewala	Called "eel's spouse"
Saltwater eel	*Tuna bogei*	Seasonal year round
Small eel	*Naginagi*	
Long fish that "bites toes"	*Borueda*	
Octopus (*Octupus*)	*Giriboda*	Seasonal in August
Freshwater crustaceans	*Wagura wairei*	Seasonal year round especially December–April
Shrimp, prawn	*Wagura*	
Shrimp, prawn	*Gaiduru*	
Crab	*Gwaga*	
Unidentified	*Kabarema*	
Crustacean in lagoon	*Gabuko*	
Crustacean in lagoon	*Bedama*	
Shrimp, prawn	*Waraida*	
Unidentified	*Wagura didiwaga*	January–April
Unidentified	*Raum*	
Unidentified	*Peua*	

161

Appendix B. *Animal foods (3% of total diet) (cont.)*

Name or description	Local name	Local varieties	Comments
Saltwater crustaceans	*Wagura bogei*		Seasonal year round especially December–April
Small prawn, shrimp		*Waguwagura*	
Unidentified		*Givi*	
Large crab		*Gwaga Gogobuna*	
Crayfish		*Wagura*	
Freshwater shellfish	*Kepokepo wairei*		Seasonal year round
Snail with round shell		*Gibu*	
Snail with pointed shell		*Ei*	
Unidentified		*Tutube*	
Unidentified		*Didika*	
Unidentified		*Imo*	
Unidentified		*Keitutu*	
Saltwater shellfish	*Kepokepo bogei*		Seasonal year round
Large scalloped clam		*Poapoa*	
Unidentified		*Matabara*	
Unidentified		*Umewa*	
Unidentified		*Nunuai*	
Unidentified		*Uviuvi*	
Unidentified		*Gibu*	
Unidentified		*Mogeo*	
Unidentified		*Bokiau*	
Unidentified		*Awalago*	
Unidentified		*Upi*	
Unidentified		*Raga*	
Unidentified		*Gibuarara*	
Unidentified		*Loikipira*	
Unidentified		*Kururu*	

Food	Wamiran name	Notes
Roe of flying fish	*Gelaruru*	Also called *iana taena* (fish excrement), seasonal November–December
Human flesh	*Rava*	No longer eaten
Pig (*Sus scrofa*)	*Poro*	Feast food only
Wallaby (*Macropus*)	*Nawala*	Feast food only
Bandicoot	*Olapa*	Feast food only
		Available only in dry season
Birds and birds' eggs	*Kiu*	Taboo to those people who have the bird as their lineage totem
Dove	*Gabubu*	Ewa totem
Black cockatoo (*Kakatoe*)	*Kapikoa*	Lavarata and Diguma totem
Green dove	*Bunebune*	Iriki totem
Bush turkey	*Nabiri*	
Cassowary (*Casuarius*)	*Matagumai*	Aurana, Manigabadi, and Labolabo totem
Chicken (*Gallus domesticus*)	*Kamkam*	Iriki totem
Cockerel	*Kokorereko*	Iriki totem
Parrot	*Gewara*	Logaloga totem
Unidentified	*Kakua*	
White cockatoo (*Kakatoe*)	*Keloi*	
Fish hawk	*Manubada*	
Hawk	*Kitave*	Aurana totem
Osprey (*Haliaetus*)	*Maidunari*	Nabunabu totem
Osprey (*Haliaetus*)	*Beulo*	Radava totem
Snakes	*Mota*	Eaten mainly by boys and young men "to make their bones grow strong"
Black snake	*Dubo*	
Large snake	*Gabadi*	Eaten only by lactating women
Snake with colorful designs	*Anauri*	Eaten together with seaweed
Ants	*Ginauri*	
Dog	*Auwou*	Not eaten by Wamirans, traded to inland and island people
Cattle (*Bos taurus, Bos indicus*)	*Bulamakau*	

Appendix B. *Vegetable foods* (97% of total diet)

Name or description	Local name	Local varieties	Comments
Unidentified	*Ladima*		Small wild red arboreal fruit, September–October
Unidentified	*Durubi*		Medium-sized, wild arboreal fruit, August
Unidentified	*Dauro*		Large wild red arboreal fruit
Queensland arrowroot (*Canna edulis*)	*Kunumona*		Wild and cultivated, seasonal year round
Passionfruit (*Passiflora edulis flavicarpa*)	Passionfruit		Wild and cultivated, October–February
Pandanus (*Pandanus krauelianus*)	*Dula*		Wild
Licorice root	*Patuma*		Wild, famine food, August–February
Cycas palm fruit	*Natuela*		Wild, famine food
Unidentified	*Mola*		Small arboreal seed, wild, famine food; January–February
Wild chestnut	*Daginawa*		Wild, famine food
Unidentified	*Kumika*		Sour wild fruit, rarely eaten, seasonal year round
Seaweed	*Larewama*		June–July
Seaweed	*Aula*		
Seaweed	*Gaogao*		
Coconut (*Cocos nucifera*)	*Pa*		Seasonal year round, mainly cultivated
		Waduwadu	White skin
		Aigavigavina	Green skin
		Ailebalebarina	Orange skin
Breadfruit (*Artocarpus altilis*)	*Kunori*		October–February, cultivated
		Wanagorogorova	
		Wanakaikaiu	
		Berekwarekwarere	Soft, not as desirable as others
		Rawa	Also not as desirable
		Petipeti	
Chestnut (*Inocarpus fagiferus*)	*Iaga*		October–December
Java almond (*Terminalia catappa*)	*Mapa*		February–May

Crop	Local name	Variety	Notes
Malay apple (*Eugenia megacarpa*)	Natu		December–February
Mango (*Mangifera indica*)	Mogari		October–January
Banana/plantain	Akova		Seasonal year round, cultivated
Plantain (*Musa paradisiaca*)	Garo	Waibuku	Big fruit
		Reiwaita	Big fruit
		Amira	Big fruit
		Rugusama	Long fruit
		Guguini	Short fruit
	Akova	Unuana	Big, fat fruit
		Kune	Long fruit
		Duladula	Short fruit
		Nawaria	Small fruit
		Murumurua	Small, thin fruit
		German banana	Red skin
		Bodaboda	Medium fruit
		Gida	Medium fruit
		Repapulo	Feast food, from Maramatana area
Eating banana (*Musa sapientum*)	Kwaria	Samoa	Big fruit, eaten raw
	Awawara	Mitiruki	Medium fruit, eaten raw
		Memeki	Small, thin fruit, eaten raw
Giant taro (*Alocasia macrorrhiza*)		Awawara	Seasonal year round, feast food
Wild taro / elephant yam (*Amorphophallus campanulatus*)		Paiata	Seasonal year round
		Awapoa	Light-yellow corm, taboo to children
			Dark-yellow corm, food for chiefs only
			Small white corm, not eaten because it irritates one's mouth
Taro (*Colocasia esculenta*)	Uri	Kanitaki	Seasonal year round, cultivated
		Nakwaria tarana	Red stalk
		Rawaiai (*giriboda*)	Red stalk
		Aumakeakea	Red stalk
			Green stalk

Appendix B. *Vegetable foods (97% of total diet) (cont.)*

Name or description	Local name	Local varieties	Comments
		Gogorapi	Green stalk
		Pavuna	Green stalk
		Uriuri ragaragana	Green stalk
		Obeobe ragaragana	Yellow stalk
		Porokawai	Brown stalk
		Dubo	Black stalk
		Taunekwa	White stalk
		Abaua	White stalk
		Nakwaria duma	Black stalk
		Nakwaria kawakiruma	White stalk
		Nakwaria adevona	Red and black striped stalk
		Tiwalai	Yellow or green and yellow stalk
		Taukopua	Black stalk
		Reiparara	White stalk
		Ipatapa ragaraga	White stalk
		Dagege ragaraga	White stalk
		Raira	
		Mataraumoi	
		Kitave	
Yam (*Dioscorea sp.*)	*Laba*		May–September, cultivated
Greater yam (*Dioscorea alata*)		*Laba*	
Greater yam (*Dioscorea alata*)		*Giridona*	Red leaves
Greater yam (*Dioscorea alata*)		*Mudubaro*	Green leaves
Lesser yam (*Dioscorea esculenta*)		*Modara*	
Aerial yam (*Dioscorea bulbifera*)		*Morewa*	
Yam (*Dioscorea nummularia*)		*Kwalawa*	Feast food
Wild yam (*Dioscorea sp.*)		*Garela*	Famine food
Wild yam (*Dioscorea sp.*)		*Goida*	Famine food

Sweet potato (Ipomoea batatas)	Kanukanuma	Seasonal year round, cultivated
	Gogoutata	Red skin, white center
	Pupua	White skin
	Raborabo	Yellow center
	Alotau	From Alotau area
	Samarai	From Samarai area
Tapioca, cassava, manioc (Manihot esculenta)	Tapioko	Seasonal year round, cultivated
		Undesirable, called "pig's food"
"Pitpit" (Saccharum edule)	Orabu	February–April, cultivated
	Keiwatana	
	Kabatom	
	Waikena	
	Gogore	Feast food
	Raberabe	
	Obiobiu	
	Wago	
	Diwewela	
Sugarcane (Saccharum officinarum)	Tom	February–May, cultivated
	Dibowani	
	Ganuberererei	
	Lagaru	
	Kovelagaru	
	Wadana	
	Riga	
	Lakalaka	
	Gwaga	
	Kanidogodogo	
	Mapa	
	Lawainai	
	Keketa	
	Tanigapawapawa	
	Bunara	
	Doboidamana	
	Urauraga	

Appendix B. *Vegetable foods (97% of total diet) (cont.)*

Name or description	Local name	Local varieties	Comments
Squash (*Cucurbita pepo*)	*Bonubonu*	*Raukum* *Molobua* *Vovogi* *Dokidoki*	August–March, cultivated
Maize (*Zea mays*)	*Pegapega*		Seasonal year round, cultivated
Papaya, Pawpaw (*Carica papaya*)	*Kaiokira*		Seasonal year round, cultivated
Green leaves	Cabbage	*Kire*	Seasonal year round, especially September–April
Leaves (*Abelmoschus manihot*)		*Gova*	Cultivated
Squash leaves		*Bonubonu ruguna*	Cultivated
Taro leaves		*Tipeni*	Cultivated, feast food
Fig leaves (*Ficus sp.*)		*Damala*	Wild
Fig leaves (*Ficus sp.*)		*Ogiogi*	Wild
Beans and peas	*Koriti*		September–April, cultivated
Pigeon pea (*Cajanus cajan*)		Pigeon pea	
Bean (*Phaseolus*)		Bean	
Snake bean		Snake bean	
Winged bean (*Psophocarpus tetragonolobus*)		Winged bean	
Oranges, lemons (*Citrus sp.*)	*Kamokuku*		February–May, cultivated
Pineapple (*Ananas comosus*)	Pineapple		August–December, cultivated
Watermelon (*Citrullus vulgaris*)	Watermelon		August–March, cultivated
Tomato	Tomato		Cultivated
Scallion	Scallion		Cultivated
Peanut (*Arachis hypogaea*)	Peanut		Cultivated
Ginger (*Zingiber officinale*)	*Naia*		Cooked with feast food, often used ritually in conjunction with magic

Appendix C. *Weekly trade store purchases*[a]

Gender of Shopper	Rice	Tinned fish	Tinned meat	Tea	Sugar	Hard biscuits	Sweet biscuits	Cheese-pop, candy	Butter	Cigarettes	Tobacco	Matches	Kerosene	Soap	Batteries	Envelopes	Total
M										.50							.50
M													5.25				5.25
M										.50							.50
F		.45		.35	.50						.20		.25				1.75
F					1.00			.20		1.00	.20		.40			.20	3.25
F					1.00								.25	.50			1.25
F													.40				.40
F				.35		.20				.50			.40				1.45
F		.90															.90
F					.50												.50
F										.50	.20		.40				1.10
F					.50								.25				.75
F					.50												.50
F											.20		.40				.60
F				.35	1.00												1.35
F													.40			.20	.60
M	.50	.45			.50								.40				1.85
F	.50	.45											.40				1.35
F							.45										.45
F	.50							.20									.70
F													.40				.40
F					.50								.40				.90
F					.50							.05					.55
F										.50				.20			.70
F												.05		.50			.55
F													.40				.40
F													.40				.40
F										.25			.40				.65
F		.45			1.00	.15	.45	.20	1.40								3.65

Appendix C. *Weekly trade store purchases*[a] *(cont.)*

Gender of Shopper	Rice	Tinned fish	Tinned meat	Tea	Sugar	Hard biscuits	Sweet biscuits	Cheese-pop, candy	Butter	Cigarettes	Tobacco	Matches	Kerosene	Soap	Batteries	Envelopes	Total
M											.40						.40
F	.50				.50	.30							.40				1.70
F					.50			.20							.20		.90
F											.20		.40				.60
F					.50	.30							.40				1.20
F					.50								.40				.90
F													.40				.40
M[b]										3.65	10.00			2.00			15.65
F					.50								.40				.90
F		.45		.35	.50												1.30
F	.50	.45		.35	.50												1.80
F				.35	.50												.85
M				.35													.35
F								.25					.40				.65
F		.45			1.00			.25									1.70
F			.55			.15		.20			.40	.05					1.35
F	2.00																2.00
F	.50			.35	.50	.30											1.65
Total	5.00	4.05	.55	2.80	13.00	1.55	.45	1.50	1.40	7.40	11.80	.15	14.55	2.70	.20	.40	67.50

[a] Figures are expressed in PNG kina.
[b] Owner of Wamiran trade store.
Source: Data gathered at Dogura trade store, 1982.

Appendix D. *Soil samples*

	Bulk density (g/ml)	pH	Phosphorus (μg/ml)	Extractable cations				Cation exchange capacity (me/100g)	Percentage saturation				Available nitrogen (kg/ha)	Total nitrogen
				Potassium (me/100g)	Calcium (me/100g)	Magnesium (me/100g)	Sodium (me/100g)		Potassium	Calcium	Magnesium	Sodium		
Ola Buibui – uata (newly turned soil)	.98	6.8	7	.21	36.0	18.0	.51	58	.4	63	31	.9	99	.21
Ola Buibui – uri (planted with taro)	.96	7.2	9	.21	37.0	23.0	.46	62	.3	59	37	.7	91	.19
Ola Buibui – debagau (fallow)	.99	7.1	7	.23	39.0	20.0	.52	62	.4	63	32	.8	97	.18
Kwaviu – uata (newly turned soil)	.97	6.9	6	.23	40.0	21.0	.53	65	.4	61	33	.8	140	.17
Kwaviu – uri (planted with taro)	.99	6.6	7	.17	40.0	20.0	.55	64	.3	62	31	.9	130	.16
Kawakio – uri[a] (planted with taro)	1.10	6.6	9	.35	31.0	14.0	.38	49	.7	62	29	.8	65	.17
Maikwei – uata[a] (newly turned soil)	1.10	6.6	4	.17	32.0	15.0	.48	51	.3	62	30	.9	76	.15
Tamodukorokoro – uata[b] (newly turned soil)	—	6.7	—	.20	55.6	18.3	—	63	—	—	—	—	—	—

[a]Hamlet gardens. All others are on open plain.
[b]Taken in 1976. All others taken in 1982.

171

Appendix E. *Food composition table*[a]

	Calories (g/100g)	Protein (g/100g)	Fat (g/100g)	Carbohydrates (g/100g)	Calcium (mg/100g)	Iron (mg/100g)	Vitamin A (IU)	Thiamine (mg/100g)	Riboflavin (mg/100g)	Niacin (mg/100g)	Ascorbic acid (mg/100g)
Taro	165	1.4	.5	39.0	22	—	5	.27	.04	.2	.5
Yam	161	1.4	.1	38.7	23	.5	0	.14	—	.2	8
Sweet potato	120	.8	.1	29.0	30	.6	600	.07	.05	.2	65
Tapioca	362	.5	.3	86.9	0	0	0	0	0	0	0
Plantain	113	1.2	.5	29.2	7	.8	32	.06	.04	.6	16
Breadfruit	102	1.7	.3	26.2	33	1.2	40	.11	.03	.9	29
Squash	33	1.3	.3	7.7	18	.6	4000	.06	.03	.4	11
Maize	92	3.4	1.2	20.7	5	.6	350	.15	.09	1.7	14
Beans	35	2.4	.2	7.6	57	.8	400	.08	.12	.5	17
Peas	350	21.0	2.5	61.0	90	7.0	120	.70	.18	2.2	2
Taro leaves	57	5.0	2.5	6.6	—	—	—	—	—	—	—
Green leaves	25	2.0	.3	4.8	80	2.5	1000	.08	.02	.5	50
Java almonds	644	14.2	68.5	5.5	119	2.6	45	.95	.12	.4	T
Coconut cream	351	4.2	34.0	12.8	9	1.7	0	.06	.03	.6	2
Banana	94	1.3	.5	29.2	7	.8	200	.04	.05	.7	11
Mango	65	.7	.2	17.0	11	.4	1900	.05	.06	.6	48
Papaya	39	.6	.1	10.0	24	.4	1000	.03	.04	.4	64
Pineapple	47	.5	.2	12.2	18	.5	90	.08	.03	.2	40
Sugar	387	—	—	—	T	T	0	0	0	0	0
Pork fat	816	3.0	89.0	0	0	0	0	0	0	0	0
Pork meat	364	12.0	35.0	0	6	6.5	0	.58	.14	3.1	0
Fish (fresh)	104	19.0	2.5	0	28	.8	T	.06	.08	2.2	T
Shellfish	96	19.6	.8	2.5	146	1.1	250	.07	.04	3.6	—
Fish (tinned)	314	22.0	24.0	1.0	44	1.3	100	.06	.20	2.6	0
Beef (tinned)	224	18.6	16.5	0	20	4.3	0	.02	.24	3.4	0
Rice	360	6.7	.7	78.9	10	.9	0	.08	.03	1.6	0
White bread	430	10.7	.9	68.7	92	1.8	0	.18	—	—	0

[a]Symbols: —, no data; T, trace only. *Source:* World Health Organization, Pacific.

172

Appendix F. *Average daily consumption*

Foods	Male Weight[a]	Calories	Protein	Female Weight[a]	Calories	Protein
Dry season						
Taro	480	792	6.7	410	677	5.7
Yam	425	684	6.0	380	612	5.3
Sweet potato	650	780	5.2	600	720	4.8
Plantain	160	181	1.9	150	170	1.8
Rice	60	216	4.0	20	72	1.3
Green leaves	50	13	1.0	40	10	.8
Peas	40	140	8.4	30	105	6.3
Banana	90	85	1.2	90	85	1.2
Java almonds	75	483	10.7	75	483	10.7
Coconut cream	20	70	.8	10	35	.4
Total		3,444	45.9		2,969	38.3
Wet season						
Taro	645	1,064	9.0	440	726	6.2
Sweet potato	775	930	6.0	630	756	5.0
Tapioca	135	489	.7	100	362	.5
Plantain	200	226	2.4	150	170	1.8
Breadfruit	120	122	2.0	90	92	1.5
Squash	210	69	2.7	200	66	2.6
Green leaves	58	15	1.2	46	12	.9
Banana	90	85	1.2	90	85	1.2
Pineapple	140	66	.7	120	56	.6
Mango	300	195	2.1	350	228	2.5
Coconut cream	20	70	.8	10	35	.4
Fish	100	104	19.0	100	104	19.0
Total		3,435	47.8		2,692	42.2

[a] In grams.

References

Appadurai, Arjun (1981). "Gastro-politics in Hindu South Asia." *American Ethnologist* 8:494–511.

Arnott, Margaret L. (1975). *Gastronomy: The Anthropology of Food and Food Habits*. The Hague: Mouton Publishers.

Baniara Patrol Reports (1924–62). Alotau, Milne Bay Province, Papua New Guinea.

Barrau, Jacques (1958). *Subsistence Agriculture in Melanesia*. Bernice P. Bishop Museum Bulletin No. 219. Honolulu: Bernice P. Bishop Museum.

———— (1965). "Witnesses of the Past: Notes on Some Food Plants of Oceania." *Ethnology* 4:282–94.

Barth, Fredrik (1966). *Models of Social Organization*. Royal Anthropological Institute Occasional Paper No. 23. London.

———— (1975). *Ritual and Knowledge Among the Baktaman of New Guinea*. New Haven: Yale University Press.

Bates, Marston (1958). *Gluttons and Libertines*. New York: Random House.

Bateson, Gregory (1972). *Steps to an Ecology of the Mind*. San Francisco: Chandler Publishing.

Battaglia, Debbora (1983). "Projecting Personhood in Melanesia: The Dialectics of Artefact Symbolism on Sabarl Island." *Man* 18:289–304.

Bayliss-Smith, Timothy, and Richard Feachem (1977). *Subsistence and Survival: Rural Ecology in the Pacific*. New York: Academic Press.

Bell, F. L. S. (1946). "The Place of Food in the Social Life of the Tanga." *Oceania* 17:139–72.

Bonnemaison, Joël (1974). "Espaces et Paysages Agraires des Nouvelles-Hébrides." *Journal de la Société des Océanistes* 30:163–232, 259–81.

British New Guinea Annual Reports (1888–1903). Victoria: Government Printer.

Brookfield, Harold C., and Paula Brown (1963). *Struggle for Land: Agriculture and Group Territories Among the Chimbu of the New Guinea Highlands*. Melbourne: Oxford University Press.

Brookfield, Harold C., and Doreen Hart (1971). *Melanesia: A Geographical Interpretation of an Island World*. London: Methuen.

Brown, Paula (1978). *Highland Peoples of New Guinea*. Cambridge: Cambridge University Press.

Burridge, Kenelm (1969). *Tangu Traditions*. Oxford: Oxford University Press (Clarendon Press).

Carneiro, Robert L. (1961). "Slash-and-Burn Cultivation Among the Kuikuru and Its Implications for Cultural Development in the Amazon Basin," in J. Wilbert (ed.), *The Evolution of Horticultural Systems in Native South America. Antropológica* (Supplement No. 2), pp. 47–67.

Chagnon, Napoleon (1968). *Yǫnomamö: The Fierce People*. New York: Holt, Rinehart and Winston.

Chateaubriand, François Auguste René (1803). *Voyages en Italie*. Paris: Minard. (1969 edition).

Clarke, William C. (1971). *Place and People: An Ecology of a New Guinean Community*. Berkeley: University of California Press.

Conklin, Harold C. (1957). *Hanunóo Agriculture: A Report on an Integral System of Shifting Cultivation in the Philippines*. Forestry Development Paper 12. Rome: Food and Agriculture Organization.

Coyne, Terry (1981). *The Effect of Urbanization and Western Diet on the Health of Pacific Island Populations*. Noumea: South Pacific Commission.

DeCoppet, Daniel (1981). "The Life-Giving Death," in S. C. Humphreys and H. King (eds.), *Mortality and Immortality: The Anthropology and Archaeology of Death*. New York: Academic Press, pp. 175–204.

Department of Provincial Affairs (1980). "Food Shortage in Wamira Village." Letter from Michael Miro, District Officer in Charge. Alotau, September 23, 1980.

Dogura Hospital Records (1978). Milne Bay Province, Papua New Guinea.

Douglas, Mary (1970). *Natural Symbols*. New York: Vintage Press.

Douglas, Mary, and Michael Nicod (1974). "Taking the Biscuit: The Structure of British Meals." *New Society* 30:744–7.

Errington, Frederick (1974). *Karavar: Masks and Power in a Melanesian Ritual*. Ithaca: Cornell University Press.

Farb, Peter, and George Armelagos (1980). *Consuming Passions: The Anthropology of Eating*. Boston: Houghton Mifflin.

Ferro-Luzzi, Anna, Nicholas G. Norgan, and John V. G. A. Durnin (1975). "Food Intake, Its Relationship to Body Weight and Age, and Its Apparent Nutritional Adequacy in New Guinean Children." *American Journal of Clinical Nutrition* 28:1443–53.

Firth, Raymond (1926). "Proverbs in Native Life, with Special Reference to Those of the Maori." *Folklore* 37:134–53, 245–70.

——— (1939). *Primitive Polynesian Economy*. London: George Routledge and Sons.

Food and Agriculture Organization of the United Nations (1957). *Calorie Requirements*. Report of the Second Committee on Calorie Requirements. Food and Agriculture Organization Nutritional Studies, No. 15. Rome: Food and Agriculture Organization.

——— (1964). *Protein: At the Heart of the World Food Problem*. World Food Problems, No. 5. Rome: Food and Agriculture Organization.

Forge, J. Anthony (1965). "Art and Environment in the Sepik." *Proceedings of the Royal Anthropological Institute*, pp. 23–31.

Fortune, Reo (1932). *Sorcerers of Dobu*. Prospect Heights, IL: Waveland Press.

Frake, Charles O. (1964). "How to Ask for a Drink in Subanun," in J. Gumperz and D. Hymes (eds.), *The Ethnography of Communication*. American Anthropologist Special Publication, Vol. 66, No. 6, Part 2, pp. 127–32.

Freedman, Robert L. (1981). *Human Food Uses: A Cross-Cultural, Comprehensive Annotated Bibliography*. Westport, Conn.: Greenwood Press.

Freeman, J. D. (1955). *Iban Agriculture*. Colonial Research Studies, 18. London: Her Majesty's Stationery Office.

Freud, Sigmund (1938). *Basic Writings of Sigmund Freud.* New York: Modern Library.

Geertz, Clifford (1972). "Deep Play: Notes on the Balinese Cockfight." *Daedalus* 101(1):1–38.

Gell, Alfred (1975). *Metamorphosis of the Cassowaries: Umeda Society, Language and Ritual.* London: Athlone.

Gerbrands, Adrianus A. (1967). *Wow-Ipits: Eight Asmat Woodcarvers of New Guinea.* The Hague: Mouton.

Gewertz, Deborah B. (1982). "The Father Who Bore Me: The Role of *Tsambunwuro* During Chambri Initiation Ceremonies," in G. Herdt (ed.), *Rituals of Manhood: Male Initiation in Papua New Guinea.* Berkeley: University of California Press, pp. 286–320.

Giddens, Anthony (1979). *Central Problems in Social Theory: Action, Structure, and Contradiction in Social Analysis.* Berkeley: University of California Press.

Gillison, Gillian (1980). "Images of Nature in Gimi Thought," in C. MacCormack and M. Strathern (eds.), *Nature, Culture and Gender.* Cambridge: Cambridge University Press, pp. 143–73.

   (1983). "Cannibalism Among Women in the Eastern Highlands of Papua New Guinea," in P. Brown and D. Tuzin (eds.), *The Ethnography of Cannibalism.* A Special Publication of the Society for Psychological Anthropology, pp. 33–51.

Giurina, Pamela (1976). "To Dogura from America." *Holy Name News* No. 118, p. 4, Dogura, Papua New Guinea: Anglican Mission Library.

Golson, Jack (1976). "Archaeology and Agricultural History in the New Guinea Highlands," in G. deG. Sieveking, I. H. Longworth, and K. E. Wilson (eds.), *Problems in Social and Economic Achaeology.* London: Duckworth, pp. 201–20.

   (1977). "No Room at the Top: Agricultural Intensification in the New Guinea Highlands," in J. Allen, J. Golson, and R. Jones (eds.), *Sunda and Sahul.* New York: Academic Press, pp. 602–38.

Goodale, Jane C. (1985). "Pig's Teeth and Skull Cycles: Both Sides of the Face of Humanity." *American Ethnologist* 12:228–44.

Goody, Jack (1982). *Cooking, Cuisine and Class: A Study in Comparative Sociology.* Cambridge: Cambridge University Press.

Gregor, Thomas (1985). *Anxious Pleasures: The Sexual Lives of an Amazonian People.* Chicago: University of Chicago Press.

Hallowell, A. Irving (1955). *Culture and Experience.* New York: Schocken Books.

   (1965). "The History of Anthropology as an Anthropological Problem." *Journal of the History of the Behavioral Sciences* 1:24–38.

Hanks, Lucien (1972). *Rice and Man: Agricultural Ecology in Southeast Asia.* Arlington Heights, Ill.: A. H. M. Publishing.

Harner, Michael (1977). "The Ecological Basis for Aztec Sacrifice." *American Ethnologist* 4:117–35.

Harris, Marvin (1974). *Cows, Pigs, Wars, and Witches: The Riddles of Culture.* New York: Vintage Books.

Hays, Terence E., and Patricia H. Hays (1982). "Opposition and Complementarity of the Sexes in Ndumba Initiation," in G. Herdt (ed.), *Rituals of Manhood: Male Initiation in Papua New Guinea.* Berkeley: University of California Press, pp. 201–38.

Henry, Jules (1941). *Jungle People: A Kaingáng Tribe of the Highlands of Brazil.* New York: J. J. Augustin.

Herdt, Gilbert (1981). *Guardians of the Flutes: Idioms of Masculinity*. New York: McGraw Hill.

(1982). "Fetish and Fantasy in Sambia Initiation," in G. Herdt (ed.), *Rituals of Manhood: Male Initiation in Papua New Guinea*. Berkeley: University of California Press, pp. 44–98.

Hipsley, E., and F. W. Clements (eds.) (1947). *Report of the New Guinea Nutrition Survey Expedition, 1947*. Canberra: Department of External Territories.

Hipsley, E., and N. Kirk (1965). *Studies of Dietary Intake and the Expenditure of Energy by New Guineans*. South Pacific Commission Technical Paper, No. 147. Noumea: South Pacific Commission.

Hogbin, Ian (1970a). "Food Festivals and Politics in Wogeo." *Oceania* 40:304–28.

(1970b). *The Island of Menstruating Men: Religion in Wogeo, New Guinea*. Scranton: Chandler Publishing.

Johnson, S. Ragnar (1982). "Food, Other Valuables, Payment, and the Relative Scale of Ommura Ceremonies (New Guinea)." *Anthropos* 77:509–23.

Jones, Barbara (1980). *Consuming Society: Food and Illness Among the Faiwol*. Ann Arbor: University Microfilms. Ph.D. thesis, University of Virginia.

Jorgensen, Daniel W. (1985). "Femsep's Last Garden: A Telefol Response to Mortality," in D. Counts and D. E. A. Counts (eds.), *Aging and Its Transformations: Moving Toward Death in Pacific Societies*. New York: University Press of America, pp. 209–26.

Kaberry, Phyllis M. (1941). "The Abelam Tribe, Sepik District, New Guinea." *Oceania* 11:233–58, 345–67.

(1942). "Law and Political Organization in the Abelam Tribe, New Guinea." *Oceania* 12:79–95, 209–25, 331–63.

(1965). "Political Organization Among the Northern Abelam," *Anthropological Forum* 1:334–72.

Kahn, Miriam (1983). "Sunday Christians, Monday Sorcerers: Selective Adaptation to Missionization in Wamira." *The Journal of Pacific History* 18:96–112.

(1984). "Taro Irrigation: A Descriptive Account from Wamira, Papua New Guinea." *Oceania* 54:204–23.

(1985). "A Sabotaged Aqueduct: Sociopolitical Parameters of Agricultural Intensification in Lowland Papua New Guinea." *British Archaeological Report*, International Series, No. 232, I. S. Farrington (ed.), *Prehistoric Intensive Agriculture in the Tropics*, pp. 683–98.

Keen, Samuel (1978). "Eating Our Way to Enlightenment." *Psychology Today* 12 (October) :62–6, 79–87.

Kelly, Raymond C. (1976). "Witchcraft and Sexual Relations: An Exploration in the Social and Semantic Implications of the Structure of Belief," in P. Brown and G. Buchbinder (eds.), *Man and Woman in the New Guinea Highlands*. American Anthropological Association Publication, No. 8, pp. 36–53.

(1977). *Etoro Social Structure: A Study in Structural Contradiction*. Ann Arbor: University of Michigan Press.

Ker, Annie (1910). *Papuan Fairy Tales*. London: Macmillan.

King, Copland (1899). *A History of the New Guinea Mission*. Sydney: W. A. Pepperday.

(1901). *Grammar and Dictionary of the Wedau Language*. Sydney: W. A. Pepperday.

Kottak, Conrad P. (1978). "Ritual at McDonald's." *Natural History Magazine* 87 (January) :75–82.

Laing, R. D. (1970). *Knots*. New York: Vintage Books.

Lea, David A. M. (1964). *Abelam Land and Sustenance*. Ph.D. thesis, Australian National University, Canberra.

(1969). "Some Non-Nutritive Functions of Food in New Guinea," in F. Gale and G. H. Lawton (eds.), *Settlement and Encounter: Geographical Studies Presented to Sir Grenfell Price*. Melbourne: Oxford University Press, pp. 173–84.

Leach, Edmund R. (1961). "Two Essays Concerning the Symbolic Representation of Time," in *Rethinking Anthropology*. London: Athlone, pp. 124–36.

(1964). "Anthropological Aspects of Language: Animal Categories and Verbal Abuse," in E. H. Lenneberg (ed.), *New Directions in the Study of Language*. Cambridge, Mass.: M.I.T. Press, pp. 23–63.

(1976). *Culture and Communication: The Logic by Which Symbols Are Connected*. Cambridge: Cambridge University Press.

Lepowsky, Maria (1985). "Food Taboos, Malaria and Dietary Change: Infant Feeding and Cultural Adaptation on a Papua New Guinea Island." *Ecology of Food and Nutrition* 16(2):105–26.

Lévi-Strauss, Claude (1962a). *La Pensée Sauvage*. Paris: Librairie Plon. (1966 English edition: *The Savage Mind*. Chicago: University of Chicago Press).

(1962b). *Totémisme Aujourd'hui*. Paris: Librairie Plon. (1962 English edition: *Totemism*. Boston: Beacon Press.)

(1964). *Mythologiques I: Le Cru et le Cuit*. Paris: Librairie Plon. (*1969 English edition: The Raw and the Cooked: Introduction to a Science of Mythology*, Vol. I. New York: Harper and Row).

(1965). "Le Triangle Culinaire." *L'Arc* 26:19–29. (1966 English edition: "The Culinary Triangle." *Partisan Review* 33:586–95).

Lindenbaum, Shirley (1976). "A Wife is the Hand of Man," in P. Brown and G. Buchbinder (eds.), *Man and Woman in the New Guinea Highlands*. American Anthropological Association Publication, No. 8, pp. 54–62.

McAlpine, John R., Gael Keig, and Karen Short (1975). *Climatic Tables for Papua New Guinea*, Division of Land Use Research Technical Paper, No. 37. Melbourne: Commonwealth Scientific and Industrial Research Organization.

McClean, Paul D. (1963). "Phylogenesis," in P. H. Knapp (ed.), *Expression of the Emotions in Man*. New York: International Universities Press, pp. 16–35.

McKnight, David (1973). "Sexual Symbolism of Food Among the Wik-Mungkan." *Man* 8:194–209.

Maclaren, Albert (1891a). "Letter to the Primate, 19 August 1891." *Anglican Archives*.

(1891b). "Letter to Friends, 25 August 1891." *Anglican Archives*.

Malinowski, Bronislaw (1922). *Argonauts of the Western Pacific*. Prospect Heights, IL: Waveland Press.

(1935a). *Coral Gardens and Their Magic*, Vol. I, *The Description of Gardening*. New York: American Book Company.

(1935b). *Coral Gardens and Their Magic*, Vol. II, *The Language of Magic and Gardening*. New York: American Book Company.

Matheson, Richard (1954). "F———," in *Born of Man and Woman*. Philadelphia: Chamberlain Press.

Maurois, André (1934). "An Idea for a Story." *Esquire* (July), pp. 26, 138.

Meggitt, Mervyn (1964). "Male–Female Relations in the Highlands of New Guinea." *American Anthropologist*, Special Publication 66:204–24.

Meigs, Anna S. (1976). "Male Pregnancy and the Reduction of Sexual Opposition in a New Guinea Highlands Society." *Ethnology* 15:393–407.

(1984). *Food, Sex, and Pollution: A New Guinea Religion*. New Brunswick: Rutgers University Press.

Myerhoff, Barbara (1978). *Number Our Days*. New York: Simon and Schuster.

Nadelson, Leslee (1981). "Pigs, Women, and the Men's House in Amazonia: An Analysis of Six Mundurucú Myths," in S. Ortner and H. Whitehead (eds.), *Sexual Meanings: The Cultural Construction of Gender and Sexuality*. Cambridge: Cambridge University Press, pp. 240–72.

Newman, Philip (1965). *Knowing the Gururumba*. New York: Holt, Rinehart and Winston.

Newman, Philip, and David Boyd (1982). "The Making of Men: Ritual and Meaning in Awa Male Initiation," in G. Herdt (ed.), *Rituals of Manhood: Male Initiation in Papua New Guinea*. Berkeley: University of California Press, pp. 239–85.

Newsweek (1981). "The Survival Summit." October 26, 1981, pp. 36–56.

Newton, Henry (1914). *In Far New Guinea*. Philadelphia: J. B. Lippincott.

Norgan, Nicholas G., Anna Ferro-Luzzi, and John V. G. A. Durnin (1974). "The Energy and Nutrient Intake and the Energy Expenditure of 204 New Guinean Adults." *Philosophical Transactions of the Royal Society of London*, Series B, 268:309–48.

Oliver, Douglas (1955). *A Solomon Island Society*. Boston: Beacon Press.

Paine, Robert (1976). "Two Modes of Exchange and Mediation," in B. Kapferer (ed.), *Transaction and Meaning: Directions in the Anthropology of Exchange and Symbolic Behaviour*. Philadelphia: Institute for the Study of Human Issues, pp. 63–85.

Panoff, Françoise (1969). "Some Facets of Maenge Horticulture." *Oceania* 40:20–31.

(1970). "Food and Faeces: A Melanesian Rite." *Man* 5:237–52.

(1971). "The Language of Plants." Unpublished.

Panoff, Michel (1968). "The Notion of the Double Self Among the Maenge." *Journal of the Polynesian Society* 77:275–95.

Papua Annual Reports (1911–50). Victoria: Government Printer.

Papua New Guinea Bureau of Meteorology (1978). Dogura Station, Milne Bay Province.

Papuan Villager, The (1930). "The Story of the Two Sisters" by Andrew Uware. January 1930, p. 7.

Parkinson, Susan (1982). "Nutrition in the South Pacific, Past and Present." *Journal of Food and Nutrition* 39:121–5.

Paz, Octavio (1970). *Claude Lévi-Strauss: An Introduction*. Ithaca: Cornell University Press.

Poole, Fitz John Porter (1982). "The Ritual Forging of Identity: Aspects of Person and Self in Bimin–Kuskusmin Male Initiation," in G. Herdt (ed.), *Rituals of Manhood: Male Initiation in Papua New Guinea*. Berkeley: University of California Press, pp. 99–154.

Pospisil, Leopold (1963). *Kapauku Papuan Economy*. Publications in Anthropology, No. 67. New Haven: Yale University, Department of Anthropology.

Powdermaker, Hortense (1932). "Feasts in New Ireland: The Social Function of Eating." *American Anthropologist* 34:236–47.

Rabaraba Patrol Reports (1972–74). Rabaraba, Milne Bay Province, Papua New Guinea.

Rappaport, Roy (1968). *Pigs for the Ancestors: Ritual in the Ecology of a New Guinea People*. New Haven: Yale University Press.

Read, Kenneth (1954). "Cultures of the Central Highlands of New Guinea." *Southwestern Journal of Anthropology* 10:1–43.

(1965). *The High Valley*. New York: Scribner.

Reay, Marie (1959). *The Kuma*. Melbourne: University Press.

Reichel-Dolmatoff, Gerado (1976). "Cosmology as Ecological Analysis: A View from the Rain Forest." *Man* 2:307–18.

Richards, Audrey I. (1932). *Hunger and Work in a Savage Tribe: A Functional Study of Nutrition Among the Southern Bantu*. London: George Routledge and Sons.

(1939). *Land, Labor and Diet in Northern Rhodesia*. London: Oxford University Press.

Rubel, Paula, and Abraham Rosman (1978). *Your Own Pigs You May Not Eat*. Chicago: University of Chicago Press.

Rubinstein, Robert L. (1981). "Knowledge and Political Process on Malo," in M. Allen (ed.), *Vanuatu: Politics, Economics and Ritual in Island Melanesia*. New York: Academic Press, pp. 135–72.

Sahlins, Marshall D. (1972). *Stone Age Economics*. Chicago: Aldine-Atherton.

(1976). *Culture and Practical Reason*. Chicago: University of Chicago Press.

(1978). "Culture as Protein and Profit." *The New York Review of Books*, November 23, 1978, pp. 45–53.

Salisbury, Richard F. (1962). *From Stone to Steel*. Melbourne: Melbourne University Press.

Scaglion, Richard (1978). "Seasonal Births in a Western Abelam Village, Papua New Guinea." *Human Biology* 50:313–23.

(1981). "Samukundi Abelam Conflict Management: Implications for Legal Planning in Papua New Guinea." *Oceania* 52:28–38.

Schieffelin, Edward L. (1976). *The Sorrow of the Lonely and the Burning of the Dancers*. New York: St. Martin's Press.

(1982). "The *Bau A* Ceremonial Hunting Lodge: An Alternative to Initiation," in G. Herdt (ed.), *Rituals of Manhood: Male Initiation in Papua New Guinea*. Berkeley: University of California Press, pp. 155–200.

Schwimmer, Eric. (1973). *Exchange in the Social Structure of the Orokaiva*. London: C. Hurst.

Seligmann, Carl G. (1910). *The Melanesians of British New Guinea*. Cambridge: Cambridge University Press.

Serpenti, Laurentius M. (1965). *Cultivators in the Swamps: Social Structure and Horticulture in a New Guinea Society*. Assen: Van Gorcum.

Sillitoe, Paul (1979). "Man-Eating Women: Fears of Sexual Pollution in the Papua New Guinea Highlands." *Journal of the Polynesian Society* 88:77–97.

Somerville, Ena (1976). *Brown Skins – Brown Paper*. Sydney: Lutheran Publishing.

Spriggs, Matthew (1980). "Taro Irrigation in the Pacific: A Call for More Research." *South Pacific Bulletin* 30:15–18.

(1984). "Taro Irrigation Techniques in the Pacific," in S. Chandra (ed.), *Edible Aroids*. Oxford: Oxford University Press (Clarendon Press), pp. 123–35.

Steensberg, Axel (1980). *New Guinea Gardens: A Study of Husbandry with Parallels in Prehistoric Europe*. New York: Academic Press.

Strathern, Andrew (1971). *The Rope of Moka: Big-Men and Ceremonial Exchange in Mount Hagen*. Cambridge: Cambridge University Press.

(1975). "Veiled Speech in Mount Hagen," in M. Bloch (ed.), *Political Language and Oratory in Traditional Society*. New York: Academic Press, pp. 185–203.

(1977). "Melpa Food-Names as an Expression of Ideas on Identity and Substance." *Journal of the Polynesian Society* 86:503–11.

(1979). "Men's House, Women's House: The Efficacy of Opposition, Reversal, and Pairing in the Melpa *Amb Kor* Cult." *Journal of the Polynesian Society* 88:37–51.

Strathern, Andrew, and Marilyn Strathern (1971). *Self-Decoration in Mount Hagen.* Toronto: University of Toronto Press.

Strathern, Marilyn (1972). *Women in Between, Female Roles in a Male World: Mount Hagen, New Guinea.* London: Seminar Press.

Tambiah, Stanley J. (1969). "Animals are Good to Think and Good to Prohibit." *Ethnology* 8:423–59.

Thaman, Randy R. (1982). "Deterioration of Traditional Food Systems, Increasing Malnutrition and Food Dependency in the Pacific Islands." *Journal of Food and Nutrition* 39:109–21.

Turnbull, Colin (1965). *Wayward Servants.* New York: Natural History Press.

(1972). *The Mountain People.* New York: Simon and Schuster.

Tuzin, Donald F. (1972). "Yam Symbolism in the Sepik: An Interpretive Account." *Southwestern Journal of Anthropology* 28:230–54.

(1978). "Sex and Meat-Eating in Ilahita: A Symbolic Study." *Canberra Anthropology* 1:82–93.

Waddell, Eric (1972). *The Mound Builders: Agricultural Practices, Environment and Society in the Central Highlands of New Guinea.* Seattle: University of Washington Press.

Wagner, Roy (1972). *Habu.* Chicago: University of Chicago Press.

(1978). *Lethal Speech: Daribi Myth as Symbolic Obviation.* Ithaca: Cornell University Press.

Watson, James B. (1977). "Pigs, Fodder and the Jones Effect in Post-Ipomoean New Guinea." *Ethnology* 16:57–70.

Weiner, Annette B. (1976). *Women of Value, Men of Renown: New Perspectives in Trobriand Exchange.* Austin: University of Texas Press.

(1977). "Trobriand Descent: Female/Male Domains." *Ethnos* 5:54–70.

(1978). "The Reproductive Model in Trobriand Society." *Mankind* 2:175–86. Special Issue on *Trade and Exchange in Oceania and Australia.*

(1979). "Trobriand Kinship from Another View: The Reproductive Power of Women and Men." *Man* 14:328–48.

Whiteman, J. (1965). "Change and Tradition in an Abelam Village." *Oceania* 36:102–20.

Wilson, E., K. Fisher, and M. Fuqua (1965). *Principles of Nutrition.* New York: Wiley.

Woodburn, James (1968). "An Introduction to Hadza Ecology," in R. Lee and I. DeVore (eds.), *Man the Hunter.* Chicago: Aldine Publishing Company, pp. 49–55.

Young, Michael W. (1971). *Fighting with Food: Leadership, Values and Social Control in a Massim Society.* Cambridge: Cambridge University Press.

(1977). "Bursting with Laughter: Obscenity, Values and Sexual Control in a Massim Society." *Canberra Anthropology* 1:75–87.

(1983). *Magicians of Manumanua: Living Myth in Kalauna.* Berkeley: University of California Press.

(1985). "On Refusing Gifts: Aspects of Ceremonial Exchange in Kalauna," in D. Barwick, J. Beckett, and M. Reay (eds.), *Metaphors of Interpretation: Festschrift for W. E. H. Stanner.* Canberra: Australian National University Press, pp. 76–87.

Index

abortion, 100
adultery, 26, 99, 111
affines
    need for, 70–3
    tensions between, 71–2, 74–5, 78–81,
        81–6, 90
age groups, 25, 125
agriculture, tropical, 3
Aidan Gadiona, xiv, 32
Aimutuara, 64
Alice Dobunaba, xiv, xv, xvi, 1, 40, 62n,
        140, 141, 142, 143, 144
Alotau, xi, 20
ancestors, *see konaga* (ancestors, spirits)
Anglican mission, 14, 22
    see also mission, missionaries
animals
    domesticated, 48–9
    wild, 48
anona (inner substance), 97, 102, 103, 111
Appadurai, Arjun, 61
aqueduct, xiii
Aranda, 90
Arapesh, Ilahita, 61
'Are 'Are, 114
areca nut, 30, 32, 43, 51, 63, 63n, 64, 65n,
        67, 69, 82, 84
Armelagos, George, 2n
Arnott, Margaret L., 2n
arua (shadow double), 101, 102
asexual regeneration, 88, 91
Australia, 61
Ayres, Mary, 113–14

Baktaman, 117
bananas (plantain), 132, 135, 165, 172, 173
    as male symbols, 62, 71

Bank of New South Wales, 14
bariawa (spirits), 112
Barrau, Jacques, 3
barrenness, 69, 69n
Barth, Fredrik, 117–18, 119, 124, 147
Bates, Marston, 61, 153
Bateson, Gregory, 75
Battaglia, Debbora, 88n
Bayliss-Smith, Timothy, 3
beer, 51
Bell, F. L. S., 5
Bemba, 2, 35n
biological needs, Wamirans' perception of, 1,
        38–9
birth, 101
blood, 88, 90, 91, 99, 100, 102–3, 118, 119,
        120f
    menstrual, 63n, 100, 119
Boianai village, xiii, 11, 15, 16, 35, 56, 67
bones, 86, 87, 88, 88n, 89, 100, 113, 118
Bonnemaison, Joël, 3
Boyd, David, 7
breadfruit, 49, 164, 172, 173
breast milk, 92, 99, 101
Brookfield, Harold C., 3
Brown, Paula, 3
Burridge, Kenelm, 6

cannibalism, 48, 56, 57, 86–8, 112, 114n,
        115n, 153
    Aztec, 2
Cape Frère, 11, 13, 15
Cape Vogel, 13
Carneiro, Robert L., 35t
cash, *see* money
Cathedral of St. Peter and St. Paul, 14
cattle project, 49, 139

Chagnon, Napoleon, 61
Chambri, 74
Chateaubriand, François Auguste René, xvii
chickens, 49, 132–3
child bearing, 90, 99–101, 114–16, 118
Christmas, 19, 137
Clarke, William C., xi, 3, 53t, 54
Clements, F. W., 54
climate, 14–17
coconut, 49, 164, 172, 173
conception, 100
Conklin, Harold C., 53t
control, 1, 2, 33, 39–41, 44, 58–9, 68–70,
    72–3, 75, 80, 85–6, 88, 147, 151,
    153
cow, 139, 141, 142, 163
    and sacredness in India, 2–3
Coyne, Terry, 50n, 155
crop yield, 45, 53–4

Damaladona, 20, 22, 48, 76, 93, 127, 139,
    141, 142, 143, 144, 145, 146
dancing, traditional, 20–1, 83
Davudavu village, 82
death, 100, 102, 102n, 111–12, 113–14
    see also feasts, death
DeCoppett, Daniel, 114
D'Entrecasteaux Islands, 58
development, international, 155–6
digestion, idiom of, 2, 110–22, 151–3
Divari village, 13, 16, 65, 79, 82
diwara (bundled taro), 104, 109, 132, 144,
    147
dogs, 49, 163
Dogura, xi, 14, 22, 27, 55, 141
Dogura House, 14
double bind, 75, 89, 90, 150
Douglas, Mary, 4, 153
dreams, 102
drought, 16, 45, 56–8
Durnin, John V. G. A., 3

East Cape, 11
eating, 8, 38–9, 134–5
    see also food, consumption of
education, 19
eel, 48, 62, 66–8, 71, 152, 161
egubedu (term for sharing areca nut), 65,
    65n, 70
Egypt, 61
empathy, 26, 27
Errington, Frederick, 61, 152–3
ethnoscience, 4
euphemisms, use of, 30–1, 131, 137–8
exogamy, lineage, 24

Faiwol, 112n
famine, 10, 16, 33, 34–5, 36, 44, 45, 56–9,
    60, 65–6, 70–3, 150–1, 153
    ecological analysis of, 45–58
    as psychological adaptation, 58–9
Farb, Peter, 2n
Feachem, Richard, 3
feasts, 123–7, 131–48, 150
    behavior at, 42, 108–9
    death, 24, 125, 125n
    importance of, 1, 10
    leadership and, 23, 108–9, 127, 130,
        131–48
    life cycle, 24, 125, 126t
    marking stages of gardening, 24, 108–9,
        125–7, 131–48
    symbolic messages at, 123, 133, 135–6,
        146–8
    torela, see torela (feast)
    types of, 124–7, 140, 147, *see also torela*
        (feast), types of
Fergusson Island, 13, 65
Ferro-Luzzi, Anna, 3
fertility, 69, 69n, 75
field methology, xiv–xvi
fieldsite, choice of, xiii
Fiji, 54
Firth, Raymond, 35n, 36n
fish, 36–7, 47–8, 159–63, 172, 173
Fisher, K., 54
fishing, 43, 47–8, 116t, 119, 136–7
food
    abundance of, 35, 36, 44
    animal, 47–9, 159–63
    anthropological approaches to, 2–7
    attitudes toward, 33–44
    beliefs about, 2, 9, 33–44
    caloric and nutritional value of, 45, 54,
        172, 173
    categories of, 46–51, 159–68
    concealing, 33, 42–4
    consumption of, 29, 31–2, 54, 173, *see*
        also eating
    exchange of, 1, 4, 10, 108–9, 123–7,
        131–48, *see also* feasts; pigs, ex-
        change of; pork; taro, exchange of
    as expression of emotions, 1, 80
    as expression of gender qualities, 1, 9,
        75, 91, 108–9, 144–5, 149–50
    as expression of political tension, 1, 9,
        91, 108–9, 149–50
    as expression of sexual relations, 1, 6–7,
        9, 61–2, 63n, 66–73, 81–6, 91–2,
        101–9, 110–22, 149–50
    humor about, 26–7
    importance of, xviii, 1
    imported, 50–1, 169–70

food (*cont.*)
  labor input, 45, 51–2, 52f, 53f
  materialist studies of, 2–4
  mythology about, *see* myth and food
  perceptions of, 33–44
  preparation of, 28–9
  seasonal availability of, 45, 46f, 46–51
  and sex, relationship between, 8
  sharing, 33, 41–2, 47, 142
  stealing, 98, 99
  symbolic studies of, 4–7
  taboo, *see* taboo, food
  vegetable, 49–50, 164–8
Fore, 113
Forge, J. Anthony, 5, 149n
Fortune, Reo, 5, 58, 101
Frake, Charles O., 4
Freedman, Robert L., 2n
Freeman, J. D., 53t
Freud, Sigmund, 61
Fuqua, M., 54

Garala hamlet, 62
gardening techniques, 36–7, 104–7
gardens, *see* taro, and gardens
Garuai
  language, 17
  village, xiii
Geertz, Clifford, 7n
Gell, Alfred, 5
gender relations, 6–7, 25–6, 68–73, 74–5,
    81–6, 90–2, 99–101, 104–7, 110–
    22, 133, 135, 144, 146, 149–50
  see also food as expression of sexual rela
    tions
generosity, 37, 41, 44
geography, Wamiran, 11–13
Gerbrands, Adrianus A., 5
Gewertz, Deborah B., 74–5
Giddens, Anthony, 5n
Gillison, Gillian, 6, 88n, 92n, 115n, 149,
    152
Gimi, 115n
Giurina, Pamela, xiv
God, Christian, 98
Golson, Jack, 3
Goodale, Jane C., 88n, 152
Goodenough Island, xiii, 13, 40, 58, 84n,
    147, 153
  Kalauna, 152
Goody, Jack, 2n, 5n
government
  councillors of local, 23–4
  Milne Bay Provincial, xvi, xvii, 57
grease, 116t, 118–19, 120f
greed, 1, 33, 37, 39, 40–1, 44, 111, 141,
    142, 144, 145, 147, 152–3
Gregor, Thomas, 4, 61

Hadza, 34n
Hallowell, A. Irving, xi, 7
hamlets, 22, 91, 92–6, 127
Hanks, Lucien, 4
Harner, Michael, 2
Harris, Marvin, 2
Hart, Doreen, 3
Hays, Patricia H., 25n
Hays, Terence E., 25n
health, Wamiran, 54–6
  see also nutritional status
height, Wamiran, 54n
Henry, Jules, 61
Herdt, Gilbert, 6, 25n, 61, 92n, 100n, 149
Hipsley, E., 3, 54
Hogbin, Ian, 5, 6
Holy Name High School, 14
houses, 24, 28, 125
human nature, Wamiran definition of, 1, 2, 7,
    33, 34, 151–3
  see also self, definition of
humor, 26–8
Hung, Manming, 55
hunger, 1, 16, 33, 36, 39, 44, 153
hunting, 48

Idei, 64, 87
Ik, 2
illness, 40, 111
India, 2–3
ingestion, 111–12, 113
Inibuena hamlet, xv, 75–6, 127, 131–45,
    146
initiation, male, 7, 25n
intercourse, sexual, 61–2, 110, 116t, 121
irrigation, xiii, xvi, xvii, 13, 16, 29, 57, 93,
    99, 104, 106, 134, 136, 138

Jeremiah Watiwati, 129–31, 132, 134, 135,
    136, 138, 139, 140, 141, 142, 143,
    144, 146
jobs in towns, 19
Johnson, S. Ragnar, 5
Jones, Barbara, 6, 111, 112n
Jorgensen, Daniel W., 111

Kaberry, Phyllis M., 5, 149n
Kahn, Miriam, xiiin, 14n, 87n, 98n
Kaluli, 41n
Kapauku, 34n
Karavar, 152–3
Keen, Samuel, 156
Keig, Gael, 15, 15n
Kelly, Raymond C., 61, 100n, 111
Ker, Annie, 62n
King, Copland, xiii, 14, 17, 87n, 157
Kirk, N., 3, 54

konaga (ancestors, spirits), 102
Kottak, Conrad P., 4
kumika (food), 65, 65n, 70
Kwabunaki village, 13, 17

labor, wage, 19
Lae, 20
Laing, R. D., 61, 62
language
    Garuai, 17
    Taupota, 17
    Tawara, 17
    Wedau, xiii, 16–18, 157–8
latana (stone oven), 65n, 66
Lavora village, 16
Lea, David A. M., 5, 149n
Leach, Edmund R., 4, 9, 61, 116, 117f, 121
leadership, 22–4, 105, 127–31, 133, 135–6, 146–8, 151
Lepowsky, Maria, 3
Lévi-Strauss, Claude, 4, 5, 5n, 6, 9, 61, 62, 72, 90, 109, 116
life cycle, 24, 112
    see also feasts, life cycle
Lindenbaum, Shirley, 113
lineages, 24–5
    see also matrilineality
Loimara hamlet, 65

McAlpine, John R., 15, 15n
McClean, Paul D., 61
McKnight, David, 61
Maclaren, Albert, 14, 87n
Maenge, 97n. 103n, 113, 152
Magavara village, 14, 82
magic, 64, 67–8, 69n, 88, 89, 96–9, 98n, 100, 101, 102, 113, 132, 134
    fishing, 48
    hunger suppression, 82, 84, 86
    hunting, 48
    taro, 91, 96–9, 105, 106, 107, 108–9, 132
malaria, 3, 55
Malcolm Motewa, 129, 131, 132, 133–4, 135
male cult houses, 6, 25n
Malinowski, Bronislaw, 5, 43n, 58, 101
manioc, Mehinaku belief about, 4
Maori, 35n
market, local, 14, 51
marriage, 7, 24–5, 72–3, 78, 81, 81n, 86
materialism in anthropology, 2–4
Matheson, Richard, 61
matrilineality, 24–5, 92, 99, 100, 101
Maurois, André, 61
meat, 40, 61, 70–2, 83–5, 116t, 119, 134, 145

meeting
    hamlet, 131–2, 133, 134, 136–8, 139, 140, 141, 144–5
    village, 30–1
Meggitt, Mervyn, 6
Mehinaku, 4
Meigs, Anna S., 6, 61, 149
men (*see also* feasts, leadership and; leadership)
    behavior of, 25–6, 124
    tensions among, 91, 104–7, 108–9, 123, 124, 127, 131–9, 143–5, 146–7, 150, *see also* food, as expression of political tension
menstrual huts, 6, 25n
mentalism, 2, 4–6
metaphor between humans and plants, 5–6
    see also sago as human metaphor; taro, as human metaphor; yams, as human metaphor
methodology, field, xiv–xvi
Mexico, 2, 156
migration to town, *see* towns, Wamiran residents in
mission, missionaries, 14, 17, 86
    see also Anglican mission
money, 19, 57, 130, 154–5, 156, 169–70
mouth, 151–3
    lack of, 62, 71
Myerhoff, Barbara, 3n
myth, 6, 7, 151–3
    Adam and Eve, 7
    and food, 38, 40–1, 60–73, 86–9, 90–1, 102–3, 111, 112–13, 114–15, 151–3, *see also* pigs, myth of origin of; taro, myth of origin of

Nadelson, Leslee, 7n, 61
names of people and animals, origins of, 38, 77–8
narrative style, 38
New Guinea Highlands, 6, 100n, 149
Newman, Philip, 7, 149
Newton, Henry, 56, 84n, 87n
Nicod, Michael, 4
Norgan, Nicholas G., 3
Norman Tolewa, 62n
Normanby Island, 13
nutritional needs, 3
nutritional status, 45, 54–6

Oliver, Douglas, 5
Orokaiva, 77, 79, 104n
Osborne Kaimou, 62n, 86n, 90n, 129, 131, 132, 135, 136, 138, 140, 143
Owen Stanley Range, 13

Paine, Robert, 124–5
Panoff, Françoise, xi, 5, 97n, 103n, 113, 152

Panoff, Michel, 5, 63n
paradox, 72
Parkinson, Susan, 50n
Paz, Octavio, 5n
pigs, 9, 31, 48–9, 74–89, 90, 118, 150
    behavior of, 32
    butchering, method of, 83, 84f
    castration of, 49, 76
    domestication of, 75–8
    earmarking of, 77, 78
    exchange of, 75, 76–7, 78–81, 132, 133,
        135, 138, 140
    feeding of, 31, 32, 49, 76
    female sexuality, as symbols of, 9, 75–7,
        78–81, 81–6, 89
    myth of origin of, 86–9, 113, 114–15
    names of, 77–8
    as phallic symbols, 5
    types of, 76, 87, 88
politeness, 27–8
political structure, 20–4, 127–31
pollution, female, 6, 25n
Poole, Fitz John Porter, 149
population, xiii, 18f, 18–20, 19f
    dynamics of, 3
pork, 9, 75, 81–6, 118, 119, 123–4, 125,
    126t, 148
    as taboo in Middle East, 2
Port Moresby, xi
Pospisil, Leopold, 34n, 53t
Pova village, 13, 14, 64, 79, 81, 82
Powdermaker, Hortense, 5
pregnancy, 100, 116t
protein, 3, 54, 75, 172, 173
Pygmies, Ituri, 35n

rainfall, 14–16, 15f, 17f, 57
Rappaport, Roy, 3, 54, 78n
Read, Kenneth, 6, 149
Reay, Marie, 5
reductionism, 4–5
Reichel-Dolmatoff, Gerado, 61
residence, 24, 25, 127
    see also hamlets
respect, 27–8
rice, 134, 137, 141, 169–70, 172, 173
    as famine relief food, 56–7
    Thai beliefs about, 4
Richards, Audrey I., 2, 35n, 61
Rosman, Abraham, 5
Rubel, Paula, 5
Rubinstein, Robert L., 5
Rumaruma, xvi, 20, 22, 49, 76, 93, 127,
    139, 141, 142, 143, 145, 146

sago as human metaphor, 5
Sahlins, Marshall D., 2–3, 3n, 35n

St. Barnabas Hospital, 14, 57
St. Paul's Community School, 14
Salisbury, Richard F., 54, 78
salt, 116t, 118–19, 120f
Scaglion, Richard, 149n
Schieffelin, Edward L., 5, 7, 41n, 65n, 100n
Schwimmer, Eric, 5, 77, 79, 104n
seasons, 14–16
self, definition of, 7, 8, 151–3
    see also human nature, Wamiran defini-
        tion of
Seligmann, Carl G., xi, 62n, 84n, 86n, 87n
semen, 100, 100n, 118, 120f
Sepik River, 6, 149
Serpenti, Laurentius M., 3, 61
sexual relations, *see* gender relations
shame, 39, 140, 142, 144, 145, 147, 148
Short, Karen, 15, 15n
Sillitoe, Paul, 6, 61
Simon Darita, 86n, 129, 131, 132, 138, 143
Sirisiri village, 11
skin, 100
snakes, 48, 63, 63n, 66–8, 71, 152, 163
soil content, 45, 52–3, 171
Somerville, Ena, 42
sorcery, 37, 84, 85, 91, 97, 98, 99, 102,
        104, 106, 108, 112, 131, 132, 133,
        134, 136–7
South America, 61
South Asia, 61
space as symbolic indicator of social relation-
        ships, 25, 85–6, 99, 134–5, 136–7,
        138, 143, 145
spirits, 102, 112
Spriggs, Matthew, 3, 53–4
Steensberg, Axel, 3
stinginess, 37
stones
    people turning into, 41, 65, 73
    prehumans and, 151, 152
stores, trade, 14, 51, 130–1, 138, 169–70
Strathern, Andrew, 6, 65n, 92n, 119, 137n,
        149
Strathern, Marilyn, 61, 119
sweet potato, 3, 132, 135, 167, 172, 173
Sybil Gisewa, xiv, 32, 40
symbolism in anthropology, 2, 4–7

taboo, 114–22
    food, 3, 4, 9, 24, 48, 98, 110, 111
    irrigation, 93, 99
    taro cultivation, 105
    at *torela*, 83, 84, 85
Tambiah, Stanley J., 4
Tamodukorokoro, 8–9, 60–73, 74, 82, 96n,
        109, 150–1, 152, 153
Tanopota village, 64

taro, 31, 34, 90–109, 112–14, 115–16, 118,
    119, 122, 123–4, 125, 126t, 137,
    138, 148, 150, 152, 154, 155, 156,
    165–6, 172, 173
  see also diwara (bundled taro)
  availability of, 36–7
  beliefs about, 9, 92
  characteristics of, 92
  cultivation of, 91, 97, 99, 101, 104–7,
    116t, *see also* feasts, marking stages
    of gardening
  customs relating to, xi
  euphemisms for, 43, 131, 137–8
  exchange of, 82, 85, 108–9, 112, 123–4,
    125, 126t, 133, 148
  and gardens, 22, 50, 64–5, 86, 91, 92–6,
    104–7
  harvest of, 92, 98, 101, 104, 107, 108–9,
    108n, 111, 125, 126t, 139–48
  as human metaphor, 5, 91, 101–4, 108–
    9, 112–14. 115–16
  importance of, xv, 92, 154, 155
  magic of, *see* magic, taro
  masculinity, as symbols of, 144–5
  myth of origin of, 66–7, 88, 90–1, 102–
    3, 112–13
  planting of, 99, 106, 125, 126t, 136
  regenerative stalks of, 103–4, 109, 112,
    125, 126t, 142–3
  taro pudding *(gwada),* 64, 68, 68n, 82,
    83, 134
Tauaga village, 62, 70
Taupota
  language, 17
  village, 56
Tawara, 17
taxation, 19
teeth, blackened, 63, 63n
Thailand, 4
Thaman, Randy R., 50n
Tikopia, 36n
tobacco, 30, 51, 169–70
torela (feast), 81–6, 89
  types of, 84n
towns, Wamiran residents in, 19–20, 57
Trobriand Islands, 43n, 123

Turnbull, Colin, 2, 35n
Tuzin, Donald F., 5, 61, 149n

unification, village resistance to, *see* wards,
    antagonism between
Uruam River, 20, 57

Vagakusime, 152
Vasey, Daniel, 52
Vurolagalaga, 65
Vuvura, 64

Waddell, Eric, 3, 53t
Wagner, Roy, 5, 6, 61
Waiko, John, 153
Wamira
  day in, typical, 28–32
  name, meaning of, 13n
Wamira River, 20
Wanama village, 87
wards, antagonism between, 20–2, 24, 139–
    45, 146
warfare, 25
Watson, James B., 3
wealth, 77
Wedau
  language, xiii, 16–18, 157–8
  village, 13, 13n, 14, 16, 19, 20, 82
weight, Wamiran, 54n
Weiner, Annette B., 6, 92n, 123, 149
Werau hamlet, 140
Whiteman, J., 5
Wilson, E., 54
winds, 16
witchcraft, witches, 101, 102, 104, 112, 124
women
  attire of, 29
  behavior of, 25–6, 30, 31, 124
Wood, Andrew, 52–3
Woodburn, James, 34n

yams, 132, 135, 166, 172, 173
  as human metaphor, 5, 149n
Young, Michael W., 5, 6, 40n, 58, 61, 70n,
    84n, 147, 149n, 152, 153